Horace
A Poet for a New Age

Keith Maclennan

CAMBRIDGE
UNIVERSITY PRESS

Cambridge University Press

Cambridge, New York, Melbourne, Madrid, Cape Town, Singapore,
São Paulo, Delhi, Dubai, Tokyo

Cambridge University Press
The Edinburgh Building, Cambridge CB2 8RU, UK

www.cambridge.org
Information on this title: www.cambridge.org/9780521757461

First published 2010

Printed in the United Kingdom at the University Press, Cambridge

A catalogue record for this publication is available from the British Library

ISBN 978-0-521-75746-1 Paperback

Cambridge University Press has no responsibility for the persistence or accuracy of URLs
for external or third-party internet websites referred to in this publication, and does not
guarantee that any content on such websites is, or will remain, accurate or appropriate.

Contents

In grateful memory of Andrew Dixon, whose hard work, acute observations and friendly editorial support contributed so much to this book.

Preface

My copy of the *Oxford Dictionary of Quotations* devotes 13 columns to Horace, far more than any other foreign writer, roughly the same as Byron, and more than Burns, Chaucer, Coleridge or Dickens. This certainly is in part the result of Horace having become over the centuries, as we are constantly told, the property of the comfortable freemasonry of white educated middle-class and middle-aged males. But perhaps it is worth considering what the qualities were which made him become not only this but one of the most important writers of antiquity.

Horace was a complex character living in a complex situation in a very complex culture. He was as near the centre of action as a literary person can well be, and his intelligence and education made him aware of the difficulties, the dangers, the excitement and the promise of the world in which he lived. Of the four types of poetry which he wrote, in only one, satire, did he have a Latin predecessor. Epodes and lyric odes were adapted to Latin and to Rome by him, and the verse epistle as a form was created by him. His Latin is intricate, economical and varied to such an extent that his injunction 'Write, but don't publish for nine years' does not seem surprising. I have not taken nine years, but I hope something of the original may nonetheless come through.

As a pupil many years ago of Robin Nisbet's, I must acknowledge that debt and the illumination that comes from reading the commentaries on *Odes* 1–3 by him and his collaborators. Eric Dugdale has made very valuable suggestions. I have trespassed endlessly on the time, the patience and the library of David West. But the principal burden has been borne by James Morwood, who has corrected, encouraged and cajoled over very many months. These last two, by their scholarship and understanding, have enormously deepened mine.

In the translations which follow I have kept as close as I could to the vocabulary, the grammar, the order of ideas and to the line-structures of the original, trying at the same time to make the result intelligible and comfortable to say. No one could hope to write English in anything like a close reproduction of Horace's metres. The best I can say is that I hope an iambic rhythm, even if often irregular and broken, is perceptible.

It is impossible to make a satisfactory selection for translation. Everyone who knows Horace at all will have his or her favourites, and all such readers will regret that many of these favourites have been omitted. I hope everyone will find that at least some have been included.

Introduction

Are you so mad as to want to have your poems turned into dictation exercises at downmarket schools?

(Satires 1.10.74–5)

If Europe in the twenty-first century is formally united at all, it is because of the Treaty of Rome, 1957. Why Rome? Rome is a symbol of European civilization. It was a centre of empire. But not simply of political control. The forms, the architecture, the language and even the ideology of the Roman empire passed to the Roman Catholic Church, whose authority still represents in sketchy and ghostly form the magnificence of its predecessor. In both we see a mighty organization responsible to a single supreme director at its centre and sharing a belief, often a sense of mission, with that controller. If any single person can be credited with the invention of this system, it is Julius Caesar's great-nephew, the emperor Augustus. Single-minded, determined, often ruthless, he rescued Rome when it seemed on the verge of collapsing in the uncontrolled competition of its leading citizens. He brought back peace and order. He had an idea of what Rome ought to be. Horace and Virgil, both of them well known to the emperor as people and as poets, took part in the creation of this idea and in its dissemination to that literate class of citizens which held the empire together.

If I put it like this, I risk making Horace seem impossibly remote and lofty. There certainly are grand passages in his poetry. But anyone who reads Horace will come to see him in a very different light. He speaks directly to his reader in a huge variety of registers from solemnity to fun and from abstraction to the most down-to-earth realism. The personality he presents in his poems is one with which the reader can easily feel on familiar terms. In fact the risk is not that he may seem remote, but that we shall feel too confident that we know him. Horace himself warns us against this: he sets traps, such as the passage where he seems to be recording confidential advice from his father – which turns out to be a re-presentation of a scene from one of Terence's comedies of 150 years before. He is a poet whom it is always necessary to read, as the great Horatian scholar Eduard Fraenkel said, *perpurigatis auribus* – with ears most thoroughly cleaned out.[1]

---

1 A great deal has been written in recent years to discourage us from taking apparently autobiographical statements by poets at face value. But, as Philip Hills says, 'what Horace wrote about himself, although highly stylized, was part of a wider social "performance" that he could not simply disown once published' (p. 11). That is, Horace had said 'I' so often that he could not very easily say to his contemporaries, 'Actually, I meant someone else, quite imaginary.'

Horace's life

Horace (his full name was Quintus Horatius Flaccus) was born on 8 December 65 BC at Venusia in south-eastern Italy.[2] His father was a freedman (freed slave: *libertus*), a fact Horace tells us was much used against him when he was making his way in life. The name, however, shows no sign of origin as a non-citizen, nor is there any suggestion that the family depended on a patron, as freedmen did upon the person who had given them freedom. It is very possible that Horace's father was in origin a free citizen of Venusia, but suffered temporary enslavement as a boy or very young man when the town was captured by the Roman army in the war of 91–88 BC between Rome and the Italian communities, the so-called Social War.

His father was in fact reasonably well off, with a 'small' farm and a trade as *coactor* ('financial manager in an auctioneering business' is a clumsy translation). He was able to move his son to Rome for most of his schooling and subsequently to send him to university in Athens. He was there in 44 BC when Marcus Brutus, one of the assassins of Julius Caesar, was also in Athens raising an army to fight in the name of the republic against Mark Antony and Caesar's adoptive son, his great-nephew, Octavian. Horace joined Brutus and during the following two years became a senior legionary officer (*tribunus militum*). At the battle of Philippi in 42 he shared in the defeat of the republican forces. Returning penniless (so he suggests) to Rome, he nonetheless secured appointment as a treasury clerk (*scriba quaestorius*). (One can make guesses at whose patronage helped him secure this place, but all Romans had friends on both sides in the civil wars of the period.) As a friend of Virgil he was introduced to Gaius Maecenas, one of Octavian's most powerful assistants. Maecenas took Horace into his wide circle of patronage and his personal friendship. Through Maecenas Horace came to the attention of Octavian, who treated him with familiarity and at one stage proposed that he should become one of his confidential secretaries. Octavian (who was perhaps Augustus by now) did not resent it, says his biographer Suetonius, when Horace refused. He wished to remain independent. A symbol of this independence was the small estate in the hills near Rome which he acquired, probably with the help of Maecenas, some time in the 30s.

---

2 Details of Horace's life are given in a short biography attached to some of the medieval manuscripts, which is recognized to be based on the *Life of Horace* written by the imperial biographer Suetonius at the beginning of the second century AD. These details can be supplemented by (and are often themselves based on) information in the poems themselves, a few of which come in this selection. Freedman's son: *Satires* 1.6.6, 45, 46; Venusia: *Satires* 2.1.35; farm, schooling, *coactor*: *Satires* 1.6.71–82; Athens, Philippi, return to Rome: *Epistles* **2.2.43–52**, pp. 166–7; *scriba*: *Satires* **2.6.36–7**, p. 44; introduction to Maecenas: *Satires* 1.6.54–62; Sabine estate: *Epistles* 1.16.1–16; *Carmen Saeculare* and its effect on Horace's reputation, *Odes* 4.3.16–24.

Horace's earliest published writings are the *Epodes*[3] and the two books of *Satires*, all of which seem to have appeared by 30 BC. During the 20s he was working on the first three books of lyric odes, probably published in 23. These seem not to have found great public favour, and perhaps because of this he turned his attention to a development of the *Satires* in the form of verse epistles, one book of which was published in 20 or 19. In 17 he was asked by the emperor to compose the hymn very publicly sung in celebration of the Secular Games, Augustus' great festival of national rededication. This seems to have directed rather more sympathetic public attention to his lyric poems generally, and a year or two later he accepted Augustus' commission to write a fourth book of *Odes*. Not long after this, at Augustus' personal request, he wrote him a substantial epistle dealing with literary topics. There are also two other long epistles concerned with literature, one perhaps written about 20 BC, one (the *Art of Poetry*) perhaps ten years later.

Maecenas appears somewhat less conspicuously in Horace's latest writings, but there is little doubt that their friendship continued until Maecenas' death in 8 BC, which was followed by Horace's own death on 28 November of the same year.

Rome in the age of Augustus

This short account of Horace's career has largely ignored the fact that the time until 30 BC was one of catastrophic troubles for the Roman state, in fact for the whole Mediterranean world. From 91 onwards there was intermittent conflict in Italy. In 49 this became full-scale civil war. There were relatively peaceful interludes, but it is not unreasonable to count eight separate outbreaks of civil war before the final conflict. The climax of this was Octavian's great naval victory at Actium over Mark Antony and the Egyptian queen Cleopatra, 2 September 31 BC. Antony and Cleopatra fled to Alexandria, where they committed suicide in 30. The period 50–30 was described by the later historian Tacitus (*Annals* 3.28.2) as one where neither law nor moral principle carried any weight.

When Octavian returned to Italy in 29 BC he had decisively defeated all identifiable opposition. This did not in itself make him immediately welcome to everyone. Fifty years earlier Sulla, returning from Greece and defeating his enemies, had celebrated that victory with the mass-murder of his opponents. Nor did it mean that opposition was permanently overcome. Fifteen years earlier Julius Caesar had returned victorious from Spain, only to be murdered himself within six months. It certainly did not mean that there was automatic acceptance of Octavian as a permanently established sole ruler. In considering what title to have himself awarded, Octavian is said to have considered 'Romulus' as a possibility, but to have rejected it on the grounds that one story of Romulus' death was that he had been murdered by senators.

---

3 The significance of this and of the other names given to the types of poetry written by Horace is discussed at appropriate places in the text which follows.

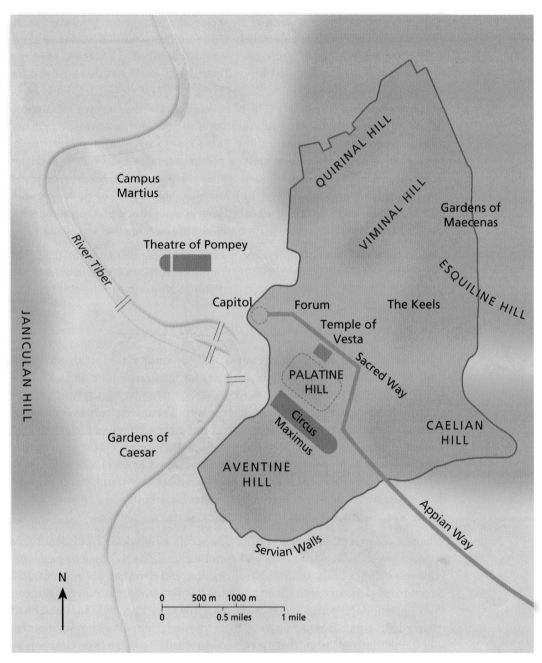

Campus
Martius

Theatre of Pompey

River Tiber

JANICULAN HILL

Capitol

Forum

The Keels

Temple of
Vesta

Sacred Way

QUIRINAL HILL

VIMINAL HILL

Gardens of
Maecenas

ESQUILINE HILL

PALATINE
HILL

Circus
Maximus

Gardens of
Caesar

AVENTINE
HILL

CAELIAN
HILL

Appian Way

Servian Walls

N

| 0 | 500 m | 1000 m |
| 0 | 0.5 miles | 1 mile |

Rome as Horace knew it.

In fact Octavian proceeded with great caution. He was determined not to be another Sulla, and took trouble to advertise his 'clemency' towards his former enemies. He took careful steps to make his power legitimate while not curtailing it. This was the delicate process of framing it within previously existing legislation which is often called 'The Restoration of the Republic'. It was not a straightforward process, but involved a great deal of experimentation and alteration. At the very moment when it was declared that the old laws were once more valid, in January 27 BC, Octavian was given the title of 'Augustus', a complete innovation. The title carried the idea of qualities reserved for the gods, already suggesting that its holder was more than just a citizen among citizens.

Under the previous arrangement ('the Republic'), Rome had been ruled by annually elected officials, of whom the most prestigious were the two consuls. These elections were strongly, often violently, contested. Elections continued under Augustus, and for at least the first ten years continued to attract fierce partisanship, though fortunately for Augustus some of the fiercest was that of his own supporters wanting to elect him consul against his wishes. But on at least two occasions, in 23 and in 19 BC, activity by disaffected opponents was dangerous enough for those opponents to be executed.

In 20 BC Augustus was in the East engaged in negotiation with the Parthian king which resulted in the return of legionary standards lost by the Romans in campaigns in 53 and 36. When he returned to Rome in 19, he treated this success, in effect, as a military victory. (Words and imagery used at this time suggest 'the conquest of Parthia'.) Only now does he seem to have regarded his efforts to establish a new order as having reached some definite conclusion. It is clear that his ambition had always been not merely to bring to Rome peace and the rule of law, but also to begin a process of social and moral regeneration. There seem to have been tentative efforts in this direction in the years immediately following Actium, but they came to nothing. Now, in 18, he put through a series of laws designed to regulate marriage, increase the birth rate and formalize a 'proper' hierarchy of social order. This done, he celebrated the renewal of Rome with the Secular Games of 17 BC.

The following years of Augustus' long reign had their difficulties and their successes, but for the most part these occurred after Horace's death. In the last book of *Odes*, we do hear something of one of the most important of these problems: how would Rome be ruled after Augustus? The emperor was determined to establish a dynasty. His earliest efforts had come to nothing when his nephew Marcellus, recently married to his daughter Julia, died in 23 BC. His wife Livia had two sons of her own, Tiberius and Drusus. These young men were put in charge of the armies which in 15 BC brought the Alpine regions under Roman control. Horace celebrates these victories in terms which speak of Tiberius and Drusus as if they were Augustus' direct family and potential successors. Horace did not live to see the many twists which this story took before Tiberius did in fact succeed Augustus in AD 14.

The literary background

Horace wrote in a combined Greek and Latin literary tradition with which he expected his audience to be familiar.[4] He draws on Homer, the lyric and iambic poets of the sixth and fifth centuries BC, the tragedians and comic poets of Athens, and some of the writers of the vast literature of the post-classical and Hellenistic periods. In Latin he has read the epics and dramatic works of Livius Andronicus, Naevius and Ennius, the comedies of Plautus, Terence and Caecilius, the tragedies of Accius and Pacuvius, the satires of Lucilius, and recent poets such as Calvus and Catullus. He does not have much good to say about most of his Latin predecessors. He acknowledges a great debt to Lucilius (see p. 17 and p. 20n) as his forerunner in satirical verse, but Lucilius and the rest are scolded for their careless and hasty writing and lack of critical standards. He expresses general admiration for Greek literature ('keep turning over your Greek models by day and by night', *Ars Poetica* 268–9), and he is especially respectful of Alcaeus, Sappho and Pindar as models for lyric poetry, of Archilochus and Hipponax for 'iambics', and in general for Homer. He says little about the Greek literature of recent times, and he only mentions in passing one of the most important influences on him and on Virgil, the third-century Alexandrian poet Callimachus (*Epistles* 2.2.100).

Callimachus wrote in reaction against what he regarded as the self-indulgent conventionality of his contemporaries. 'It is not mine to thunder, but Zeus" (*Aetia* 20); 'Poet, make fat the animal you sacrifice, but make your Muse slender' (23–4); 'Go not by the roads made flat by wagon wheels, and do not drive your chariot along the tracks made by others' (25–6); 'Everything available to the public disgusts me' (*Epigram* 30.4); 'Big book, big mischief' (Fragment 359). His inventiveness, his very precise technique and his expressed contempt for popular approval all appealed to Horace.

Horace was also familiar with the world of philosophy, which he tells us he had studied in his time at Athens. The two world-views most in vogue at the time, about which educated people in general could be expected to know at least enough to conduct a conversation over dinner, were those of the Stoics and Epicureans. It is the ethical aspect of these philosophies which figures most in Horace.

Stoicism went back to the teaching of Zeno of Citium (335–263 BC) and his follower Chrysippus (*c.*280–207 BC). As it appears in Roman literature, the philosophy lays great stress on the idea of moral virtue: virtue leads to happiness, only the wise man can be virtuous, only the virtuous man is wise. Unless directly conducive to virtue, everything else is either indifferent or evil.

---

4 Many of the names in the following lines appear in the text and notes, but for a brief introduction to each, see *OCD*. Given that much the greater part of this literature has been lost, we have to accept that many of the references made by Horace are simply inaccessible to us. Fortunately this does not invalidate the poems.

The world is governed by laws which are collectively identified with Fate and a divine Providence. Such an outlook, by which the wise man pursues a course of action undeterred and undistracted by other people and other things, had a strong appeal to some Roman aristocrats. Marcus Brutus' last words, as he died at Philippi ('O wretched Virtue, you were but a word. I followed you, but you were Fortune's slave' – Dio 47.49.2), were said to have been a lament for the failure of Stoic virtue to bring about the realization of his own ideals, and there is an element of Stoicism in Horace's expression of Augustan ideas and references to Augustus himself.

Epicurus (341–270 BC), the founder of the other school, taught that happiness is defined by pleasure. Pleasure consists in the state of having one's desires fulfilled. If therefore one can limit the nature and extent of desire, pleasure can be more reliably achieved. Merely physical pleasures are unreliable, because in achieving them one must always fear losing them, so that pleasure is not secure. The ideal state is 'being untroubled' (*ataraxia*). To achieve this state, it is necessary to recognize that everything in the universe, including the gods, is a temporary combination of atoms.[5] The gods, if they exist, exist in a world remote from ours, neither troubling it nor troubled by it. There is therefore no need for fear of the hereafter. Epicureans tended to separate themselves from the world and live in communities which re-created the original community of Epicurus, 'The Garden'. A famous maxim of the school was 'Live unnoticed'.

Several other views are identifiable. The ancient school of Plato, the Academy, in its later years preached a systematic scepticism, a 'suspension of judgement'. The followers of Plato's pupil Aristotle, 'Peripatetics', were particularly identified with the idea of avoidance of extremes, the 'golden mean'.[6] Diogenes was the original Cynic ('doggish') sage: he and his followers attempted to live according to nature, rejecting all systems and all societies as unnatural. Plato, his older contemporary, called him 'the mad Socrates'. Horace himself was influenced by the sermons ('diatribes') of the generally cynical Bion of Borysthenes.

All these attitudes can be taken to extremes and made the subject of mockery. Readers of Horace quickly realize that he is an adept at this. If he has a philosophy of his own, it is one which is influenced by philosophical teaching but not in thrall to it (see *Epistles* **1.1.13–15**, p. 150). If there is one influence which can be detected more than another, it is that of the Stoic Panaetius, who spent some time in Rome in the second century BC and did much to spread Stoic ideas among the Roman nobility. His was a Stoicism adapted to the requirements of ordinary life. His

---

5 This doctrine is expressed with tremendous force and vividness by Lucretius in his great poem *On the Nature of Things* (*De Rerum Natura*), especially Book 3. Horace knew this poem well.

6 *Aurea mediocritas.* Gold is the extreme of brilliance and value, which makes the phrase an oxymoron: 'Extreme moderation'.

views are reflected closely in Cicero's work *On Duties*, which Horace clearly read and incorporated in several passages of the *Epistles*. But Horace likes to present himself as lurching from high Stoicism at one moment to the most degraded form of pleasure-seeking at another and, while giving thoughtful, rational, untechnical advice to a friend, to lead us to see himself as 'one from Epicurus' herd: a glossy pig' (*Epistles* **1.1.16–18,** p. 150 and **1.4.15–16,** p. 152).

Translations and imitations

Horace has been translated and imitated as much as, and perhaps more than, any other poet. To allow space for translations by other poets in this book would simply reduce the space available for Horace himself. But many of these Horatian poems are easily accessible. The best known of them are the translations and imitations of *Satires, Epistles* and the *Art of Poetry* by Dryden, Pope and Swift. But many others from the seventeenth to the twentieth centuries have tried their hand at these poems of Horace: Ben Jonson and William Cowper; lesser-known names such as Philip Francis, Francis Howes, John Conington from the eighteenth and nineteenth centuries. Really successful translations of the *Odes* are rarer. Demanding metres, compressed ideas and a genius for expressing high thought in plain speech tend to lead the translator into triviality, wordiness or leaden literalness.[7] Milton's famous version of *Odes* 1.5 is only partly successful. Samuel Johnson's *Odes* 1.22 and 4.7 are worthy of their author. The scholar Richard Porson succeeds with *Odes* 1.27. A. E. Housman's version of his favourite *Odes* 4.7 is a fine poem in its own right. James Michie's 1963 collection contains many excellent versions, among them 1.20 and 3.10. Then there are those who have adapted rather than translated. Allan Ramsay's Scottish versions seem to prepare the way for Robert Burns. John Quincy Adams, sixth president of the United States, produced a spirited adaptation of *Odes* 1.22, C. H. Sisson a sardonic version of the *Carmen Saeculare*, and 'Horace, Odes Book V' by Kipling is well worth reading. It would be hard to do better than Byron's *Hints from Horace*, a re-presentation of the *Art of Poetry*. But readers will make their own judgements, undeterred by these opinions, favourable or otherwise.

---

7 Into all of these traps the present translator knows himself only too likely to stumble.

1 The poet on the attack: *Epodes* and *Satires*

The published work of Horace's early years appears in one book of *Epodes* and two books of *Satires*. It is likely that *Satires* 1 was the first collection to be published, in 35 BC (Brown, p. 3). *Satires* 2 and the *Epodes* seem both to have appeared after the battle of Actium in September 31 BC. (Two of the *Epodes* refer to the battle, and *Satires* **2.6** (pp. 42–9) is set during the time when Maecenas was in charge in Rome after the battle.)

Epodes

'Epode' is our word, dating from the Middle Ages, for a verse form which Horace called '**iambics**'. He claimed to be the first (*Epistles* 1.19.23–5) to write Latin poems in imitation of the sixth-century Greek iambic poet Archilochus of Paros. The word 'iambic' is said to be derived from a word meaning 'to hurl (a missile)', and the word is used by both Catullus (36.5) and Horace (*Odes* 1.16.1–4) of deliberately insulting poems. Archilochus wrote poems at the expense of Lycambes and his daughter Neobule. Apparently Lycambes had promised Neobule to Archilochus and gone back on his word. By his poems, Archilochus, it was said, drove the two to suicide. Horace claims that he will follow Archilochus in rhythm and spirit but 'not in subject-matter nor the words which had harassed Lycambes' (*Epistles* 1.19.25).

There is one poem in the collection which appears to attack a named individual. Epode 10 prays that one Maevius may suffer a horrible death by shipwreck. It seems to be closely modelled on a poem of similar theme by **Hipponax of Ephesus**. No historical 'Maevius' has been identified. Epode 4

---

iambics almost all traditional English poetry is basically iambic in metre, i.e. unstressed syllable alternating with stressed syllable, unstressed first: 'He léft it déad, and wíth its héad / He wént galúmphing báck.' Lacking as we do the great variety of different standard metres which the Greeks had and Horace introduced to Latin, we do not easily understand that a particular metre is appropriate for one sort of subject-matter and not for another. But you would not rewrite *Paradise Lost* in limericks.

Hipponax of Ephesus (sixth century BC) another model for Horace's iambics. Epode 6 contains the name Bupalus, the equivalent in Hipponax' verse of Lycambes. More recent, and unmentioned, was Callimachus (see Introduction, p. 6).

is written at the expense of an unidentified freedman promoted to military tribune. (It has been suggested that in this poem Horace puts into the mouth of an enemy the insults which were often directed at himself.) Epode 6 is an invitation to his enemies to attack him and thereby justify him in retaliation (compare *Satires* 2.1.46). Epode 5 is a long plea by a small boy to two witches, that they should refrain from murdering him as part of their effort to make a love-potion; 12 is a rant against a girl who has abandoned Horace. Epode 2 is a poem of praise to country life which in the last four lines turns out to be uttered by a banker who has no intention of changing his lifestyle.

Epode 9 is printed after *Ode* **1.37**, p. 83.

Epode 3

Horace has eaten some garlic and is feeling very much the worse for it. The setting is established by 'these greens' (7) and 'the horrid meal' (8). It is a dinner party. From line 20 it seems that Maecenas was there. At this point we see that the poem is in fact addressed to Maecenas, who seems to have noticed that the garlic has not agreed with Horace and to be teasing him about it.

Whoever with wicked hand once broke
his father's aged neck – let *him*
eat garlic, **poison worse than any hemlock** –
aah, reapers, with your guts of steel!
What venom rages here beneath my diaphragm?   5

Jason and the 'yet unbroken bull' (Epode 3.11)

---

poison worse than any hemlock   the traditional punishment for killing one's father was to be sewn into a sack and drowned. Hemlock was a standard method of execution in classical Athens, famous for its victim Socrates, but it also figures as an instrument of murder in *Satires* 2.1.56.

aah, reapers   reapers eat garlic for lunch on a very hot day in Virgil, *Eclogues* 2.10–11. They are at the bottom of the social scale: their insides can presumably cope with anything. Horace cannot, and groans with the discomfort.

Did I miss viper's blood boiled up
among these greens? or did **Canidia**
have a hand in the horrid meal?
Medea gazed upon the Argonauts
and on their leader, fairest of them all,   10
off to yoke the yet unbroken bulls,
and this she rubbed all over Jason.

In this she soaked her gifts as she took revenge
on his mistress, then fled on the winged dragon.
No heat from the skies so fierce has ever settled   15
on thirst-racked **Apulia**.
Nor did the gift burn more scorchingly
into the shoulders of **Hercules the Achiever**.
And if you ever **make a wish like this**,
Maecenas, witty friend, I pray   20
your girl may fend your kiss off with a hand
and fall asleep on the edge of the bed-frame.

---

1   Is this 'a deliberately insulting poem', like the iambic poems of Archilochus?
2   What is the effect of the mythological allusions in it?

Canidia   a bloodthirsty witch and hag who crops up several times in the *Epodes* and *Satires*, and is given surprising prominence by her place in the last line of the last satire.

Medea   princess of Colchis, from whose king, Aeëtes, Jason and the Argonauts were pledged to win the Golden Fleece. Aeëtes tested Jason by telling him to yoke two fire-breathing bulls and plough a field with them. Medea used a drug to protect Jason. Later, when she and Jason were living in Corinth, Jason wished to marry the king's daughter. Medea in jealousy gave her as a gift a robe soaked in poison which burned away her flesh; Medea then murdered her own children by Jason and fled from Corinth on a chariot drawn by winged dragons. Medea's drug – i.e. for the present purposes, the garlic which poor Horace has eaten – is useful for protection and destruction, as also is hemlock (destruction here; in *Epistles* 2.2.53 a protection for poets against falling asleep).

Apulia   for Horace's own experience here, see p. 35n.

Hercules the Achiever   Hercules' wife Deianira, in Sophocles' play *Women of Trachis*, sent her husband a shirt soaked in what she hoped was a love-charm in order to win back his affections from the young Iole. The effect was similar to Medea's robe (above). The Latin word for 'Achiever' is extremely prosaic, and has the effect that we take a sardonic look at Hercules' glory, reckoning also that success in this last labour was something he could not achieve.

make a wish like this   if we take this as 'If you ever have this idea (*again*)', it is clearly Maecenas who has played a practical joke on Horace with the garlic. If we take it as 'If *you* ever have this idea', it seems that Horace and Maecenas are fellow-guests at a party with a (for Horace) ill-planned menu, while Maecenas is with him and mocking him.

Epode 4

This poem seems to preserve the true spirit of the iambus: a withering attack on an individual offender. The individual is not named, but a number of points tempted ancient scholars to identify him as Pompeius Menas. Menas was a freed slave of Sextus Pompeius. Sextus put him in command of his fleet and made him governor of Sardinia. In 38 BC Menas deserted Sextus and joined Octavian (see line 17), thereby contributing substantially to Sextus' defeat in 36. Menas was rewarded by Octavian with the status of a knight. He seems to fit most of the requirements of the offender described below, except that there is no reason to believe that he ever held the post of *tribunus militum* (see line 20).

Who is the speaker? Is Horace speaking for himself? If so, he is exposing himself to criticism in attacking the offender for holding high military rank in spite of his origin as a slave. 'Horace himself was only one generation better' (Syme, p. 354); and Horace acknowledges (*Satires* 1.6.46) that he was the object of spiteful attacks for his social promotion. And if Menas is the butt, Horace may be taking a risk in attacking him: it might be construed as showing sympathy with Sextus.

Perhaps Horace is adopting a separate *persona* for himself (see the Introduction to the *Satires* pp. 17–18). It was a characteristic of Archilochus that he 'said the very worst things about himself' (Fragment 295 West). Possibly it is just in this that Horace revives the spirit of 'iambics'.

To **wolves and sheep** there fell by lot a destiny:
to hate each other. So I do you,
your back entirely seared with **Spanish rope**,
your legs calloused with irons.
Though in the arrogance of wealth you strut about,   5
fortune cannot change birth.
And can you see, as you mince along **the Sacred Way**

---

wolves and sheep   traditional enemies, as in Aesop's fable, also appearing in Homer *Iliad* 22.262–5, where Achilles says to Hector, whom he is about to kill in battle, 'as there are no pacts between lions and men, nor do wolves and sheep have agreement, but they always hate each other, so it is not for me and you to be friends'.

Spanish rope   in the many references to beatings in Latin literature, the rope is rarely used as a weapon, and may be particularly associated with seafaring. That the man has been beaten and put in irons shows that he was formerly a slave. 'Spanish' may hint at his origin.

the Sacred Way   (see map, p. 4) runs the whole length of the Forum. Important people made themselves known as they walked along it.

'Now we must drink'
(Odes *1.37.1*)

in **a toga three feet times three**:
to you, to you the faces of the passers-by
are turned in generous rage?
'This man, whom **Justices** have flayed with whips,
disgusts the auctioneer
ploughing **Falernian lands** a mile across,

10

---

a toga three feet times three   the toga was a semicircular piece of woollen cloth, peculiar to Roman citizens and often worn only reluctantly by them. But it was a status symbol. According to *OCD*, there was at this period a fashion for wearing a larger and larger toga, reaching by the 1st century AD a size of 19 x 10 feet. In fact, there is debate about the meaning of Horace's terms of measurement: it is in any case a garment of fantastic size.

Justices   the *tresviri capitales* had responsibility for order in the streets, and could have slaves beaten.

disgusts the auctioneer, Falernian lands   'auctioneer' translates a word which has various meanings. If this is the right one, the idea is that the offender has used ill-gotten riches to buy up a large estate in the best wine-producing region, between Rome and Naples (see *Odes* **1.20.9–12** and p. 70n, and **2.6.19–20**, p. 114). Even the auctioneer who knocks it down to him is shocked to do so.

---

abrades **the Appia** with his colts,

and in **the foremost rows, a mighty knight,**   15

(so much for **Otho!**) takes his seat.

What is the good of taking all those **ships**, their bows

weighted with heavy rams,

to fight with **bandits** and a troop of **slaves**,

when *he*, when *he* is **Colonel of the Guard**?'   20

---

1   On how many different grounds does the speaker attack his 'enemy'?
    What are the grounds? Does there seem to be any development, such (for
    example) that the worst offences come last?

2   'It is possible that the speaker is not Horace at all: the opinion of ex-slaves
    is quite different from Horace's own ...' (In *Satires* 1.6.6–11 Horace speaks
    approvingly of Maecenas for his refusal to judge people by their family
    origins, whether slave or free.) '... and the resentment against the man's
    military tribunate resembles that experienced by Horace himself. Perhaps
    [the speaker] is supposed to "represent" narrow-minded snobs whose
    loathing for fellow-Romans would be particularly disturbing and dangerous
    in a time of civil strife' (Mankin, pp. 99–100). Is there anything to be said for
    this assessment of the poem?

3   Compare *Epode* 3 with *Epode* 4 as 'attack' poems.

---

the Appia   the Appian Way, the main road south from Rome. For Horace's journey along
it, see *Satires* **1.5**, pp. 28–37.

the foremost rows, a mighty knight; Otho   in 67 BC Lucius Roscius Otho, as tribune of
the people, proposed and carried a law by which the first fourteen rows in the theatre
were restricted to members of the equestrian class, the 'knights'. (On them, see on the
Art of Poetry **113**, p. 180.)   To be a knight, one had to have substantial property. Otho is
limiting his privilege to those who do. Our offender clearly has so much that he doesn't
need to bother about Otho and his limits at all.

ships, bandits, slaves   Octavian won two great naval battles in the course of establishing
his power, one at Naulochus in 36 BC against Sextus, the son of Julius Caesar's old enemy
Pompey the Great, the other at Actium against Mark Antony and Cleopatra in 31 BC. There
is debate about which of these is referred to here. In favour of Naulochus is the reference
to 'slaves'. In *Res Gestae* 25.1 Augustus records that in the war against Sextus Pompeius
he captured 50,000 slaves who were fighting for Sextus. In favour of Actium is the fact
that the dramatic date of *Epodes* 1 appears to be the prelude to Actium, combined with
the belief that Horace has presented the *Epodes* in chronological sequence of reference
(Mankin, pp. 10–12). For Antony as a slave (to Cleopatra) see *Epodes* **9.11–14**, p. 84.

Colonel of the Guard   the phrase translates *tribunus militum*, a post normally held by
young men with prospects, but one of considerable military authority. Horace himself
had held the rank in Brutus' army, and he speaks of its importance in *Satires* 1.6.48: 'a
Roman legion did what I told it'.

Epode 7

The dramatic date of this poem is the later 30s BC, after the defeat of Sextus Pompeius in 36, when the next round of civil fighting was looming – the struggle between Octavian and Mark Antony. Horace represents himself as addressing a public meeting, perhaps in the Forum. Terrifyingly, his audience is incapable of listening to words of peace and reason: they are set on fighting and can hardly wait to begin.

Where now, you madmen, where? And why are your hands
closing on hidden swords?
Too little, then, the **Latin blood that's shed**
on land and on the sea?
and not for jealous **Carthage**'s proud towers 5
to fall in flames to Rome,
or **untouched Britons** to process in chains
along **the Sacred Way**,
but for our City, as the **Parthian** prays,
to fall by its own hand? 10
Lions and wolves are better: they are cruel
only to other kinds.

Latin blood that's shed on land and on the sea   since Caesar's murder in 44 BC there had been at least four civil wars: in early 43, when Octavian combined with the republican Senate to defeat Antony; in 42, when Octavian and Antony defeated Brutus and Cassius; in 41–40, when Italians rebelled, enraged that their land was being confiscated to satisfy soldiers; and in 36. This year saw the defeat of Sextus Pompeius, who had occupied Sicily and blockaded Rome, describing himself as 'son of Neptune'. As the result of a gigantic programme of training and engineering organized by the formidable Marcus Agrippa, his fleet was destroyed at the battle of Naulochus.

Carthage   the Phoenician city in North Africa, Rome's rival for supremacy in the western Mediterranean for some two centuries until her destruction in 146 BC. Hannibal, her greatest leader, came close to capturing Rome in 217–215 BC.

untouched Britons, the Sacred Way   'untouched' in the sense of 'not previously conquered'. Julius Caesar's raids on Britain of 55 and 54 were evidently recognized as not having any long-term significance. The Sacred Way (see map, p. 4) through the Forum is the standard route for a triumphal procession.

Parthian   the eastern frontier of the Roman empire was the western frontier of the Parthian empire. There was age-old, deadly rivalry between the two.

*Two barbarian captives, chained at the neck and ankle, are led on an open cart through the streets of Rome (*Epodes *7.7).*

Is it blind madness? or some stronger force?
or guilt? Give me an answer!
Silence. Their faces turn both blank and pale   15
their minds bemused and shattered.
It's so: a bitter doom pursues the Romans:
a crime, a murdered brother,
once **Remus**' guiltless blood flowed on the ground,
a curse upon his children.   20

1	What role does Horace seem to be imagining for himself?
2	What is his implied answer to the questions he asks in lines 1–2?
3	Would Horace's words seem relevant anywhere in today's world?

Remus Romulus killed his brother Remus in a dispute over the foundation of Rome. Civil conflict is seen to be endemic to the Roman community.

Satires

Origins of Horace's *Satires*

To a modern ear, 'satire' refers to a form of writing which holds up follies and vices to ridicule. The word is Latin (*satura*), and the first writers of satire were the poets Ennius and Naevius, 150 years earlier than Horace. They, and their great successor Lucilius (see note on p. 20), whom Horace used both as a model and as a standard from which to differentiate his own writing, used the term more broadly, including personal anecdotes, fantastic narrative and discussion of practical philosophy. A likely derivation of the Latin word is *satura lanx*, 'a dish mixed from a great variety of ingredients'. Their writing was mostly but not entirely in verse, while Horace's immediate predecessor, the scholar Varro, composed his *Menippean Satires* entirely in prose. Horace, writing in the 30s, acknowledged 'satire' as the genre within which he was writing, but called the poems themselves *sermones*: 'conversations' or 'talks'. The title is a translation of *diatribē* (non-academic moral/philosophical harangue), several of which were written by Bion of Borysthenes, a Greek author of the third century BC whom Horace refers to as a model in *Epistles* 2.2.60. But one of Horace's principal sources is the philosopher-poet Lucretius, who in the 50s BC had written *On the Nature of Things*, a great poem in six books designed to persuade, charm and cajole the reader into accepting the truth of the philosophy of Epicurus (see Introduction, p. 7).

Of the names in the *Satires* likely to be those of real people, apart from those of major historical characters, we are most likely to be able to identify Horace's colleagues and competitors in the literary world. These apart, it is noticeable how few references there are in a volume of satires to identifiable individual people who are guilty of the failings attacked by the author. The period is 40–30 BC, which other sources indicate was an age of crime and excess not equalled for a long time after; therefore, the decision not to name offenders seems likely to have been deliberate.

Persona

There are 18 poems in the two books of Horace's *Satires*. In the great majority of them the poet speaks as 'I', and provides weaker or stronger reasons for the reader to identify that 'I' with Horace. But Susanna Braund (*The Roman Satirists*, pp. 5–9) warns us against taking everything said by this 'I' as autobiographically true of Quintus Horatius Flaccus. There is a close

---

satura   the meaning of the term was debated: the most likely derivation connected it with a dish which contained a great miscellany of different foods. Quintilian, author of an important work on education and literature, discussing various genres, said 'Satire at least is entirely Roman' (*An Orator's Education* 10.1.93).

A poet, watched by a Muse, tries out several masks. From Pompeii.

connection between satire, drama and rhetoric. In drama 'I' will be determined by which character is speaking. In many forms of drama the actor wore a mask (*persona*), which would give a general idea of the character represented (compare *Art of Poetry* **156–78**, p. 183–4). Cicero speaks (*On Duties* 1.107–15) of four *personae* which everyone must 'wear' on different occasions and for different purposes. There is also some evidence that the character in which satirists speak is substantially influenced by the rules laid down for rhetorical presentation. The *persona* adopted by the satirist is therefore likely to be determined or at least influenced by the argument he seeks to present. Of the three *personae* which Braund identifies – 'angry', 'mocking' and 'smiling' – Horace is sometimes mocking and sometimes smiling. 'The mocking satirist … can easily alienate us because of his superiority, [while] the smiling satirist seems seductively unthreatening and because of that the power of his criticism is increased.'

Peter White (*CCH* pp. 200–6) takes this a stage further. It is not only the poet who takes on the *persona*, it is the addressee of the poem – and any other characters who appear in it. That is to say, it is not just Horace-the-satirist addressing Maecenas in *Satires* 1.1 and Horace-the-lyricist addressing him in *Odes* **1.1** (p. 58–62) but (perhaps) Maecenas-the-source-of-good-sense in the one case and Maecenas-the-benefactor in the other. Each named person, whether historically identifiable or not, plays a role in each poem which is entirely defined by the poem and not by external biographical details. There is certainly some value in this approach, in that one does not allow one's judgement of a poem to be clouded in advance by what one thinks one knows of the characters concerned, or indeed, allow one's opinion of a historical character to be determined by the role he or she plays in a particular poem.

Metre

The metre Horace uses throughout the *Satires* and *Epistles* is the hexameter, which is also the metre of epic poetry, such as Virgil's *Aeneid*. ('The seminal shape of the genre of verse satire is as the antidote to epic' (Llewelyn Morgan in *The Times Literary Supplement*, 21 and 28 August 2009).) Here is, as an example, Homer, *Iliad* 1.3 translated into hexameters by Henry Dart in 1865. It gives a tolerable sense of the metre.

> Mány the soúls of the míghty, the soúls of redoúbtable héroes.

Satires 1.1–3: the 'diatribe-satires'

These satires are sermons in the English sense of the word: 1.1 is directed at those who cannot be contented with what life offers them and those who aim to get rich by any available means; 1.2, directed against extreme behaviour, focuses luridly on the undesirability of affairs with married women; 1.3, beginning with general observations on inconsistency of behaviour, turns to the particular inconsistency whereby people judge others by standards different from those by which they judge themselves, and finally becomes an argument against fundamentalist Stoics who have only one absolute standard, 'right or wrong', with no gradations, from which it follows that 'all mistakes are equal'. Having thus given three examples of what he is doing in writing satire, in 1.4 Horace justifies it against imagined critics.

Satires 1.4

1.4.1–64

Cratínus, Eupolis and Aristophanes
and others, good men and poets of ancient comedy,
if any earned the mark of 'wicked' or of 'thief',
of 'lecher', 'murderer' or some other form

Cratinus, Eupolis and Aristophanes the names of three of the most famous writers of comedy in Athens in the fifth century BC. The style in which they wrote acquired the name 'Old Comedy'. Their plots tended to be fantastic, and the interest of the drama lay in the spectacle, in the songs and dances of the chorus, in the frequent interaction of actors with the audience, and above all, from Horace's point of view, in the involvement of the plays with contemporary life. Actors could represent political leaders or people otherwise well known in society. These people could be subjected to the most abusive attacks or represented in the most ridiculous situations. Though some attempts were made to limit this freedom of speech, they do not seem to have had much success until, at the end of the century, comedy turned away from public affairs. Hence 'Middle' and 'New Comedy', which are represented in Greek largely by the extensive fragments of Menander (c.344–292) and in Latin by the Greek-derived plays of Plautus (active c.205–185) and Terence (d. 159). See lines 48–52.

---

of disrepute, they **damned him unrestrainedly**.   5
Hence all **Lucílius**. Them it was he followed
changing but **rhythm and metre**. He was witty,
keen-scented too, but, writing verses, clumsy.
A fault: in one hour he'd dictate two hundred lines
standing on one foot, and be proud of it;   10
a muddy torrent: one you'd want to strain:
loquacious, lazy at the drudgery of writing
– of writing *well*; as for writing *a lot*, forget it. Look!
A **challenge** from **Crispinus**: 'Here, sir, if you please,
here are some tablets. Let's arrange a place, a time,   15
some referees. Let's see now who can write the more.'
By heaven's grace, I'm made with an impoverished
and puny spirit, seldom speaking, saying little.
You'd ape the winds closed tight in goatskin **bellows**,
labouring on till iron grows soft in fire –   20

---

damned him unrestrainedly in his *Clouds*, Aristophanes presents Socrates, his contemporary (and perhaps friend: see Plato's *Symposium*), as an intellectual fraud who runs the 'Thinking Shop' and trains the young to reject moral standards. In *Wasps* the highly influential statesman Cleon appears as a corrupt bully.

Lucilius c.180–102, author of 30 books of 'Satires', of which only some 1,300 lines survive. These covered a great variety of topics, including autobiographical episodes, literary discussions, parodies and attacks on individuals. For points of direct comparison between him and Horace, see *Satires* **1.5.57n**, p. 34 and **1.5.77n**, p. 35.

rhythm and metre the standard metre of spoken drama is iambic (p. 9n), though Old Comedy used a wider range. In his earlier books Lucilius used both iambic and other metres, but in his later ones he settled on the hexameter, the metre of epic (p. 19), in which he is followed by Horace.

keen-scented the Latin term suggests a highly developed critical sense, both artistically and morally speaking: compare Quintilian's remark in the second note below.

standing on one foot a proverb for things done very easily.

a muddy torrent: one you'd want to strain writing in about AD 90, the Roman orator, educator and critic Quintilian had this comment: 'I do not agree with these [people who think Lucilius the best poet of all], but nor do I agree with Horace, who speaks of Lucilius as "a muddy torrent", with parts which could well be removed. We find in Lucilius wide knowledge and freedom of speech, with the severity of judgement and biting wit which arise from that' (10.1.94).

challenge there is a word in Horace describing this challenge: *minimo* ('with a very small [amount?]'). There is no agreement on what it means.

Crispinus appeared in *Satires* 1.1.120 as a collector of maxims; here he is a wordy poet.

bellows Plautus also used the image of bellows in a forge to suggest a person who can shout too long and too loud (*Bacchides* 10).

Do so! And good for **Fannius** if **people bring him**
bookshelves and portrait bust unasked, while nobody
reads what I write, and **I won't give a public reading**, since
satire's what they most hate. Why? Most of them
are culpable. Pick anyone among the crowd: 25
he'll be in trouble with greed or with ambition.
One's mad for married women, one for boys;
He's gripped by gleaming silver; **Albius** gapes at **bronze**.
He's trading goods from **rising sun to that which warms
the lands of evening**; yes, he's hurrying   30
from bad to bad like whirlwind sand, in fear
his pile may shrink, or eager it should grow.

All these are scared of verses; poets they hate.
'**There's hay on his horns**. Keep clear. If he can force a laugh
he'll raise one at himself or **at his closest friend**.   35
And what he's once splashed on his paper, all must know
while walking home **from bakehouse or from tank**,
old women, servants.' Right then. Here's my brief reply.
First now, from those to whom I'd grant the name of poet,
I'd count myself out. Writing a line that scans is not,   40
you'd say, enough. And if there's one whose style, like mine,
is nearer talk, he can't be called a poet.

Fannius   Fannius appears in *Satires* 1.10.80 as a dinner companion of the Tigellius whose sweaty hands receive comment in line 72 of this poem. He is also a poet.

people bring him   the Latin could mean 'he gives people'. Even in antiquity scholars were uncertain. Here Fannius' admirers have presented him with a set of bookshelves and a bust of himself as a reward. But it could be that Fannius has offered bookshelves and bust to purchasers in order to encourage them to come to his readings.

I won't give a public reading   in *Epistles* 1.19.37 Horace speaks again, 10 or 15 years later, of his reluctance to appear in public. His ostensible reason in this satire is that people are afraid of what he will say.

Albius   possibly the same person as in line 109. Otherwise unknown.

bronze   probably statues; it sounds as if Albius is an antique dealer like Damasippus in *Satires* 2.3, whose business collapsed.

rising sun to that which warms / the lands of evening   in this expression Horace combines the idea 'from dawn till dusk' with 'from farthest east to utmost west'.

There's hay on his horns   farmers were said to wrap hay round the horns of dangerous cattle as a warning.

at his closest friend   from line 78 this becomes an important theme.

from bakehouse or from tank   publicly available resources for cooking and water supply, therefore centres of gossip. While men might get their gossip from the barber, these would be used by women taking their slaves with them. To court popularity among this audience is really sinking low!

He must have genius, lofty spirit, a tongue
of mighty sound: then the fair name is his.
And therefore some have questioned: '**Comedy**:   45
true poetry, or not? No **violent inspiration**,
no strength in word or matter. If not by rhythm
distinct from talk, mere talk.' '**But furious father
rages at spendthrift son**, who, mad with passion
for a hired mistress, spurns a well-dowried wife,   50
and, tipsy, strolls before it's dark (for shame!)
with torches.' Would **Pomponius**, did his father live,
endure a less intemperate reproach? And so
a line of common speech is **not enough**,
when, if you **split** it, anyone might moan   55
in the **masked** father's matter. From what I now
am writing, as Lucilius once, if you removed

Comedy   it is perhaps worth mentioning that, so far as we know, all the spoken language of the theatre was in verse, none in prose. Horace is implying the distinction between tragedy (definitely poetry) and comedy (perhaps not). Horace seems here to be quoting Cicero (*Orator* 67): '[comic poets] whose writings are no different from everyday speech, except that they are presented as separate lines'.

violent inspiration   for a description of such possession see Virgil, *Aeneid* 6.77–80, where the god Apollo takes over his priestess, the Sibyl. 'In Phoebus' cave the Sibyl raves wildly, not yet tamed: she tries to shake off the mighty god. All the more does he wear her down, controlling her foaming mouth and her fierce heart, shaping them as he presses.' Horace treats the idea in *Odes* **2.19** (pp. 63–6), perhaps with a touch of irony, since he is the one possessed.

But furious father / rages at spendthrift son   an imaginary objector to the view 'Comedy is not poetry'. He is referring to a stock scene from comedy of the type familiar to us from Plautus and Terence. Young men in love with predatory mistresses, old men angry at their wayward sons, anxious to get them married off, are part of the standard repertoire. The opponent's point is that, in scenes like this, there is the language of strong feeling and that this may qualify as 'poetry'. In the Preface to *Lyrical Ballads* (1798) Wordsworth described poetry as the spontaneous overflow of powerful feelings.

Pomponius   an unknown person. He is mentioned to suggest the thought: 'This type of strong feeling is commonplace. Poetry deals with the unusual, the imaginary.'

not enough   i.e. not enough to qualify for the description 'poetry'. In one sense, Horace is right about his own satires, because very little of the diction is in any way unusual or elevated; you could expect to find any of the words in prose. But in another way he is being consciously ironic. The ideas, the grammatical structure, the word-order within the sentence, the relation of sentences and words to metrical lines: these all make of the *Satires* something special.

split   by 'split the line', Horace means to break it up so that it loses its rhythm and becomes a line of prose.

masked   making the point that the father is a character on stage.

scansion and metre, and an earlier word
you brought in later, making the last first,
you wouldn't (as by splitting 'When foul Discord   60
War's steely posts and portals shear'd asunder')
find the assembled fragments made a poet.
I'll go no further. 'Proper poem or not?' I'll ask
another time.

---

1   In summarizing the history of satire, Horace presents a simple sequence:
    the idea began with Greek Old Comedy (see note on line 1), was inherited
    by Lucilius (line 6) and passed on directly to himself. The real picture is
    more complicated (see p. 17). What does Horace's motive seem to be in
    presenting the history as he does?

2   By what standards are the desires and activities referred to in lines 27–32 to
    be thought equally objectionable?

3   Think about the distinction Horace draws in lines 39–64 between the poet
    and the not-poet. It seems to have something in common with the image of
    the poet expressed by Coleridge (*Kubla Khan* 49–54): 'Beware! Beware! / His
    flashing eyes, his floating hair! / Weave a circle round him thrice, / And close
    your eyes with holy dread, / For he on honey-dew hath fed, / And drunk the
    milk of Paradise.' In what important ways is the poet different from the lay
    person? And how serious is either Horace or Coleridge in thus marking the
    poet off from others? (Compare *Odes* **2.19**, pp. 63–6; **3.30**, pp. 67–8; *Epistles*
    2.2.109–26, and the *Carmen Saeculare*, pp. 98–102.)

4   The whole sentence 'From what I now … made a poet' (56–62) is a
    convoluted structure with the quotation from Ennius making a bizarre
    contrast. What is Horace trying to achieve?

---

scansion and metre   Latin and Greek verse depend very heavily, much more than English,
on the division of syllables into those which are long and those which are short. 'Scansion'
is the process of identifying this distinction. 'Metre' refers to the rhythmic pattern of the
resulting line or stanza.

'When foul Discord / War's steely posts and portals shear'd asunder'   a quotation from
the early Latin epic poet Ennius. In his historical epic *Annales* Ennius is referring to the
Roman practice of opening the temple of Janus to mark the outbreak of war – thus the god
Janus becomes equated with War. Solemn subject-matter, the presence of gods, elevated
words, assonance, chiasmus, alliteration are all characteristic of 'poetry'. However, given
that the point is 'clever rhythm can't make prose into poetry', it is amusing that Horace
has chosen a line and a half of epic verse which he would certainly have regarded as old-
fashioned, lumbering and unacceptable. (For Horace's attitude to his Latin predecessors,
see pp. 6, 17 and *Epistles* **2.1.34–75**, pp. 171–2.)

assembled fragments   Horace is surely encouraging us to think of some grisly scene such
as that in Virgil, *Georgics* 4.520, when the poet Orpheus is torn to pieces by the women
of Thrace.

'Proper poem or not?'   the question is 'Can Satire be called proper poetry?' Horace's
point is that mere linguistic complexity does *not* constitute poetry. He has written a
passage of linguistic complexity sufficient to baffle any reader, precisely (it seems) so that
the reader will impatiently say 'This is just word-juggling, not poetry.'

1.4.64–143   For now: this type of writing:
should it alarm you? Savage **Sulcius**   65
and **Caprius** prowl, loud-mouthed, **booklets in hand**,
a terror, both, to crooks. But he who has clean hands
and lives life well may disregard them both.
If you're like **Birrius and Caelius** the robbers,
a Caprius or a Sulcius I'll never be.   70
Why fear me then? No shop, no pillar can flaunt my books
for vulgar hands, **Tigellius'** hands, to sweat on.
I read for friends alone (and they must force me),
not anywhere, to anyone. Of those who read their words
in Forum or while bathing, there are plenty.   75
It echoes well, the indoor space. This is the fun
of fools, who never ask if their performance is
tactful or timely. But 'You love to hurt,'
he says; '**That puts you in the wrong.**' This dart
you've hurled, where is it from? Is it supplied   80
by my companions? He who slanders absent friends,

Sulcius and Caprius   unknown, but they must be professional prosecutors. In Roman social ethics, prosecutors were a rather coarse and self-promoting type, as opposed to the nobility of the defence advocate. They seem to be real names, but are probably chosen to represent a coarse type of person; *sulcus* a furrow, *caper* a he-goat.

booklets in hand   Michael Brown's phrase, from his edition of *Satires* 1. Sulcius and Caprius have this in common with Horace, that they are a terror to villains. They also all three have booklets: in Sulcius' and Caprius' case the booklets are full of lists of people to prosecute. In Horace's case the booklet (like the poet's booklet in Catullus 1.1) will contain his verse, which, in reality, indicts few people by name (see p. 17).

Birrius and Caelius   bandits. Horace perhaps gets the name of Birrius from a real gladiator, Birria, who took part in a notorious political murder in 52 BC.

Tigellius   Horace gives his full name as Hermogenes Tigellius. He was a singer (see *Satires* **1.9.25**, p. 39). The pillar seems to be part of a bookshop, to which books on sale are attached for advertisement purposes. Tigellius is perhaps too mean to buy the books, so merely paws the promotional copies.

It echoes well, the indoor space   in a letter (56) the first-century AD philosopher Seneca speaks disparagingly of the man 'who likes the sound of his own voice in a bath-house'.

That puts you in the wrong   it is suggested that, whatever Horace's professed motives for writing satire may be, in fact he does it with malice. This allows him to make a strong counter-attack on his opponent. Richard Rutherford notes that with this presentation of the argument Horace shifts the question from public (should satire attack public vices?) to private (should one show personal malice?): 'satire becomes personal and ethical, less antagonistic and less political', reflecting 'Horace's low status and the uncertainty of the times' (*CCH*, p. 258).

who won't stand by them when attacked, who seeks
an easy laugh, who wants to be thought witty,
who makes up what he hasn't seen, who cannot keep
a secret: he is the evil one; **him, Roman, flee.**   85
Three couches and four guests on each you'll often see,
with one who's glad of any chance to damn them all
but him **who's given the water**; then him too, when drunk,
when truthful Bacchus opens the hidden heart.
To you does *he* sound pleasant, civilized and open,   90
you evil-hater? If I mock silly **Rufillus for**
his scent of pastilles, and Gargonius' of goat,
does that seem spite and malice? If you hear the words
'**Petílius Capitolínus and his thefts**',
you would defend him in your usual way: 95
'Since we were boys, Petilius and I have been
companions, friends. Those many things I've asked of him
he's done. That he's alive and well in Rome, I'm glad.
But still, I'm baffled how that trial ended with
"Not guilty".' Here's the **black ink of the cuttlefish**,   100
here is neat poison! Here's a vice I promise, as before,
if I can promise true, will from my writings
and from my thoughts be far. Now if I speak too free
and flippantly, you'll grant the right, the pardon.
My excellent father formed in me this habit.   105
For every vice he gave an instance to deter me;
urged me to live with thrift and frugally,
and be content with what he had provided.

---

him, Roman, flee   the adjective 'Roman', used thus to address someone, is very rare and solemn, occurring only twice in Horace and twice in Virgil. It is all the more forceful for appearing as a surprising universal command in what reads like a particular context.

Three couches and four guests on each   this is the standard arrangement (*triclinium*) for a Roman dinner party.

who's given the water   i.e. the host.

Rufilus for / his scent of pastilles, and Gargonius' of goat   the identical line occurs at *Satires* 1.2.27. If this is the later passage, Horace is using this as shorthand for all the satirical attacks he makes.

Petilius Capitolinus   he sounds like a real defendant in a real case, which is mentioned again in *Satires* 1.10.26 as especially difficult.

black ink of the cuttlefish   'evil' in lines 85 and 91 represents the word 'black' in the Latin. Horace now picks this up with the blackest substance he can think of.

'See what a bad life **Albius**' son is living
and penniless **Baius**. Learn from it not to waste   110
what you inherit.' To keep me clear of shame
or falling for a whore: 'Don't ape **Scetanus**.'
Some love's permitted, some – adultery – is not.
'**Trebonius** was caught; his name's not good,'
he'd say; 'some things are better sought, some shunned.   115
Philosophy will tell you why. Enough for me
if I preserve the ways our fathers left us,
and, while you need a guardian, keep your life
and reputation safe. When time makes firm your limbs
and spirit, you'll swim without **support**.' So he   120
shaped me, a boy, by words. When telling me
what I should do, he'd say 'You've one to follow'
and offer some selected **juryman**;
then, when forbidding, 'Can you doubt how wicked,
how damaging this is, when *he* and *he*   125
are quite disgraced?' A funeral next door means fear
of death for **greedy invalids**: they spare themselves.
So with young spirits: other folk reproached
keep them from vices. Hence I am clear of those
which bring destruction, though perhaps in thrall   130
to lesser, pardonable faults. Of these, maybe,
long life or candid friends may shrink the number;
my own thoughts too. Alone in **couch or colonnade**
I don't desert myself. 'Here's a more honest way',
'Like this I'll be living better', 'This is how   135
I'll please my friends', 'So Someone does. Not pretty!
Might I, unknowing, be like him?' Thus, pursing my lips,
I cogitate. And in an idle moment
I'll play with paper. Of those lesser faults

Albius, Baius, Scetanus, Trebonius   all unknown, unless Albius is son of the Albius in line 28.

support   Horace's word is 'cork', a piece of which was evidently used as water-wings.

juryman   there was an official list of all those liable and entitled to sit on juries. The names on the list were picked by the praetor, according to Cicero (*Pro Cluentio* 121), on the grounds of their flawless moral character.

greedy invalids   they have evidently been put on a diet by their doctor, but are going weakly back to their former gluttony when they are reminded of mortality by the death next door.

couch or colonnade   places where one could hope to be on one's own for private reflection, either relaxing in bed or taking a stroll under the colonnade (Wordsworth, 'Daffodils': 'For oft when on my couch I lie / In vacant or in pensive mood').

that's one. For which, if you won't make allowance
there'll come a mighty company of poets
to aid me (**we're the great majority**) and like
the Jews, we'll make you come and join our crowd.

> • In Satire 1.4, Horace has set out to justify the writing of satire in general, his
> own literary standards, and his own position as a satirist. How has he gone
> about it? Has he succeeded in his aim?

Horace's father – the original

In Terence's play *The Brothers* (lines 407–21) the old man Demea is told by his servant Syrus
how his son Ctesipho has reacted to seeing his nephew Aeschinus behaving irresponsibly:

SYRUS   Ctesipho started shouting: 'Aeschinus! The idea that you're doing these shocking
things! You're letting the family down!'

DEMEA   I weep for joy.

SYRUS   'It's not your money you're wasting, it's your life.'

DEMEA   Bless him. I do hope he's like his ancestors.

SYRUS   Hah!

DEMEA   Syrus, Ctesipho is chock-full of those principles.

SYRUS   Bah! he had a stock at home to learn from.

DEMEA   It's all done properly. I leave nothing out; I give him the habit. I tell him to look
into other people's lives as in a mirror, and to take an example from others for
himself – 'Do this'.

SYRUS   Quite right.

DEMEA   'Avoid this.'

SYRUS   Clever.

DEMEA   'This will do you credit.'

SYRUS   That's the thing.

DEMEA   'This leads to moral harm.'

SYRUS   Very proper.

DEMEA   And, what's more …

SYRUS   I haven't the time to spend listening to you. These fish are at their best. I mustn't
let them go off.

Syrus' story is in fact a collection of lies. Aeschinus and Ctesipho have been engaged in a
plot to kidnap a girl without their fathers knowing.

• This scene is clearly in the background to Horace's description of his father's educational
practice. Does it put what Horace says in a different light?

---

we're the great majority   because, no doubt, of the universal craze for writing verse to
which Horace refers in *Epistles* **2.1.108–13**, pp. 173–4.

Jews   compare Jesus' own satirical comment at the expense of the Pharisees: 'Ye compass
sea and land to make one proselyte.' (Matthew 23.15)

Satires 1.5

The satire describes a journey from Rome to Brundisium, modern Brindisi. The travellers are listed below. The purpose of the journey is given in lines 27–9: it is a diplomatic mission designed to patch up differences. The presence of Maecenas, always a spokesman for Octavian/Augustus, and of Fonteius Capito, Antony's friend, suggests one of the high-level missions of the early 30s BC when the two **triumvirs** Octavian and Antony were keeping up the appearance and perhaps attempting the reality of cooperation. From *Satires* **2.6.40–2** we know that Horace did not first meet Maecenas until 38, and from *Satires* 1.6.54–62 that there was an eight-month gap between the first meeting and Horace being formally accepted as a friend of Maecenas. The occasion is therefore likely to be spring 37. At this time, according to Plutarch (*Antony* 35), Antony sailed from Greece to Italy with a large fleet and aggressive intention. Denied permission to land at Brundisium, he sailed round to Tarentum. Meanwhile Antony's wife, Octavian's sister Octavia, persuaded her brother not to react belligerently to Antony's arrival.

An entirely different approach to the origin of the satire is a literary one. Horace will have known of the *Journey to Sicily* by his predecessor and model **Lucilius**. An ancient scholar says 'In this satire Horace is imitating Lucilius.' In the surviving fragments of Lucilius' *Journey* there are two passages which have clearly influenced Horace (see on lines 56–7 and 77–9). It is reasonable to ask how much of the narrative, if any, is autobiographical and how much a literary exercise.

As far as Beneventum the party follows the Via Appia, the most ancient of the great Roman public roads. In the late republic there was an alternative route from Beneventum through Canusium and Bari called the Via Minucia; it took a more direct route through the mountains, and it is this branch which Horace and his party take. (In a later poem, *Epistles* 1.18, Horace gives as an instance of a point of supreme unimportance the question of which of the two routes to Brundisium is better.)

---

triumvirs   in the summer of 43 BC it became plain that Mark Antony could not establish uncontested power over Octavian, nor vice versa. They therefore set up a three-man commission nominally to reform and re-establish the constitution, but in practice to perpetuate their own supremacy. This commission we somewhat misleadingly call the Second Triumvirate. (On the First, see *Odes* **2.1n**, pp. 86–90.) The third member of the triumvirate, Marcus Lepidus, was an aristocratic supporter of Julius Caesar who held his place chiefly because it suited the other two to have someone who could appear to hold the balance. Lepidus was discarded in 36, but in some form the arrangement survived until shortly before the battle of Actium in 31.

Lucilius   see *Satires* **1.4.6n**, p. 20.

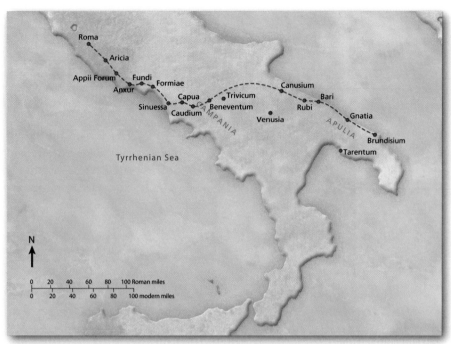

The journey from Rome to Brundisium.

The journey to Brundisium

In his 1883 edition of the *Satires*, Arthur Palmer offered the following as an itinerary:

Day	Place	Distance in Roman miles
1	*Aricia*	*16*
2	*Forum Appii*	*20*
3	*Fanum Feroniae–Anxur*	*17 + 3 = 20*
4	*Fundi–Formiae*	*12 + 13 = 25*
5	*Sinuessa, the Campanian crossing*	*18 + 3 = 21*
6	*Capua*	*22*
7	*Caudium*	*21*
8	*Beneventum*	*12*
9	*Trivicum*	*?25*
10	*(Unsayable town)*	*24*
11	*Canusium*	*?35*
12	*Rubi*	*30*
13	*Bari*	*22*
14 (or 14 and 15)	*Gnatia*	*37*
15 (or 16 and 17)	*Brundisium*	*44*
		374 Roman miles total

(1 Roman mile = 0.92 modern miles or 1.48 km.)

The old Via Appia, not far outside the walls of Rome. The road surface is ancient.

I left **Great Rome**: **Aricia** welcomed me –
at a low inn. With me, **the *rhetor* Heliodorus**;
in Greece, no scholar greater. **Appii Forum** next,
jam-packed with sailors and with mean hoteliers.
(**Idlers, we split this stage** in two. If dressed for it   5
– we weren't – you'll make it one. Best take the **Appia** slow.)
Bad water here made me declare a war
on my insides. The others dined. Impatient, I

Great Rome   in the Latin the name of Rome is the last word of the first line as *Brundisium* is the first word of the last line. 'Great Rome' immediately points up the smallness of its neighbour Aricia.

Aricia   a small hill-town 16 miles from Rome. (Distances in the notes are given in Roman miles.)

the *rhetor* Heliodorus   see the list of Horace's fellow travellers, p. 33.

Appii Forum, Appia   for the Via Appia, see above. From Rome it led due south-east to the sea at Anxur. For at least the second half of this distance it passed through the Pomptine marshes, a stretch made disagreeable and dangerous by malarial mosquitoes and bandits. Appii Forum was a settlement 27 miles from Aricia in the marshes. From it a canal led 17 miles parallel to the road as far as the sea. It could be less trouble to travel by barge, as Horace does.

Idlers, we split this stage   but not *very* idle – 43 miles (38 modern miles) is a long journey for a single day, even if it makes two quite short ones.

awaited them. Now night prepared to spread
the world with shadow, and to sprinkle heaven with stars.   10
Then insults flew, slaves cursing sailors, sailors slaves.
'In here now!' 'Hey, you're packing them hundreds in!
Enough now!' Gathering fares and harnessing the mule
took a whole hour. The hellish midges and the marsh-frogs
kept sleep away, while, drowned in booze, 'My bonny lies   15
beyond the ocean' sang traveller and boatman
in rivalry. Sleep overcame the traveller
at last. The mule was sent to grass; its reins
the lazy boatman fixed, then fell on his back and snored.
Day was upon us when we felt the barge was making   20
no progress, till one hothead, leaping up,
batters the **mule and boatman**, head and haunches,
with a willow cudgel. Ten o'clock, at last, we land
to wash our face and hands, **Feronia**, in your streams.
Breakfasting then, we crawl three miles and come   25
to **Anxur** on its far-seen shining cliff.
Here we would meet **Maecenas** and the excellent
Cocceius, both on a mission of great gravity:
envoys **adept at reuniting friends estranged**.
Here I apply, for inflammation of the eyes,   30
black ointment. Then Maecenas comes, and with him
Cocceius, **Capito Fonteius**, flawless man
and friend as no one else to Antony.
Fundi, Aufidius Luscus praetor, we with joy

---

mule and boatman   the canal by the Via Appia carried barges, hauled by mules, which walked along a path beside it. It carried heavy goods traffic as well as passengers.

Feronia   a goddess, one of whose shrines lay by the end of the canal, near **Anxur** (also named Terracina) on the coast.

Maecenas, Cocceius, Capito Fonteius   see the list of Horace's fellow travellers, p. 33.

adept at reuniting friends estranged   in 40 BC, during an earlier crisis in the relations between Antony and Octavian, Maecenas and Cocceius had been part of the group which helped engineer a reconciliation.

Fundi, Aufidius Luscus praetor   the translation attempts to pick up the formal character of the expression, like the proper way of referring to naval ships – 'HMS *Surprise*, Captain Aubrey' – because this is part of the mockery of Luscus' pretensions. Luscus is evidently proud of the idea that in the annals of Fundi this year will be dated by his name, as Roman years are dated by the consuls. Apparently the governing officials of Fundi at this time went in fact by the lesser title of 'aedile'; if Luscus has usurped 'praetor' he is the more absurd.

Looking from the acropolis at Anxur (Satires 1.5.26). Fundi with its lake is on the left and Formiae is just beyond the distant hills on the right.

abandon, mocking **the crazy clerk's regalia:**   35
edged toga, broad-stripe tunic, pan of coals.
Then, tired, we rested in **Mamurra's capital:**
the house **Murena**'s, Capito's the cooking.
The next day's dawn was far the best: and why?
At Sinuessa **Plotius, Virgil, Varius**   40
were with us, friends than whom there are none finer seen
on earth, nor any linked in closer bond to me.
What glad embraces, what delight we shared!
Good friends come first, in wise men's reckoning.

---

the crazy clerk's regalia   the 'regalia' consisted of (a) the toga with a purple edge, worn by senior magistrates: Luscus was perhaps entitled to this; (b) a tunic with a broad purple stripe: this was the prerogative of Roman senators, which Luscus was not; (c) a pan of coals to sacrifice or to burn incense on, in honour of his distinguished visitors.

Mamurra's capital   the town is Formiae. It cannot be accommodated in a Horatian line (compare lines 1 and 87), so an epic-style periphrasis is used which turns out to be not so grand, since Mamurra, the 'epic hero' commemorated, was a grossly extravagant and disreputable associate of Julius Caesar.

Murena   Maecenas' brother-in-law. Much later, in 23 BC, he became consul but was executed for participating in a conspiracy against Augustus.

Plotius, Virgil, Varius   see the list of Horace's fellow travellers, p. 33.

The **lodgings** where you cross into Campania   45
gave shelter, the **providers** wood and salt, their due.
At Capua next the mules unloaded, early;
Maecenas went to play; Virgil and I to sleep:
ball games are bad for ailing eyes and stomachs.
Cocceius' well-stocked villa next received us,   50
above the inns of **Caudium**.

Horace's companions

The *rhetor* Heliodorus. A *rhetor* was a teacher of public speaking. He would
preside over the third stage of a young man's education, and might well
be known in public for his rhetorical performances. No one is known of
exactly this name, but it has been suggested that Heliodorus is the name
given by Horace to Apollodorus, the teacher chosen by Julius Caesar for
his great-nephew who became Octavian, then Augustus. (It would be
impossible to fit 'Apollodorus' into the hexameter metre of the poem, but
'Helio-' could be a punning alternative for 'Apollo-' given that Helios is the
sun, as is Apollo under his other name Phoebus.)

Maecenas: Octavian's close associate since at least 44 BC, Horace's patron
and benefactor. On his many-sided character, see pp 68–9.

Cocceius: one of two brothers who both held the consulship in 39 and who
both appear to have been on good terms with Antony as well as Octavian.

Fonteius Capito: an officer on Antony's staff in Asia. After the date of this
journey he would be appointed to escort Cleopatra from Egypt to Syria and
later hold the consulship in 33.

Plotius and Varius: mentioned in *Satires* 1.10.81 among those whose
opinion Horace most values. Varius was himself a distinguished poet: a
writer of vigorous epic and of a famous tragedy, *Thyestes*. After Virgil's
death in 19 BC Varius and Plotius were commissioned to present the not-
yet-completed *Aeneid* for publication.

Virgil: the friend to whom Horace is chiefly grateful for his introduction to
Maecenas (*Satires* 1.6.55). At this time he is known only for the *Eclogues*.
The *Georgics* follow in about 29 BC and the *Aeneid* in 19.

---

lodgings, providers the lodgings are government guest-houses where officials on
public business may stay. Local residents ('providers') have the duty of supplying basic
necessities.

Caudium the locality famous for one of the most disastrous defeats ever suffered by a
Roman army: 'the Caudine Forks' in 321 BC during the war against the Samnites.

Now in brief song
please tell, my Muse, **the clown Sarmentus' fight
with Messius Cicirrus**: with what ancestry they **came
to question**. Messius' is glorious **Oscan** stock,
Sarmentus' owner's living. With this parentage   55
they joined the fray. Sarmentus first: 'You are, I claim,
like a wild horse.' We laugh; and Messius says
'Just so', and shakes his head. '**That horn**! Had they
not cut it from your forehead, how would you now
be acting, if so fierce when maimed?' His brow, deep scarred,   60
made hideous the left side of his bristling face.
Jesting much at his looks, at **the Campanian plague**,
'Please dance for us,' he said, '**the shepherd Cyclops**.
You need no **mask**, you need no tragic **buskins**.'

---

the clown Sarmentus' fight / with Messius Cicirrus this absurd contest between two nonentities is presented with the pomp of an epic battle: the address to the Muse, the reference to ancestry, and the formal character of the duel, with each attacking in turn, as Homeric heroes take turns to throw their spears. 'Clown' represents the Latin *scurra*, a person invited to an entertainment in order to make jokes at the expense of the guests, and even of the host when he's drunk, according to *Satires* **1.4.88** (p. 25).

came to question 'came to battle' would be epic language; the Latin here suggests 'litigation', which creates bathos.

Oscan Oscans or Opici were ancient inhabitants of many areas of southern Italy. The adjective seems to have been used as synonymous with 'stupid' (Aulus Gellius, *Attic Nights* 2.21.4), so that 'glorious Oscan stock' is an oxymoron.

like a wild horse a fragment of Lucilius (3.109–10, Warmington) suggests that there was a similar contest in the *Sicilian Journey*: two Capuan gladiators are abusing each other, and one says of the other: 'this fellow is an Ethiopian rhinoceros with his sticking-out teeth'. See the note on line 77 for the sort of comparison Horace may be inviting with Lucilius.

That horn so Messius is an unhorned unicorn.

the Campanian plague nobody knows what this is. Guesses are (a) large warts, thus Messius's scar indicates their removal; (b) something associated with the Cyclops, perhaps sexual aggression.

the shepherd Cyclops according to Homer, Odysseus was imprisoned in a cave by the one-eyed shepherd-giant Cyclops. This Cyclops had an erotic role in other stories which associated him with the sea-nymph Galatea. A character in Aristophanes' play *Wealth* (line 290) pretends to be the Cyclops performing a merrily obscene dance with his flock.

mask, buskins the suggestion is that the Cyclops will be dancing a role from a satyr play, in which, as distinct from comedy, the cast wore tragic gear: mask and high boot. As it happens, the only fully surviving satyr play is *Cyclops* by Euripides.

Cicirrus spoke at length. 'Your **chain**, have you given it,   65
as promised, to the **Lar? Clerk** you may be,
but still your **mistress' rights** are valid. Why,' he asked,
'did you ever **run away**? A single **pound
of grain** for one so thin, so stunted, is enough.'
Oh yes, we made that dinner long and merry.   70
Then straight for Beneventum where our bustling host,
turning some skinny thrushes, was all but roasted with them.
The fire fell in; and spreading o'er the cookhouse old
the flames made haste to taste the lofty roof above.
Then could you see the feasters and their fear-struck slaves   75
grabbing the food with greed, eager to douse the blaze.
Now the familiar summits of **Apulia**
showed me themselves, scorched by **Atabulus**. From there
we'd barely crawled away, when lodgings near **Trivícum**
received us, though with smoke to make one weep,   80
as soaking wood and leaves burned in the stove.

chain, Lar, Clerk, mistress' rights, run away, pound of grain Sarmentus, we are told, had been an Etruscan slave whose master, a republican, had been killed after the battle of Philippi. Maecenas had acquired him, freed him and made him a treasury clerk. Messius pretends that Sarmentus has never been properly freed. 'Mistress' refers presumably to his dead former owner's wife. The chain is a sign of his servitude, which he might dedicate to the household god (*Lar*) on liberation, as tradesmen dedicated the tools of their craft. Not having been properly set free, he will not have done this. So how does he now pass for free? Because he ran away. But he had no need to run away: he's so puny that a slave's rations (a pound of grain) would keep him well. It is curious that Sarmentus' story is so like Horace's own, even down to his size: Augustus called Horace 'lovable midget' (Suetonius, *Life of Horace*).

Apulia, Atabulus the south-eastern corner of Italy, on the northern border of which was Horace's home town of Venusia. Apulians evidently gave the name Atabulus to the Sirocco, the scorching summer wind from the south. The journey through the mountains is a feature of Lucilius' poem (102–5, Warmington):

> But this was all a game of up and down,
> all up and down, I say, and fun and games.
> But to Setinum when we came, O that was hard:
> crags goat-abandoned, Etnas all and Athoses.
> ('goat-abandoned' is a Greek word in Lucilius.)

Horace gets the hardship of the mountains into two and a half lines, and in those lines he includes his own memories of the landscape. Lucilius is rambling and repetitive and in Horace's view, self-indulgent in the inclusion of Greek words. (See *Satires* 1.10.1: 'Did I not say Lucilius' verse was uncontrolled?'; in lines 20–1 of the same poem a supporter of Lucilius says: 'He did great things by mixing Greek with Latin', to which Horace answers: 'How slow you are to learn! You think it difficult, when Rhodian Pitholeon – presumably some hack – did the same?') For Quintilian's comment, see *Satires* **1.4.11n**, p. 20.

Trivicum there is a modern Trevico, 25 miles from Benevento.

Here, like an utter fool, I waited half the night
for a deceitful girl, till sleep assailed me, still
tensed up for love. Then dreams obscene to see
stained my nightdress and stomach as I lay face up.   85
From here by coach for four and twenty miles we sped
towards a town **whose name's unsayable in verse**
though easy to suggest: you can buy water here
dirt cheap, the bread's superb. The traveller
who's canny takes an extra sackful for the road.   90
Canusium's bread is stony; while in water the place once built
by mighty **Diomede**'s no richer by a jug.
Here Varius left us, he distressed, his friends in tears.
Then we reached Rubi, worn from travelling far
on unsound roads made rougher by much rain.   95
Next morning skies were fairer, roads were worse, until
the walls of fishy Bari. Now came Gnatia, built
despite the Water-Nymphs. It offered mirth and fun,
longing to prove that **incense** on the sacred steps
will melt flame-free. **Apella** can believe, **the Jew**,   100
not I. I've learned that **gods live life untroubled**,
and natural phenomena are not the gods
hurling things down from **heaven's high roof** in rage.
Long scroll, long road. Both end at Brindisi.

---

whose name's unsayable in verse   and unsayable it must remain, in verse or prose, since no one has found a town in the area which cannot be accommodated somehow in a Horatian line.

Diomede   often called 'Diomedes'. One of the greatest fighters on the Greek side in the Trojan war. Abandoning his home in Argos after the war because of his wife's unfaithfulness, he is said to have settled in Apulia.

despite the Water-Nymphs   evidently the water-nymphs disapproved of the foundation of Gnatia, and ensured that it had a poor water supply.

incense   a local miracle, like the blood of St Januarius in Naples, which is still believed to liquefy spontaneously on his feast day.

Apella, the Jew   Apella is a name frequently used for freed Jewish slaves, perhaps used here because by a Greek/Latin pun it can be made to mean 'skinless', i.e. circumcised (compare *Satires* **1.9.70**, p. 70). The suggestion is that Jews were naturally credulous and superstitious.

gods live life untroubled   Horace is here in Epicurean mode. Epicureans believed that *if* there were gods, they lived in a remote heaven and took no interest in human affairs.

heaven's high roof   the picture of the gods hurling things from the roof must derive from the theatre, where gods were likely to appear either on the 'machine', a sort of crane, or on the 'god-walk' above the stage building. The picture is decidedly and deliberately comic.

1 The Sarmentus–Messius episode (lines 51–70) is the longest one in the satire. In his edition, Michael Brown comments on line 70 that 'the heavy rhythm seems to belie the enjoyment claimed and suggests a degree of irony in the assertion'. The translation cannot bring over that 'heaviness', but the comment encourages this question: does Horace really want us to think he found that dinner 'long and merry'?

2 How much is this satire literary exercise and how much autobiography? (Fraenkel, pp. 105–9, has an interesting passage on the topic.)

3 To judge from the names of the people taking part in it, this was a very important mission. Consider the aspects of the journey upon which Horace concentrates our attention. Do they give a picture of a group of people engaged in an important and urgent enterprise? If not, what impression do they give? And why do you think Horace deals with the journey in this way?

4 How is the spirit of friendship communicated?

5 'This poem is about "them and us". The "us" is the elite group around Maecenas, the group which Horace wishes to impress so that he will be included in it' (Braund, *The Roman Satirists*, p. 23). Does this fairly convey the spirit of the poem?

6 Consider stories of journeys in the modern world as told by others and perhaps by yourself. Is Horace's approach similar?

Satires 1.9

Horace describes a morning walk interrupted by a man who presumes on a slight acquaintance to inflict himself on the poet and engage him with unwanted conversation. In this he finally reveals his real motive: to use Horace's influence to insinuate himself into Maecenas' circle. The satire does at least three things: it presents Horace's view of Maecenas' circle, it presents the Pest as an instance of the self-seeking ambition which is the object of Horace's satire in other poems, and it presents the poet himself in an ironically comical light, as incapable of dealing with this infuriating individual. Of these, only the second comes under the heading of what 'satire' suggests in English.

Walking one day, as usual, down the **Sacred Street**,
planning a verse or two, wrapped up in them, I find
a man in front of me. I know his name – that's all.
He grabs my hand: 'How are you, dear old thing?'
'**Fine as it is,**' I say. '**I'm at your bidding.**'   5

Sacred Street   the Via Sacra, the road which runs through the Forum and up to the base of the Capitol (see map, p. 4).

Fine as it is, I'm at your bidding, Nothing more then?   these are all formulae of polite dismissal, which would make it clear to the Pest, if he were listening, that he was not wanted.

'My ears droop down, just like a stubborn donkey' (Satires 1.9.20).

He follows. I open: '**Nothing more then?**' He
says 'You should know me. I'm **a man of taste**.' 'Then good
for you,' say I, and, desperate to escape,
I walk at speed. I stop. I whisper rubbish
into my servant's ear, while sweat runs down   10
soaking my heels. 'Lucky **Bolanus** with
his temper-fits,' I mutter. He rabbits on:
'How good the city looks! The streets as well!'
I wouldn't speak. 'You're dying,' he said, 'to get away.
I saw straight off. It's no good. I'll hang on.   15
From here I'll follow all the way.' 'No need
to drag you round. I'm on a call. No one you know.
He's ill. It's miles across the river, at **Caesar's Park**.'
'I'm free just now and not a slouch. Go on. I'll follow.'
My ears droop down, just like a stubborn donkey   20
loaded too heavy. Off he goes again:
'I know myself: you'll find no better friend
in Viscus or in Varius. No one can write

---

a man of taste   Horace uses the adjective *doctus*. Literally meaning 'learned', the word
was used by poets and others of the period to describe themselves as having absorbed
the universal Greek literary tradition and therefore being able to carry it on. It conveys
the idea 'member of the cultivated in-group'.

Bolanus   an otherwise unknown choleric gentleman.

Caesar's Park   by his will Julius Caesar left to the Roman people his estate on the
Janiculan hill (see map, p. 4) as a public park. Walking there would involve going through
some of the more disreputable parts of the city. But the Pest is not to be put off.

in Viscus or in Varius   in *Satires* 1.10.81–6 Horace gives a list of those whose criticism he
seriously values, among whom are Varius and 'the two Viscuses'. The Pest has evidently
done his homework on Horace.

more lines than me in fewer minutes. No one can dance
more sexily. My singing voice might well   25
attract the envy of **Hermogenes.**'
I took my chance, broke in: 'D'you have a mother,
a family, who need you safe?' 'No one at all.
All buried.' 'Lucky them! Now it's just me.
Finish me. **That grim fate** I see, by Sabine crone   30
on **shaken urn** foretold me in my boyhood.
"Him shall no poison nor the foeman's brand destroy,
nor cough, nor heart attack, nor tardy gout.
A chatterbox shall one day end him. Those who talk,
if wise, let him avoid, when riper years shall come."'   35
Here now was Vesta's, with the **fourth part of the day**
now done. He was, it happened, **pledged to be
in court,** or failing that, to lose his case.
'Here, be a friend,' he says, 'and help.' 'Damn me, but I'm
too weak to stand, too ignorant of the law,   40
and, you know, in a rush.' 'I can't decide,' he says.

---

more lines than me in fewer minutes   mere fluency of writing is not an important ability in Horace's eyes. In *Satires* **1.4.9–16** (p. 20), both Lucilius and Crispinus are scolded for boasting of it.

Hermogenes   mentioned in *Satires* 1.10.80 as a member of a group utterly alien to Horace and his friends, and in 1.3.129 as a singer who, for the purposes of the argument there, is best when he is silent. The Pest has condemned himself by the very three points he hoped to use in his own favour.

That grim fate   Horace launches into oracular solemnity of language in describing the prophecy he claims to have received. 'Chatterbox' (line 34) in this context marks an abrupt bathos.

shaken urn   the urn would contain slips which, shaken out at random, would indicate to the fortune-teller what to prophesy.

Here now was Vesta's   Horace could have said 'we arrived at …', but he seems to avoid using 'we' to refer to himself and the Pest – in order, no doubt, to emphasize that they are not a pair. They had reached the temple of Vesta, the little round temple at the south-east end of the Forum (see map, p. 4). (Horace omits the word 'Temple' as we would say simply 'St Paul's'.) It sounds as if Horace had been walking towards the Forum down the Via Sacra from where it began on the slope known as Carinae – 'The Keels'. This at least is consistent with his claim to have been heading for the Janiculan.

the fourth part of the day   i.e. three hours of the 12 daylight hours had passed, making it about 9 a.m. Horace has got up early today, judging by *Satires* 1.6.121, where he says he usually stays in bed till 10.

pledged to be / in court   the Pest had perhaps made a tactical error in arriving in the Forum at just this moment. The third hour (9 a.m.) was the moment for legal business to begin, and the Forum would be the venue. But he is not deterred.

'Drop you, or drop my case?' 'Me, please.' 'I won't.'
And off he sets, **in front**. To fight a winner
is hard. I follow. 'You and Maecenas: how is it?'
he starts. 'A man of few friends. Pretty sound.   45
At taking chances, no one better. You'd get
a stout supporter, a good junior partner
by bringing this one in. Blow me, if you wouldn't
get rid of everyone.' 'That's not the way we live,
the way you think. There's not a house more clean,   50
more free of such corruption. I don't suffer
if one is richer, one **more learned**. Each one has
his place.' '**That sounds amazing, hard to credit.**' 'But
that's it.' 'You spur me on. I'm anxious all the more
to get in close.' 'Just want it, be the man you are.   55
You'll conquer. He's content to lose, and so
makes first approaches hard.' 'I'll do my best.
I'll bribe his slaves with presents. If today
I'm kept away, I won't give up. I'll find a time.
I'll cross his path, I'll join his train. **There's naught**   60
Life gives to mortals free of toil.' Just then up comes
Aristius Fuscus, a dear friend, who knew my man
clearly. We stop. 'You're on your way – **where from,**
where to?' he asks, and answers. I began to tweak
his unresponsive arms, to shake my head,   65
to roll my eyes: 'Help! Help!' With ill-timed humour
he laughed, looked blank. I seethed with scalding rage.
'You surely said you'd something private to discuss.'
'Yes, I remember. But I'll find a better time.

---

in front   no longer following, as in line 6. Horace is losing, as he immediately acknowledges (line 43).

more learned   the adjective is again *doctus*: 'a member of the cultural elite'.

That sounds amazing, hard to credit   the Pest simply assumes that all social relations are governed by the spirit of self-seeking competitiveness.

There's naught / Life gives to mortals free of toil   Horace is adept at putting high-sounding precepts into the mouths of very unsuitable speakers. *Epode* 2 is a long hymn to the delights of the simple country life. It is only in the last four lines that it is revealed that the speaker is a moneylender about to collect his profits.

Aristius Fuscus   another of the group from *Satires* 1.10.81–5 upon whose judgement Horace relies. An ancient commentator describes him as 'the foremost schoolteacher of his time'. A famous ode is dedicated to him (**1.22**, pp. 136–8); in *Epistles* 1.10.3 Horace describes him as 'almost my twin brother'.

where from, where to?   a routine casual greeting.

Today's **the thirtieth sabbath**. Do you want   70
to fart at **the bob-tailed Jews?**' 'I've no objection.'
'Ah, but I have. I'm not too well. Just one
among the crowd. I'm sorry. Another time.' To think
so black a day had dawned! The wretch runs off, and leaves me
under the knife. But luck puts in my way   75
the adversary. 'Where are you off to, villain?'
he cries. 'Will you be my witness?' I most gladly **offered**
my ear. Then off to court. Shouting to right and left.
Running in all directions. **Thus did Apollo save me.**

---

1   Is this a well-constructed story?

2   Horace wants to keep the Pest out of Maecenas' circle. Is he selfishly trying to stop another man doing what he had done himself?

3   J. D. Cloud (in Braund, *Satire and Society*, pp. 65–7) discusses Horace's use of the law in this satire. In failing to appear in court (line 42), the Pest has made his own defeat inevitable, so that there is in strict law no need for the arrest at the end. However, in placing the legal issue at the exact halfway point of the poem, Horace indicates that he wants it to play a structural part of the poem, and is preparing for the arrest scene. We are at liberty to invent a rational explanation for this. The law also serves as the symbol of proper conduct, and therefore rescues Horace, who represents that proper conduct.

    Do you agree with this assessment? Is it to take the poem too seriously?

4   What can we learn from this poem about proper and improper attitudes to friendship, as they are viewed by Horace?

5   What type of *persona* is the narrator adopting in this poem?

---

the thirtieth sabbath, the bob-tailed Jews   there was a large Jewish community in Rome, favoured by both Caesar, who exempted synagogues from the general prohibition on private assemblies, and Augustus. Some scholars have believed that Fuscus had a particular Jewish occasion in mind here, but in the context it is much more likely that he is made to use half-understood terms as a form of mumbo-jumbo to frustrate Horace. 'Bob-tailed' is an allusion to circumcision.

under the knife   i.e. a sacrificial victim.

offered my ear   an ancient formal procedure. If a litigant claims the right to summon another party into court, and the other party refuses to come, he is entitled to seize him and invite a bystander to witness the arrest. The agreement to witness is indicated by the litigant touching the tip of the bystander's ear.

Thus did Apollo save me   the satire ends with a reference to a battle scene from the *Iliad* (20.443) where Apollo rescues Hector from Achilles. In *Odes* **2.7.13** (p. 116) Mercury did the same for Horace at Philippi. Lucilius had used this tag but in Greek (267, Warmington); Horace, disapproving of bilingual texts (*Satires* 1.10.20–30), translates. He had also begun this satire with a reference to Lucilius (258, Warmington).

Satires 2

In the second book, the subject of the first satire is once again satire itself. As landowner now and established friend of the great, Horace finds his circumstances changed. His focus changes too. His friends will defend him from malicious attack, and if there should be a problem with the law, Caesar (Octavian) will stand up for him. In *Satires* 2.2–4 Horace is not the main speaker: different approaches to life are put (for approval or mockery) by different speakers. In *Satires* 2.5, most unexpectedly, Tiresias the blind prophet appears, giving Ulysses cynical advice from a Roman context about how to recover his fortunes.

Satires 2.6

This is one of Horace's best-known poems, containing at the end the fable of the Town and Country Mouse.

Its dramatic date can be fixed with fair certainty to 31–30 BC. In 31 Octavian sent back to Italy many of the soldiers who had fought (on each side) at the battle of Actium. Such retired soldiers were normally given land to cultivate. Lines 55–6 reflect public anxiety about where these settlements were to be made.

The poem starts and ends in the country, in fact at the country estate which the poet acquired in the mid-30s BC, probably with the help of Maecenas. He uses it to present several contrasting ideas: town/country; discontent/content; riches/poverty.

Remains of an elegant room at the villa which may well have been Horace's (Epistles *1.14.3; 16.5–7).*

2.6.1–70   For this I prayed: a piece of land – but not that big;
a garden there, and near the house a constant spring;
some little wood above. More generously and better
the gods have given. I thank them. I ask no more,
O son of Maia, but that you make these gifts my own.   5
If I have not by bad means made my wealth
the greater, nor will by **folly** make it less;
if I don't fall for this: 'That nick of land –
it makes the estate untidy – O that I had it!'
or 'May some chance present me a pot of silver',   10
like the hired hand who found the treasure,
bought the land, farmed it, by Hercules' smile
enriched! If present goods content me, this I pray:
'**Fatten the master's flock and all he has, except
his wit**, and be, as you are, my constant guardian.'   15

So, when I'm free of town, in my hill-fortress,
on what shall I make the muse of **flatfoot satire** shine?
No killing social round, no **wind from Africa**,
no fever season (**Libitina**'s goldmine) here.
Father of Morning – or do you prefer the name   20
Janus? – from you men start their daily tasks'
beginnings, as the gods will: you now shall be my song's
prelude. In Rome you hustle me **to court**: 'Come on!

O son of Maia   the son of Maia is the god Mercury, who under his Greek name Hermes is the bringer of good fortune. In *Odes* 2.17.29 Horace refers to himself as 'one of Mercury's men', and in **2.7.13–14** (p. 116), he speaks of Mercury as having rescued him from battle.

folly   Horace himself uses two words here, one indicating a practical failing (ineptitude for agricultural matters) and the other a moral one (squandering of wealth: luxury).

Fatten the master's flock and all he has, except / his wit   slender wit was a poetic ideal of Callimachus, on whom see Introduction, p. 6.

flatfoot satire   Horace's name for his own satires is 'conversation', which is distinguished from verse (*Satires* **1.4.39–62**, pp. 21–3).

wind from Africa   making the late summer climate unbearable.

Libitina   the goddess of funerals. At her shrine was kept the equipment of the undertakers, from hire of which the goddess apparently received a profit.

Janus   the god of beginnings, mentioned first at sacrifices, the god of the New Year ('January').

beginnings   the word is redundant in the Latin, as here. Horace evidently wants to make a special point of 'starting'.

to court   Horace imagines himself as faced with one of the basic duties: to appear in court on behalf of a friend and offer a financial guarantee that his friend will appear on the day appointed for a hearing. In 'the worse for me' (line 27) he imagines that he will find himself losing the money he has deposited.

Hurry, or you'll be the one who's slow to keep a promise!'
The north wind scours the land, midwinter **hauls**   25
the snowy day along the inside track. I have to go.
'Speak loud and clear' I'm told. I do – the worse for me.
Then I've to fight the crowd, tread on slowcoaches' heels.
'Hey, madman, what's up? What do you want?' I'm rudely hailed,
angrily cursed. 'You'd trample on everything in your way.   30
Run along to Maecenas. Show him what a good boy you are.'
This I like. This tastes good, it does. But when I reach
the shadowy Esquiline, a pack of other men's affairs
leaps at my head and sides. 'Be there by seven
tomorrow morning at **the Well** for Roscius.'   35
'**The Clerks** request: be back in town, Quintus, today,
on urgent College business: don't forget.'
'See to it that Maecenas signs these papers.'
'I'll try.' 'You want? You can,' he says, and won't give up.

Seven passing years have almost turned to eight   40
since first Maecenas made me one of his own,
just one of the crowd he'd have as a carriage-mate
when on the road, or share such trifling secrets
as 'What's the time?' 'Will **Thracian Chick** give **Syrus** a fight?'
'This morning chill is nippy if you don't watch out:'   45
things you can safely drop in a leaky ear.
And daily, hourly, ever since, **our fellow**'s been

---

hauls / the snowy day along the inside track   it is as if, as winter approaches, the sun goes round in smaller and smaller concentric circles like a charioteer switching successively from outer to inner lanes one after another on a racetrack.

the shadowy Esquiline   Maecenas had recently built himself a fine mansion on the Esquiline hill, in an area previously used for burying criminals and the poor (see map, p. 4).

the Well   it is not known who Roscius is or what his business was, but there is some evidence that the *Puteal Libonis* (Libo's Well) in the Forum was a meeting place for moneylenders.

The Clerks   some time after his return from Philippi, Horace had been appointed a member of the Treasury Clerks, a 'college' with partly administrative and partly social commitments.

Seven passing years have almost turned to eight   an important line for Horatian chronology. The references to land-allocation in lines 55–6 set the dramatic date of the poem in late 31–30 (see p. 42), thus placing the beginning of Horace's friendship with Maecenas in 38–37, in time for the historical circumstances of the journey to Brundisium.

Thracian Chick, Syrus   gladiators' names or nicknames. 'Thracian' refers to a type of gladiator with scimitar and small shield.

our fellow   with ironic modesty Horace refers to himself in the third person.

more plagued by spite. He's watched the games with **him**,
played on the Campus: 'Who's the lucky one?' they say.
An icy rumour creeps from the **Rostra** round the lanes.   50
They want a statement, all I meet: 'Oh sir,
you must know this, you spend your time in **Heaven**:
what news from **Dacia**?' 'None I've heard.' 'Oh come,
you're always teasing.' 'Damn me if I know
a thing.' 'Well, farms for the troops: will Caesar keep his word   55
in land from **the Triangle** or from Italy?'
I'm ignorant and swear it. They're amazed: 'On earth
there's not a single man can hold his tongue so tight.'
Meanwhile – poor me – the day goes wasted, as I pray
'My country home, when shall I see you? Will I ever   60
in **reading**, sleep and long inactive hours,
drink sweet oblivion of this life of trouble?
When will **the bean, Pythagoras' kin**,
and cabbage be set before me, bacon-greased?
O heavenly evenings, heavenly feasts! when I with mine   65

---

him   i.e. Maecenas.

played on the Campus   the Campus Martius is the flat ground in the bend of the Tiber (see map, p. 4), increasingly being taken up by various public buildings at this time, but still also used for outdoor exercise.

Rostra   the platform outside the Senate House in the Forum from which political announcements were made.

Heaven   the envious word which Horace's questioner uses to refer to his close acquaintance with the ruling elite.

Dacia   an area of modern Hungary whose people were beginning to come within the Roman sphere of interest, and therefore to be regarded as a potential threat. There were campaigns in their general area in the early 20s BC.

the Triangle   a nickname for the island of Sicily. The anxiety about this question was real. There had been many such settlements in Italy over the past 12 years, often involving confiscation of land and much violent disturbance. Virgil's *Eclogues* 1 and 9 contain moving descriptions of the consequent distress.

reading   Horace's phrase is 'in the books of the old ones' which effectively means 'reading the classics' – but this would give a false impression.

the bean, Pythagoras' kin   a complicated sideswipe at Pythagorean attitudes. In the fifth century BC the Greek philosopher Pythagoras founded a school whose members believed in the transmigration of souls. They were vegetarians and disapproved also of eating beans. One justification for vegetarianism is that one avoids eating animals because they contain the spirits of those who are to be or have been humans. Horace implies that it follows from this that beans must also be potential humans and therefore 'Pythagoras' kin'. There is a little more than a cheap joke here, in that throughout the *Satires* Horace is mocking of those who carry religious and philosophical doctrines to extremes.

sit down before **my Lar**, feeding **the skittish boys**
on what I've tasted. Suiting his whim, each guest
drains cups not predetermined, unconstrained
by senseless rules. Hard-headed, one drinks strong;
one is content to mellow slowly.

> 1   Lines 1–15. To be satisfied with what you have is one of the pillars of
> contentment for the Epicurean. How many different ways of displaying
> discontent does Horace show in these lines?
>
> 2   In Horace's scheme, what are the contrasting features of 'City' and 'Country'?
> Does this have any bearing on Horace's relationship with Maecenas?
>
> 3   The topics chosen for serious discussion include ideas which would interest
> several of the contemporary philosophical schools (see Introduction, pp. 6–8).
> What would you regard as a profitable after-dinner conversation, and would it
> be entertaining?

2.6.70–117   Then   70
there's talk, not 'What do others own in land or town?'
not Lepos as dancer: good or bad? but things
we need to know and shouldn't ignore: 'Do men
find happiness in riches or in virtue?'
or 'What makes friends? shared interests or principles?'   75
and 'What is the Good, its nature and its aim?'
Cervius my neighbour's rambling on with old wives' tales
but not ineptly. If one tries to praise
Arellius' troubled wealth, he starts:
                                                        'I'm told
a country mouse once to his humble den   80
welcomed a town mouse, two old friends together.
Thrifty, tight-fisted, still he could relax
his meanness for a friend. Yes – he was liberal
with hoarded chickpea and with bearded oat.
He brought by mouth dry raisins, half-chewed bits   85
of bacon, longing by choice of fare to quell his friend's
disdain, whose proud tooth barely touched each dish,
while he, the master, stretched out on fresh chaff,

---

my Lar the household god, protector of Horace and his people.

the skittish boys Horace's word here is *verna*, used of a slave who has been born and
brought up in the same household. Such slaves traditionally felt, and were regarded
as, more securely part of the family than other slaves, and could therefore take greater
liberties.

ate **emmer and darnel**, leaving the better dishes.
At last said Town Mouse: "Where's the joy, my dear,   90
in living – surviving – on a forest cliff?
Why not choose people, towns, before the wild, the woods?
Trust me. Let's hit the road. All things on earth
have as their portion mortal souls, nor is there any
escape from doom for great or small. So now, my friend,   95
live pleasantly, be happy, while you can.
Think on the brevity of life." These words convinced
the rustic. Out from home he lightly leapt.
Then both went on their purposed way, resolved
to creep in darkness to the city walls. Now Night   100
held the mid-vault of heaven, and they together
set foot within a wealthy mansion, where
with crimson drapes the ivory couch blush'd bright,
and there, piled high in baskets, quantities
uneaten from the evening's lavish feast.   105
He settled the rustic in his place, stretched out
in purple robes, and played the bustling host.
Dish after dish he brought, and like a butler
did all the needful, tasting whatever he offered.
His friend, ensconced, glad at his altered lot,   110
acted the merry feaster, till with sudden shock
doors crashing open struck them from their couch.
Throughout the hall they scurry, panicking
with yet more frantic terror when the roof resounds
with monstrous **dogs**. Then said the rustic: "I don't need   115
this kind of life. Goodbye. My den, my woods,
risk-free, will make me happy on plain vetch."'

---

emmer and darnel   emmer is an unproductive form of wheat, darnel a 'false wheat'
which grows as a weed in wheat fields.

dogs   Horace names the breed: Molossians – the Rottweilers of the ancient dog world.

1 Compare the country mouse's diet in these lines with Horace's preferred diet in lines 63–4. What point might Horace be making?

2 Sometimes Horace invites us to treat the mice as human beings like ourselves, and sometimes he invites us to see them as little creatures. What use does he make of these two perspectives?

3 In the fable Horace switches easily between a conversational and a grand or formal style. The translation makes an effort to reproduce these switches. Where do they occur and why?

4 To what in Aesop (see below) do the dogs in Horace (lines 114–15) correspond? Why has Horace made the change?

5 Does the story have a happy ending?

6 The story is told by Cervius (line 77). Does this affect our attitude to it?

Aesop's version of the tale of the two mice

Two mice, one a country mouse, one a house mouse, began to live their lives together. The house mouse went first to dine with the other in high summer. Munching grain and roots mixed with clods he said, 'You are living the long-suffering life of an ant. But I have lots of good things. Compared with you I am living in a horn of plenty. If you come with me, you'll live a life of all the luxury you want.' Convincing the other, he took him with him to the house. He showed him wheat-grain and barley and pulse and figs and honey and dates. The country mouse was delighted and relaxed. The house mouse brought some cheese too, dragging it out of a basket. Someone opened the door. They ran off into a little hole, squashed up against each other and squeaking. Just when they were going to sneak out again and pinch a small dried fig, another person came in to fetch something else. They went back in to hide. The country mouse, though longing for all these things, said, 'Goodbye. Enjoy your wealth and luxury, having it all but being in danger. I will eat plants and roots, and live my life frugally and without fear.' Moral: that it is better to live a frugal and peaceful life than to suffer fear and danger by living in the lap of luxury.

- Is the moral which is appended to the Aesopic version of the fable relevant to Horace's satire as a whole?

The city/country contrast appears frequently in Roman literature. It is intriguing to see it used not merely for imaginative, or perhaps didactic ends, as Horace does, but for very practical ones, as here where in a speech delivered in 80 BC Cicero uses it as evidence for the innocence of his countryman client Sextus Roscius, charged with the murder of his father. 'Just as you do not find every crop or every tree grow in every soil, so different crimes are products of different ways of life. In the city extravagance is produced; from extravagance arises avarice; from avarice aggression; from aggression is born every type of wickedness and crime. But this country life, which you [i.e. the prosecution] describe as merely boorish, is the very mistress of thrift, industry and honesty' (*For Roscius of Ameria* 75).

It sounds as if Cicero could expect his audience, a jury consisting of senators, to take the rustic ideal with some degree of seriousness.

Satires 2.7

Horace is given a moral lecture by his own slave, Davus. The main theme, 'moral instability', is very similar to those of *Satires* 1.1 and 1.3. But there it was Horace speaking to a general audience of readers, while here it is Horace's slave lecturing Horace, the similarity of subject-matter indicating that here we have Horace paying himself back in his own coin. The lecture is also given a Stoic (see p.7) slant: Horace is the slave of his desires; only the wise man is free.

'A word with you, sir. I've been **listening** some time.
Your slave, sir, slightly anxious.' **Davus**? 'Yes. **A property
wishing its master well**, and honest too, though **not
too good to live**.' Well, **it's December and you have
the freedom** by tradition. Use it and speak up.   5

'Some men rejoice in wickedness and stick to that
determinedly. Some – many – drift, now doing right,
sometimes involved in vice. Take **Priscus** now –

---

listening   listening to what? If the great eighteenth-century Cambridge scholar Richard Bentley is right, Davus has been listening to Horace spouting the previous *Satires*. This would give extra point to his own tirade. The later satirist Juvenal may be worth quoting: 'Am I to spend my whole life listening? Shall I never have the chance to answer back?' (*Satires* 1.1).

Davus   a stock name in comedy for a slave, especially the 'clever slave', who knows, as Davus does, better than his master.

A property / wishing its master well   Horace emphasizes the anonymous, impersonal character of slavery (a) by using a neuter noun for a piece of property, hence 'its'; (b) by having to be reminded of his own slave's name.

not / too good to live   there is a proverbial idea that the good die soon (Ovid, *Amores* 2.6.39: 'It is the best things which are soonest snatched away from us' – of a pet parrot). Davus plays on it with the hint that he is bad in order to survive.

it's December and you have / the freedom   at the festival of the Saturnalia (17–23 December) slaves became temporarily equal with their masters.

Priscus   a not uncommon third name for a Roman citizen, but its holder is unidentifiable.

noted for three rings often, then for a bare left hand.
Quite inconsistent. Changed his stripe from hour to hour.   10
Leaving a great house he'd go straight to where
a decent freedman couldn't get respectably away.
In Rome, seducer; then he'd rather live as scholar
in Athens. He was born under the sign Caprice.
The sponge Volanerius saw well-earned gout   15
destroy his knuckles, so he hired a boy
to pick the dice and put them in the box,
paying him by the day. In sticking to one vice
he was much less unhappy, better off than he
who strains now at a slack, now at a tautened rope.'   20

And where's this rubbish heading, rascal? Won't you say
right now? 'At you, sir.' Villain, how? 'You praise
the plebs of old, their luck, their character, and then
suppose some god said "Be like that", "No!" you'd say, "No!" –

---

noted   the Latin implies 'noted in disapproval'.

three rings   one gold ring was the sign of a member of the knights (*equites*, see p. 180n). Crassus (see p. 93) advertised his immense wealth by going so far as to wear two (Isidore, *Origines* 19.32.4). To wear none was to conceal one's proper status.

stripe   on their tunics senators wore a broad purple stripe, knights a narrow one. Other citizens had plain tunics. As with the ring, a change of costume means a change of status, and hence a change in the behaviour which might be expected of a person.

a decent freedman   a freed slave, 'freedman', was in law a citizen, but with limited rights, i.e. one step down from the plain-toga man of the previous note.

He was born under the sign Caprice   a version of Horace's actual words is 'born with all the Vertumni there are against him'. Vertumnus was god of change. Horace multiplies him to suggest Priscus' frequent changes, and 'against him' suggests that the changes were not for the better.

The sponge Volanerius   the Latin word is *scurra*, regularly (*Satires* **1.5.52**, p. 34, 'clown'; line 36 in this piece) used in Horace for the type represented by the *parasite* of comedy: a hanger-on who hopes to scrape a living by finding a wealthy person whom he can amuse and assist. Volanerius is otherwise unknown.

well-earned gout   gout is apparently not associated with over-indulgence until some time after this satire was written (Muecke, on this line). 'Well-earned' therefore suggests that it is a divine response to Volanerius' gambling, which makes Volanerius' offence worse, if he defies the gods by circumventing their punishment.

now at a slack, now at a tautened rope   the reference is unclear. The most vivid idea suggested has been of a pack-animal towing a barge. Davus implies that the slack rope too has its disadvantage – presumably that of the jolt as tension returns.

some god   the idea of the god offering a possibility which is rejected appears also in *Satires* 1.1.15–19 and is another indication of the connection of thought.

either not thinking what you preach is better, 25
or being too feeble to stand by it; stuck, in fact:
you want to get your feet out of the mud, and can't.
At Rome you want the country; there (fickle!) you laud
the city to the skies. Suppose you're not asked anywhere.
You praise **the peaceful cabbage**, and as if you never went 30
out anywhere unless compelled, you say you're lucky, glad
you haven't got to go somewhere and drink a jar. A message comes:
"Maecenas wants your company. Come late, when lamps
are lit." "Buck up, someone, and bring me oil! Is no one
listening to me?" You gibber, shout and run along. 35
The oaths of **Mulvius and the hangers-on** are unrepeatable
as they depart. "I do admit," **he**'ll say, "I'm easily
led by the stomach; my nose goes up at cooking smells.
I'm idle, weak. Just say the word! A greedy-guts!
You're just the same, and worse perhaps. And yet 40
you take the high ground, scold me, use fine words
to wrap your failing in." What if I prove you **stupider**
than me who cost you just **two thousand**? Leave aside
your death-stare. Hold your hand; **restrain your rage**:
I'll tell you what **Crispinus' doorman** taught me. 45

You fancy someone's wife. I like a hooker.
Which of us is more crucifiable? When I'm set up
by nature's urge, by light of lamp some naked girl
accepts a lashing from my swollen tail,
or as I lie back, rides the horse with bouncing bum, 50
then sends me off not shamed nor bothered that
some richer, better-looking guy may piss there too.
When you sneak out, dropping your signs of rank –

---

the peaceful cabbage   compare the menu in *Satires* **2.6.64**, p. 45.

Mulvius and the hangers-on   these are the unfortunate people who have been encouraged by Horace's 'reluctance to go out' to come and scrounge dinner off him.

he   i.e. Mulvius.

stupider   strict Stoic philosophy held that only the wise man is good or happy. 'Stupid' therefore equals 'morally bad'.

two thousand   (sesterces): a typical price for an ordinary slave of poor quality.

restrain your rage   having permitted Davus to speak, Horace, in getting angry, is showing precisely the inconsistency of which he is accused.

Crispinus' doorman   in *Satires* 1.1, Crispinus is a verbose and unintelligent verse-writer. Now Horace has to listen to a lecture deriving not even from Crispinus but from one of his underlings!

'Shut in some foul box where, knowing her mistress' crime, the slave-girl shoves you' (Satires 2.7.59-60). Bryn Terfel as Falstaff in the laundry-basket from Verdi's Falstaff, *based on Shakespeare's* Merry Wives of Windsor.

your ring as Knight, your Roman dress – **not juryman
but rotten Dama**, scented hair hid in a cloak,   55
are you not what you seem? You're scared. She lets you in.
You're shivering deep down with lust and fear by turns.
It's all one, whether you sell yourself to be scourged with rods
and stabbed to death, or end up shut in some foul box
where, knowing her mistress' crime, the slave-girl shoves you,   60
squashed up and touching head with knees. Where wife offends,
husband has **legal power**, surely, over both?

---

not juryman / but rotten Dama one of the functions of the knights was to act as members of juries. In doing so they were of course expected to represent incorruptible probity, the opposite of what Davus here describes Horace as doing. 'Dama' occurs in legal texts as a typical slave-name. Horace has reduced himself to this.

are you not what you seem i.e. slave not knight.

It's all one in entering on an adulterous liaison, Horace has shown himself willing to accept the worst consequences: at the very least, extreme humiliation. This is much the same as signing himself on as a gladiator, in which case he would have to accept beating or death.

legal power the second-century AD writer Aulus Gellius (*Attic Nights* 10.23.5) quotes the elder Cato from the second century BC: a husband may kill his wife caught in adultery. Horace hints here that the man may suffer the same, indeed deserves worse.

Davus' favourite art (Satires 2.7.95–99). A retiarius (net-fighter) has enveloped his opponent in his net and is about to use his trident on him. Graffito from Pompeii.

More rightly, over the seducer. She at least
sins without change of dress or place, and **underneath**.
And will you knowingly accept the yoke and let   65
a mad thing rule you – property, life, body, name?
You've got away. You're scared, of course. You've learned your lesson.
No. You'll be seeking to submit to fear and ruin
and re-enslavement, yet again. What beast, once free,
will cravenly surrender to the chains it broke?   70
"I'm no adulterer," you say. Nor I a thief, if I've the sense
to keep my hands off silverware. **Remove the risk**,
and wayward nature will run wild, restraint removed.
Are you my master? You, the slave of numberless

---

underneath Seneca (*Epistles* 95.21) suggests that anything other than the missionary position indicated culpable immodesty on the part of a woman.

66 the manuscripts have an extra line here, line 65: 'since the woman fears you and does not trust you as a lover'. No satisfactory way of getting sense in context out of this has yet been found, and the scholar Shackleton Bailey, followed here, decided that it was an interpolation.

a mad thing i.e. lust.

Remove the risk the Stoic Cleanthes (quoted by Muecke) observed 'Whoever longs to do something wicked, but holds back from it, will do it if he gets the opportunity.' Hence Stoics believed that irrational passions should be eliminated. (Compare Matthew 5.28: 'If a man looks on a woman with lust, he has already committed adultery with her in his heart.')

people and circumstances, who, **touched with the rod**   75
three times and four would not be free of abject fear?
Another point, as strong as all I've said: one slave
who serves another is, in your terms, "deputy"
or "fellow-slave". To you, then, what am I? I mean,
you give me orders, being an abject slave yourself,   80
dragged like a puppet, strings in another's hand.
Who then is free? The **wise man**, who commands himself,
fearing not poverty, not death, not chains,
strong to resist desire, despising honours,
and in himself so whole and smooth and rounded   85
that nothing external takes upon that polished shell,
and on him Fortune falls always enfeebled. Now,
can you, in this, see any part that's yours? A woman
demands **five talents**, plagues you, drives you from her door,
soaks you with icy water, summons you back. Shake off   90
the shameful yoke! Say "I am free, yes, free!" You can't.
You have a master in your heart firm, stern and cruel.
You're tired: he goads you; you resist: he drives you hard.
Fool! When you're gaping at a work by **Pausias**,
how is your error less than mine, when I admire   95

---

touched with the rod   the ceremony of giving a slave his freedom involved touching him with a rod (the *festuca*).

wise man   a rather different take on Stoicism is offered by Cicero in *Pro Murena*. Cicero is urging the jury to disregard the speech made by his opponent, the well-known Stoic Cato (on whom see *Odes* **2.1.24**, p. 88):

> Once there was a brilliant man called Zeno. Followers of his principles are called Stoics. This is a general idea of his philosophy. The wise man is never subject to influence and never forgives an offence. Only a fool and a lightweight will ever feel pity. A real man cannot be pacified or made to change his mind. The wise alone are handsome, however deformed, rich, however impoverished, kings, even if in slavery. The rest of us, those who are not wise, they call runaways, exiles, enemies and lunatics. All mistakes are equal, every wrongdoing is a nefarious crime, and it is no less wicked to wring a chicken's neck unnecessarily than to strangle one's father.
>
> (*Pro Murena* 61)

If one reads *Satires* 2.3, one comes away with a similar impression after Horace has been subjected to an ear-bashing from a fanatical convert to Stoicism.

five talents   an outrageous price. In the world of comedy, which Horace here presents, to buy a charming slave-girl outright costs only half a talent (e.g. Plautus, *Mostellaria* 300).

Fool!   on excessive devotion to fine art, see Seneca, *Epistles* 115.8: 'We go mad about pictures and sculpture.'

Pausias   a refined miniaturist of the fourth century BC (Pliny, *Natural History* 35.124).

with straining knees the fights of **Fulvius** or **Rutuba**
and **Pacideianus scrawled** in charcoal or in red,
just like an actual fight: blows, dodges, clash of arms,
and heroes. He's a useless idler, Davus. You
are called a subtle arbiter of ancient art.   100
I'm worthless, lured by baking cakes. Do your
virtue and strength of mind resist a gourmet feast?
Why is it worse for me to follow the belly's call?
My back gets thrashed. But don't you suffer too
from going to hunt for dishes which cost a fortune?   105
You do. Feast after endless feast turns sour,
and feet ill-treated cease to bear the damaged body.
Is the slave wrong, who steals a strigil after dark
and changes it for grapes? Is he who sells estates
to suit his stomach in no way slavish? Then again   110
you can't be on your own an hour, or plan
your leisure. You shun yourself, truant and runaway,
seeking to cheat Anxiety now with wine, now sleep.
In vain. She is the dark companion, following where you flee.'
Get me a stone! 'What for?' Bring me my **arrows**!   115
'The fellow's mad – or writing verse.' Get out! Or else
you'll find yourself **ninth man on the Sabine farm**.

Fulvius, Rutuba, Pacideianus gladiators. The only known name is Pacideianus, who appears in Lucilius (172–5, Warmington).

scrawled as graffiti on walls, as advertisements.

you can't be on your own an hour here Davus returns to the more down-to-earth criticism which he had levelled at Horace in lines 28–35.

arrows very impractical weapons, in the circumstances. But Horace is turning himself into an angry god, like Apollo in *Iliad* 1.43–5.

ninth man on the Sabine farm in his furious reponse to Davus, Horace makes a standard threat to the house-slave, i.e. punishment by being sent out to work on the farm (Plautus, *Mostellaria* 18–19). 'Ninth man' seems to suggest a pecking order where the last man gets all the worst jobs.

1   Davus had obviously prepared his lecture. Imagine that he did not have more than a small scrap of paper to write his most important points on. What did he write?

2   To what extent does the character attacked by Davus seem to be a convincing presentation of Horace himself?

3   Is Davus' advice good? Is it vitiated by the source from which it comes? Does Horace have any respect for Stoicism?

4   Is Horace's reaction consciously that of the people to whom he attempts to justify the writing of satire in *Satires* **1.4** (pp. 19–27)?

5   Davus' language is uninhibited. Is this part of the argument, or does it simply characterize him as a slave? Is it relevant that Horace dates this conversation to the Saturnalia (line 5)?

6   Who are the satirists of our place and time? What do they attack, and how? Does Horace have anything in common with them? Should satirists always take risks? Did Horace?

2 The new Alcaeus: *Odes* 1–4 and *Carmen Saeculare*

After the second book of *Satires*, Horace turned his attention to a different style of verse. Roman poetry existed in almost all the major Greek forms by now: epic (Ennius' *Annals* and other poems); didactic (Lucretius, Virgil's *Georgics*); tragic (Ennius again, Accius and others, including lately Varius, whose *Thyestes*, produced at the games in celebration of Actium, had been rewarded by Octavian with a gift of a million sesterces); comic (Plautus, Terence, etc.); pastoral (Virgil's *Eclogues*). But hardly anything had yet been attempted to challenge the great lyric poets of the sixth century BC: Sappho and Alcaeus of Lesbos, Pindar of Thebes. ('Lyric' poetry is composed in complex and varied metre and organized in stanzas, or groups of stanzas. It is accompanied by instruments and sung. It is appropriate to hymns and celebrations and to the expression of intense personal feelings.)

In the last poem of *Odes* 3, Horace makes this claim: 'I, passing from humble to mighty, / first found for Aeolic song a home / in Italian melodies' (**3.30.12–14**, pp. 67–8). 'Aeolic' because this is the Greek dialect of the north-eastern Aegean, in particular of the island of Lesbos, home of Sappho and Alcaeus. It is their themes – religious, political, military, erotic, romantic, convivial, polemical – which he seeks to reproduce, and their metres he uses. In the generation before Horace, Catullus had composed four lyric poems (11, 34, 51 and the long wedding hymn 61). Horace indicates his respect for these poems by references to them in his own work. But he sets out to do something much more substantial, by creating three whole books in this style, and hoping thereby to have effectively established a whole new genre of Latin poetry. Horace's own word for these poems is 'Song' (*carmen*, a Latin translation of the Greek *ōdē*, which is the origin of the English word), as opposed to 'Iambics' for what we call the *Epodes*, and 'Conversation' (*sermo*) for the *Satires* and *Epistles*.

Horace frequently mentions musical instruments in his poems – lyre, *cithara* (the word is the origin of 'guitar'), *barbiton*, *testudo* (all stringed instruments), *tibiae* (pipes). It is debated whether this is simply a nod to the Greek origin of lyric poetry in songs sung at *symposia*. The question is discussed by Philip Hills (p. 48).

The first three books of *Odes* are likely to have been published in 23 BC (see introduction to *Odes* **1.4**, p. 122), though the dramatic date and very likely the original composition of many of the poems are rather earlier. The earliest dramatic date (late 31 BC for **1.37**, pp. 80–83, the poem referring to the situation in the aftermath of Actium) corresponds roughly with the latest available dramatic date for the *Satires* (**2.6**, p. 42: 31–30 BC, when Maecenas is in charge in Italy while Octavian is in Egypt), suggesting that there was a fairly precise moment when Horace turned to lyric poetry. The *Carmen Saeculare*, a lyric poem for public performance, appeared in 17. *Odes* 4 was published at Augustus' request in 13.

The order in which the poems appear in the manuscripts is not chronological by the date of their dramatic setting. The dramatic order of 3.8, 3.14 and 3.29 is the reverse order. It is unlikely that it is chronological in order of composition. But some principles of order are detectable: see on **1.4** (p. 122) and, for example, on **3.29** and **4.11** (pp. 71, 146). In a small selection such as this to have presented the poems simply in the order they appear would give an impression of randomness. They are therefore grouped, rather artificially, by subject; 'artificially', because there are endless overlaps.

Many of the topics covered by the poems are conventional: hymns, prayers, invitations, congratulations, words of welcome, etc. It was recognized that poetry and rhetoric were closely related activities. There was a huge literature instructing the speaker in how to deal with the requirements of particular situations. Part of Horace's skill lies in the way he treats these conventions, emphasizing one rather than the other and combining them with personal elements. In the introductions and notes to the poems which follow, it has been impossible to deal adequately with this, but some suggestions have been made. A very detailed treatment of the subject is offered by Francis Cairns (pp. 3–33 and throughout the book).

Lyric poetry: *Odes* 1.1, 1.32, 2.19, 3.30

Odes 1.1

Horace begins his collection of *Odes*, as he does with each of his other major works, *Epodes*, *Satires* and *Epistles*, with a dedication to Maecenas (see pp. 68–9).

The poem takes the form of 'some like to do this, some like to do that, but I …'. This is not uncommon in Greek and Latin literature, and has been given the name 'priamel'. (Compare *Odes* 1.7, 4.3; Sappho, Fr. 16; Shakespeare, Sonnet 91.) Almost all the odes are divided into metrical stanzas. This one has an identical metrical form to each line, and no obvious division into equal stanzas. It is presented here in blocks, which will, it is hoped, make the structure clear.

Maecenas, descendant of ancestral kings,
O my defence and my sweet splendour,

some folk delight to raise the dust of Olympia
with speeding chariot, while the turning post,
missed by their scorching wheels, and the palm of glory   5
carry them, lords of the earth, aloft to heaven;

another, if the crowd of fickle Romans
competes to raise him up with threefold honours;
another, if he has stored in his own granary
all that is swept from Libya's threshing floors.   10

The one who's glad to take the mattock and cleave
his father's fields you'd never move by offering
the wealth of Attalus to board a Cyprian boat,

O my defence   the exclamation 'O' sounds oddly in modern English, but in the Latin it is given such striking emphasis that it has been kept as an indication of the intensity with which Horace wishes to express gratitude to his patron.

to raise the dust of Olympia   Pindar, one of Horace's great models in lyric poetry, wrote celebration odes for victories at Olympia, and of these victories the most important was the chariot race. In fact by Horace's own day the chariot race had lost its importance, so for Horace to make it the greatest symbol of sporting victory is itself a gesture of respect to Pindar.

missed   but only just missed. There were millimetres between success and disaster at the turning point in a chariot race: close would save distance, too close would mean a very dangerous accident. It is of course not the turning post which is responsible but *the fact that* the turning post has been missed.

crowd of fickle Romans / competes   for 'Romans' Horace uses a term (*Quirites*) appropriate for the Roman *plebs* in political assembly. 'Fickle' seems to make the same point as 'the weathervane choice of the people' in **3.2.20** (p. 91). Evidently the point is 'some seek political success'.

threefold honours   probably the three successive elective offices a Roman politician needed to achieve on his way to the top: being aedile, praetor and consul.

Libya's threshing floors   Libya was the Graeco-Roman term for the whole of what we call Africa. A huge quantity of grain for the Roman market was produced in Africa, especially in the area which the Romans themselves knew as 'Africa', mainly modern Tunisia.

mattock   the mattock, a heavy hoe with a substantial blade for breaking up difficult ground, is a symbol in Horace for back-breaking manual labour (*Odes* 3.6.38).

Attalus   the name of several kings of Pergamum in the second and third centuries BC. The last of the line, dying in 133 BC, left his kingdom to the Romans. His wealth was proverbial.

Cyprian   an adjective providing exotic detail – but Cyprus was in fact famous for its shipbuilding.

'The turning post [the obelisk on the right], missed by their scorching wheels' (Odes 1.1.4–5). The rider of the single horse has just passed it.

scared sailor, cutting the **Myrtoan sea**.

When the **gale from Africa** fights the **Icarian waves**,   15
the frightened trader commends the life of leisure
and his own home-town's fields; soon he repairs
his shattered ships, not schooled to live in poverty.

One man does not refuse a cup of vintage **Massic**,
and from a full day's work he'll take time off,   20
sprawling now under a green arbutus,
now at the gentle fountainhead of a holy spring.

Myrtoan sea, gale from Africa, Icarian waves 'Myrtoan' is the name for the southern Aegean. We are perhaps at the end of summer, when the waves of the Aegean tend to run north–south under the influence of the famous 'Etesian winds' – today's *meltemi* – but here are troubled further when they meet the south-westerly from Africa. This stretch of sea was much crossed by traffic from the east to Italy: St Paul had a very difficult late-season passage, described in Acts 27. 'Icarian' also adds local colour: Icaria is one of the eastern islands. Its name also reminds us of the fate of Icarus, drowned when the wax of his wings melted and he fell into the sea. (See March, p. 212.)

One man does not refuse Lying comfortably on the grass, cup of wine in hand, is not an activity entirely alien to Horace's poetic persona (see illustration, p. 13).

Massic a wine 'that brings forgetfulness' (*Odes* **2.7.21**, p. 117).

Many take pleasure in army life, where horn and bugle
sound together, and in war, which mothers
curse. Patient under the chilly sky **stays**   25
the hunter, forgetting his tender wife
if his faithful hounds have sighted the hind
or his delicate nets are torn by a **Marsian** boar.

For me, the **ivy which makes the crown for learned brows**
puts me among the gods above; for me, **cool woods**   30
and satyrs with lightly dancing nymphs –
these part me from the crowd, if **Euterpe** does not
silence her pipes nor **Polyhymnia**
shrink from tuning her **Lesbian** lyre.

But if you will put my name among the **Lyric Poets,**   35
my head will soar to strike the stars above.

- How serious is Horace in this ode – in his presentation, and in his purpose?

---

stays   i.e. out all night, which is why the tender wife might mind.

Marsian   the Marsians lived in the wildest part of the Apennines, where even the men were dangerous (*Odes* **3.5.9**, p. 95).

ivy which makes the crown for learned brows   ivy is sacred to Bacchus, god of poetic inspiration. At the end of *Odes* **3.30**, p. 68, Horace will claim a crown of the bay sacred to Apollo, a grander aspiration. 'Learning' (*doctrina*) is an important poetic qualification – the word does not sound quite so stuffy in Latin.

cool woods / and satyrs with lightly dancing nymphs   nymphs and satyrs are members of Bacchus' following and thus part of the poet's imaginative world.

these part me from the crowd   'they make me different', as all the people with particular interests are different from all the others. But he is also alluding to his own wish to appeal to a small and select elite (cf. note on *Satires* **1.9.2**, p. 38).

Euterpe, Polyhymnia, Lesbian   Euterpe and Polyhymnia are two of the nine Muses. At this time there was no generally accepted idea that individual Muses were in charge of individual types of literature. 'Lesbian' refers to Sappho and Alcaeus, both from the island of Lesbos (see introduction to this chapter, p. 57).

Lyric Poets   there was a canon of nine Greek lyric poets established by the scholars of Alexandria. Perhaps Horace aspires to being a tenth.

> ### Another selection of career choices from *Satires* 1.1.1–14
>
> *How is it, Maecenas, that no one, when once his place in life*
> *has come to him by thought or accident, contents*
> *himself with that, but praises those whose aims are different?*
> *'You lucky merchant-venturers!' the soldier says,*
> *worn out with age, limbs broken with endless toil.*   5
> *'No,' says the venturer, tossed in his gale-racked vessel,*
> *'A soldier's life for me. Why so? The battle-lines meet, and then*
> *Within the hour quick death or joy of victory.'*
> *The farmer's praised by the canny man of law*
> *whose client pounds on the door as the cock greets dawn.*   10
> *That farmer, dragged from home to town by a court's summons,*
> *exclaims 'In town alone can the Good Life be lived.'*
> *To finish this topic there's so much to say, it would quite wear out*
> *that chatterer Fabius.*
>
> - In what way is the list in this satire similar to *Odes* **1.1** and in what way different?

Odes 1.32

In this and the following poem Horace is talking about the roots of his own poetry. Both of them take, at some point, the form of a hymn to a god. Each approaches poetry from a rather different direction.

I pray: if, idle in the shade, I have
composed some trifle with you which may last
this year and more, come now,
utter a Latin song,

my **lyre**, first tuned by **Lesbos' citizen**,   5
who, fierce in war, still amid arms
or if he'd tied his **storm-tossed ship**
to the spray-soaked shore,

---

lyre here Horace uses the word *barbiton*; in 13 he uses *testudo*, a tortoiseshell. Mercury invented the lyre by fixing arms, a bridge and strings to a tortoiseshell.

Lesbos' citizen Alcaeus. He lived in the early sixth century BC and took a vigorous part in the political struggles of the island. 'Citizen' is deliberately chosen as reflecting Alcaeus' sense of duty to the community.

storm-tossed ship one of the few poems of Alcaeus which have in significant part survived imagines the poet on board ship in a storm; it is believed that the storm is a metaphor for political turmoil.

sang songs of **Liber**, of the Muses, and
of Venus with **the boy** clinging to her side;
of **Lycus** too, dark-eyed and beautiful
with his dark hair.

10

O lyre, Apollo's glory, bringing joy
to Jupiter's feasts on high; O sweet balm
for troubles, be blessed and give your blessing
whenever I call you **duly**.

15

---

1 If this poem is a hymn, which is the god to whom it is addressed?

2 The following is a prayer traditionally used by Anglican and Catholic Christians:

   Almighty God, who hast given us grace at this time with one accord to make our common supplications unto thee; and dost promise, that when two or three are gathered together in thy Name thou wilt grant their requests: Fulfil now, O Lord, the desires and petitions of thy servants, as may be most expedient for them; granting us in this world knowledge of thy truth, and in the world to come life everlasting.

   Consider on the basis of this and of the Horace poem what rules might be prescribed for the form of address to a divinity.

3 In what respects is Horace acknowledging Alcaeus as a respected predecessor?

Odes 2.19

Bacchus, the Greek Dionysus, is the god of wine, but in wider terms he is god of the inspiration to which wine can give just one sort of access, and god of the music and poetry which flow from that inspiration. (The principal festival of Athenian tragedy was the Great Dionysia, and the plays were performed in the theatre dedicated to Dionysus.) In this poem Horace is talking about his own poetic inspiration, using the language and imagery of his predecessors. For a representative of the type of ode with which Horace is working, compare Sophocles, *Antigone* 1115–52.

Liber the Italian god identified with Bacchus. His name indicates also 'The one who sets free'.

the boy Cupid, her son.

Lycus there is no trace of Lycus and virtually no trace of erotic themes in the surviving poetry of Alcaeus (D. Page, pp. 294–9).

duly or 'in due form'. Roman religion was insistent on rituals being performed with absolute precision.

Bacchus in these notes, he is referred to as either Dionysus or Bacchus interchangeably.

A Maenad, one of the 'Running Nymphs' (Odes 2.19.9). She runs barefoot and her hair is tied up with a snake (line 19). Thyrsus in right hand, leopard brandished in left, she must surely be 'untiring' (line 10).

In far-off rocky mountains I have seen
Bacchus – believe you me, you coming ages –
teaching his songs to the learning Nymphs
and goatfoot Satyrs with their pricked-up ears.

Euhoe! My heart quakes with a sudden terror;   5
my breast is full of the tumultuous joy
of Bacchus: Euhoe, be gentle, Liber,
gentle! I dread the force of your **thyrsus**.

I am empowered to sing of the Running Nymphs,
the Untiring Ones, and of their **well of wine**,   10
their flooding streams of milk; to speak once more
of honey dripping from some hollow trunk;

Euhoe!, thyrsus 'euhoe' is the cry of the Maenads, the ecstatic female followers of Bacchus; the thyrsus is their ivy-tipped staff. To be struck by it could induce inspiration or frenzy. They are 'the Running Nymphs, the Untiring Ones' because in their state of possession they could accomplish impossible feats: see the vase-painting in the illustration above.

well of wine this and the following miraculous events are associated with Bacchic possession – compare Euripides' play *Bacchae* 142: 'The earth flows with milk, wine and the nectar of bees.'

to sing too of that **blessed bride**: how with the stars
her glory was included, how the halls
of **Pentheus** were brought down in cruel ruin,   15
how Thracian **Lycurgus** met his end.

You channel rivers and the inhuman sea.
On distant ridges, drenched with wine,
you bind in viper-knots the hair
of the Bistonian women, with no hurt to them.   20

You, when the impious company of **Giants**
climbed up the steep slope to your father's realm,
forced **Rhoetus** backward, **hideous yourself**
with lion's claw and mouth;

though of you 'better at dancing and at fun   25
and games' they said; nor were you held fit
for fighting – yet in war and peace
alike you took the central part.

---

blessed bride   Ariadne, daughter of King Minos of Crete, who had helped Theseus find his way through the Labyrinth. Theseus took her with him when he left for Athens, but abandoned her on the island of Naxos, where she was found and carried away by Dionysus to become immortal. Her wedding crown was set among the stars – or in some versions she became a star herself.

Pentheus, Lycurgus   two men who came to a bad end for resisting Dionysus and preventing his worship. Pentheus, ruler of Thebes, attempted to imprison Dionysus: the god's power brought the palace walls crashing down (Euripides, *Bacchae* 585–604). The death of Pentheus himself, torn to pieces by the Maenads, is also at the back of our minds. There are several different lurid accounts of the death of Lycurgus, king of the Edonians in Thrace: see March, p. 28.

You   with the word 'You' here and in lines 19, 21 and 29 Horace switches from describing the god to addressing him. The repeated 'yous' are characteristic of hymns.

you bind ... the Bistonian women   Bistonian = Thracian. The Lycurgus story associates Thrace with Bacchus; it is a remote and outlandish region; the strange name Bistonian makes it more so. For hair tied up with snakes, see the vase-painting in the illustration on p. 64. Snake-handling is a typical feature of ecstatic religion.

Giants, Rhoetus, hideous yourself   the Giants, children of Earth, among them Rhoetus, made war on the Olympian gods. Dionysus was among the fighting gods. Sometimes he is shown as accompanied by a lion, sometimes he presents himself in the form of a lion. (Since Latin has case-endings, 'hideous' will be spelled differently depending on whether it describes Dionysus, the lion's mouth, or the Giant. Editors differ as to which Horace wrote. This is the reading of Nisbet and Hubbard.)

The Gods are fighting the helmeted Giants (Odes 2.19.21–4). One of Bacchus' lions takes a mouthful of giant. From the treasury of the Siphnians at Delphi, about 530 BC.

You went unharmed when **Cerberus** saw you, fair
and **golden-horned**: he gently rubbed   30
his tail against you, and as you departed
touched you on feet and legs with **three-tongued mouth.**

---

1   'What is there to stop me telling the truth with a smile?' (*Satires* 1.1.24–5). Are there things to smile at in this poem? If so, what are they? And is Horace here saying anything serious about his sources of inspiration?

2   In W. B. Yeats's poem 'Sailing to Byzantium', the poet comes to the city to seek inspiration and is moved to address the figures in gold mosaic as if in a hymn. Does his experience have anything in common with Horace's?

3   Compare the different views of poetry expressed in *Odes* **1.32,** pp. 62–3 and in this poem, **2.19.** Which comes nearer to your own view?

Cerberus   the guard dog of the Underworld. Dionysus' mother was Semele, a mortal. (For her death, see March, p. 353.) Dionysus went to the Underworld and brought her to Olympus. By tradition Cerberus (undoglike) fawns on new arrivals but savages those who try to depart: he abandons this practice in Dionysus' case. There is also a more mysterious aspect to Dionysus' association with the Underworld, hinted at in a fragment of the early fifth-century philosopher Heraclitus: 'Hades and Dionysus are one and the same'.

golden-horned   Dionysus also sometimes presents himself as a bull.

three-tongued mouth   Cerberus usually has three heads: this was how Aeneas encountered him in *Aeneid* 6. In *Odes* 2.13.34 he has a hundred heads. His three tongues in one mouth here are unique, otherwise the property of serpents.

Odes 3.30

With this poem Horace rounds off Books 1–3 of his lyric poetry. (The formal term is 'seal' – *sphragis*). He writes with pride in his achievement, and he writes as if there is to be no more lyric poetry.

I have raised up a monument more long-lasting than bronze,
higher than the **Pyramids** where they stand in majesty,
which no voracious rain, no wild north-easter
could bring to ruin, or the line of years
uncountable and the rout of time.   5
I shall not all die; there is much of me
will escape **Libitina**: I shall grow and grow,
fresh with each new glory, so long as **the Pontifex**
climbs up the Capitol with the silent Virgin.
Of me they will say, where the boisterous **Aufidus** roars,   10
and where **Daunus** poor in water ruled
over his peasant peoples, that I, passing from humble to mighty,
first found for **Aeolic song** a home

I have raised up a monument more long-lasting than bronze   Horace manages this in four words. To represent poetry as architecture is traditional.

Pyramids   this seems to be the first mention of the Pyramids in surviving Latin literature. Egypt had been absorbed into the Roman empire only seven years before this poem was published; knowledge of its antiquities was only just becoming commonplace. Admiration for the Pyramids as structures can be deduced from the splendid one set up in Rome by M. Cestius Epulo as a monument to himself within a few years of the writing of this poem; it is still visible where it is built into the walls by the Porta S. Paolo towering over Keats' grave.

Libitina   the goddess of funerals, who made a profit on each death (*Satires* **2.6.19**, p. 43).

the Pontifex / climbs up the Capitol with the silent Virgin   the Capitol serves as the topographical and architectural symbol of eternal Rome. The Pontifex ('priest') and the Vestal Virgin serve as the religious symbol. The virgin is 'silent' because she is evidently participating in a religious ceremony, where ill-omened (i.e. any) words might invalidate the rite. They are walking up the Clivus Capitolinus from the Forum, the route taken by religious processions and triumphing generals. But to talk about the constituent elements of this image should not detract from it as an intensely felt and envisaged part of Horace's pride.

Aufidus, Daunus   the Aufidus is the river of Horace's home country, northern Apulia; Daunus its mythical ancient king. Shortage of water in this area is noticed in *Satires* **1.5.88** and **91** (p. 36). For a king to be short of this most elementary item is poverty indeed.

Aeolic song   see the introduction to this chapter, p. 57.

in Italian melodies. Feel now the pride
which great deeds earn, and with the **Delphic bay** 15
in your goodwill, **Melpomene**, crown my hair.

---

1 It is Horace's pride to have introduced a Greek poetic form to 'Italian melodies'. In this poem, how does he stress the Italian and how the Greek elements?

2 Shortly after this poem was published, Horace's contemporary (but not, apparently, close acquaintance) Propertius addressed these lines to the girl, or more exactly, any girl, in whose honour he wrote poetry:

Whoever you are, made famous by my little book, you are blessed. Each poem of mine will be a monument to your beauty. Neither the Pyramids, lavishly raised sky high as they are, nor Jupiter's home at Olympia which imitates Heaven, nor the extravagant wealth of Mausolus' tomb will evade the terms which death imposes at the end. Fire or rain will steal their splendours away, or, victims of their own mass, they will fall to the hammering years. But fame acquired by the human spirit will not pass from recorded time. The spirit's glory is deathless.

(Elegies 3.2.17–26)

What do Horace's poem and this passage have in common? Compare also Shakespeare, Sonnet 65.

3 Assuming that Propertius wrote his lines in the knowledge of what Horace had written, in what way does he seem to be making a statement different from Horace's?

4 In writing poetry, what models would you choose, if any, and why?

Maecenas: *Odes* 1.20, 3.29

Horace's patron was, as we have seen (see especially *Satires* **2.6.15–58** pp. 43–5), a remarkable man. He came from Arretium in Etruria, a member on his mother's side of a family which already 250 years before had been conspicuous for wealth and power. A companion of Octavian from the beginning, closer to him than anyone except Agrippa, Maecenas undertook important negotiations on his behalf during the 30s BC and was several times

---

Delphic bay a wreath of bay leaves was the prize for victors at the Pythian festival at Delphi. These could be athletes or poets. The tree was particularly associated with Apollo.

Melpomene the Muse traditionally associated with lyric poetry.

Jupiter's home at Olympia the temple of Zeus (Zeus = Jupiter) at Olympia in southern Greece, built in the mid-fifth century BC and containing the great gold-and-ivory statue of Zeus, the work of the sculptor Pheidias. It was one of the Seven Wonders of the World.

Mausolus' tomb Mausolus was a king in Caria (south-western Asia Minor) in the fourth century BC. He built for himself a huge memorial tomb which became the standard for such tombs thereafter. It also established for them the name 'mausoleum'. At just this time Augustus was building his own mausoleum on the Campus Martius by the Tiber. Substantial fragments of the original Mausoleum can be seen in the British Museum.

left in charge in Rome during Octavian's absence. Sources describe him as vigorous and effective in action, but, when relaxation was possible, 'he would almost outdo a woman in giving himself up to **indolence and soft luxury**' (Velleius 2.88.2). He never sought senatorial authority, remaining a member of the knights (*equites*) throughout his life, so that his enormous power was somewhat anomalous, and by his position he was a reminder of the autocratic character of Augustus' regime. When in charge in Rome he was always informally dressed, refused an armed escort and went about accompanied by two eunuchs, says Seneca, not an admirer. 'He was reluctant to use force, abstained from shedding blood, and the only way he showed his power was in extravagant behaviour' (*Epistles* 114). He gathered writers around him from the first: Virgil, Varius, Horace and perhaps Propertius. He was a writer himself, mocked not only by later authorities (Seneca and Quintilian) but also by Augustus himself for his strained expression and fantastic vocabulary (Suetonius, *Augustus* 86.2). He suffered from a perpetual fever (Pliny, *Natural History* 7.172), and his insomnia could only be treated by the sound of music or waterfalls (Seneca, *Dialogues* 1.3.10). Horace was a client, but also a friend, and Maecenas' will contained the request to Augustus 'Remember Horatius Flaccus as you remember me.'

Odes 1.20

To give an idea of the form of a poetic invitation, here is the poem written by Philodemus to his patron the Roman aristocrat Piso (*Palatine Anthology* 11.44).

> *Tomorrow, dear Piso, your Muse-loving companion is dragging you to his humble cabin, beginning at the ninth hour, for the Annual Dinner on the Twentieth. If you give up your gastronomy and toasts in 'Bacchus' Own' from Chios, you will at least see the truest of friends, you will hear conversation sweeter than in the land of the **Phaeacians**. And if, Piso, you chance to turn your eyes on me, the Twentieth I celebrate will turn from poor to rich.*

The client (i.e. social inferior, recipient of favours) presents himself as his patron's equal, but acknowledges his relative poverty and in fact makes a virtue of it, in that for material goods are substituted spiritual and philosophical ones. He acknowledges himself privileged in the friendship of the great man. Everything said can be received as a compliment by the patron.

---

indolence and soft luxury   he was not much worried by his waistline, to judge from a poem addressed to Horace (Suetonius, *Life*): 'If I don't love you more than my own guts, may you see your friend turn scraggier than a *ninnium*' (sadly, we don't understand the word *ninnium*, which evidently indicates the very essence of scragginess).

Phaeacians   the Phaeacians were the people who entertained Odysseus splendidly after he was shipwrecked on his way back home (*Odyssey*, Books 5–8).

Cheap **Sabine** you will quaff, deep draughts
from **modest flagons**, laid down by me myself
and sealed in **a Greek jar** when in the theatre
you were applauded,

Maecenas, **noble knight**, so that the banks   5
of **your ancestral river**, and with them
the merry echo of the Vatican hill
sent back your praise.

You can drink **Caecuban**, and the grape
crushed in the presses of **Cales**: but my cups   10
are not tempered by **Falernian** vines
or the hills of **Formiae**.

Maecenas.

Sabine   an unpretentious wine (there is no mention of it in Pliny's list of good wines of Italy in *Natural History* 14.8). It is, however, grown in the vicinity of Horace's estate (though not on it, to judge by *Epistles* 1.14.23, where, it is said, pepper and frankincense would be easier to produce than wine). If Maecenas was responsible for Horace's acquisition of the estate (see Introduction, p. 2), this mention will be an expression of gratitude. 'Sabine' also conjures up the reputation which the Sabines had in Roman literature, of thrift, modesty and virtue (*Odes* 3.6.37–40).

modest flagons   flagons are big. The modesty must lie in the quality of the pottery.

a Greek jar   probably because Greek wines were frequently salted; their jars would retain the salt and act as a preservative. Horace makes it clear that this wine is special for the time of its manufacture and as such is to be kept as long as possible.

you were applauded   Maecenas' recovery from a serious illness was greeted with conspicuous applause when he appeared in the theatre on 1 March, possibly in 33 BC (*Odes* 3.8).

noble knight   'knight' was the technical designation for the second rank in Roman society, after the senators. (See the introduction to this section.) 'Noble' translates *clarus*, a regular epithet for senators, thus making a point of Maecenas' modesty.

your ancestral river   the Tiber. Maecenas came from Arretium in ancient Etruria (now Arezzo in Tuscany); Horace speaks of 'the Tuscan river' in *Odes* 3.7.28. It rises in the territory of Arretium.

the merry echo of the Vatican hill   the theatre will have been the Theatre of Pompey on the Campus Martius, not far from the Tiber bank. 'Vatican hill' refers here to the Janiculan ridge, which stretches along the far side of the Tiber from the theatre (see map, p.4).

Caecuban, Cales, Falernian, Formiae   four of the greatest wines of Italy.

> 1 Horace hopes that Maecenas will be glad to receive this poem. How many reasons, and what reasons, does he offer to Maecenas for being glad? Twelve, according to Francis Cairns, quoted by David West (1995, p. 94).
>
> 2 'Some scholars have marked this poem down as a tissue of commonplaces. Which it is. Like the music of Mozart' (West, 1995, p. 98). Is this a fair comment?

Odes 3.29

This poem comes second last in the collection *Odes* 1–3. The last poem (pp. 67–8) is Horace's seal (*sphragis*), summing up his own achievement. This poem places Maecenas in a place of honour at the end of the collection as he had been at the beginning (*Odes* **1.1**, pp. 58–61).

Maecenas' political anxieties (lines 25–8) seem to point to a date between 27 and summer 24 BC, when Augustus was absent in Gaul and Spain and Maecenas was in Rome, having, no doubt, some supervisory role, as he had had previously, during the Alexandria campaign of 30–29.

Although the poem begins in the form of an invitation, it spreads out to cover many other themes, conspicuously an ethical discussion including Stoic and Epicurean elements surely carefully calculated to appeal to their addressee: we catch a distant echo of the conversation among Maecenas' circle of friends. (Though compare *Satires* **2.6.40–59**, pp. 44–5!)

Descendant of Etruscan kings, for you,
Maecenas, I have soothing wine in a cask
as yet unpoured, with rose petals too
and balsam pressed for your hair:

I have had them here a while. Get clear of business,   5
Don't just look out for ever at watery **Tibur**,
at **Aefula**'s shelving fields and father-killer
Telegonus' mountaintop.

Give up that affluence, now wearisome,
that structure which comes close to the high clouds.   10
Stop marvelling at the smoke,
the money and the noise of glittering Rome.

Descendant of Etruscan kings   compare *Odes* **1.1.1**, p. 59.

Tibur, Aefula, Telegonus' mountaintop, that structure   Maecenas lived on the Esquiline hill, where he had built a famous tower ('that structure', line 10). We imagine him in the tower, gazing out from central Rome towards the hills where his friends, Horace included, are enjoying leisure – Tibur to the east and Aefula, a height to the south-east close to ancient Praeneste. The third place is Tusculum, described as it is because it was founded in legend by Telegonus, Odysseus' son by Circe. Telegonus became a pirate, and killed his unknown father accidentally while raiding Ithaca.

Often a change brings pleasure to the rich,
and simple meals, watched by the poor man's gods,
ungraced by drapery or purple,   15
smooth the frown from the brow.

Now the bright **father of Andromeda**
displays his hidden fire, now Prócyon
and the maddened Lion's star go wild,
as the sun brings back the days of drought.   20

Now weary shepherds with their languid flock
seek shade and water, while **Silvánus'**
bristling scrubland and the riverbank
fall silent, with no straying breeze.

But your concern is '**What form best suits the State?**'   25
Your troubled fear is for the City: 'What are they plotting
in **China**, in Cyrus' one-time kingdom of **Bactria**
and on **the fractious Don?**'

---

father of Andromeda   Cepheus, king of the Ethiopians, was father of Andromeda, who was rescued from a sea-monster by Perseus. After his death he became a constellation. Cepheus and the other stars mentioned here, Procyon and 'the Lion's star', became conspicuous in the sky during July, thus indicating the hottest time of the year, when wealthy Romans usually abandoned Rome for the coolness of the nearby hills. (For details of the astronomy and Horace's possibly cavalier attitude to details, see Nisbet and Hubbard, pp. 352–3.) The Lion is 'maddened' by the heat.

Silvanus   the Italian god of the countryside, often equated with Pan.

What form best suits the State?   in January 27 BC Octavian, according to himself, ended the period of civil wars and 'transferred the republic into the control of the senate and people of Rome' (*Res Gestae* 34.1). The definition and distribution of powers then reached survived for four years until a new arrangement was proclaimed in mid-23. There was clearly a good deal of debate at this time about constitutional arrangements, as well there might be, given that a republican system was having to adapt itself to becoming an effective monarchy.

China, Bactria, the fractious Don   a mixture of impossible and unlikely threats, parodying Maecenas' anxiety. The Don, flowing into the Black Sea in southern Russia, stands for the Scythians, who were in fact in discussion with Augustus. An embassy reached him in Spain in 26–25. Bactria is northern Afghanistan. It had once been part of the Persian empire, hence 'ruled over by Cyrus' (550–530 BC), so is now part of Parthia, the successor-empire to Persia, which did indeed have a history of serious conflict with Rome. But the reference to the very remote region of Bactria downplays the threat. The Chinese occur on two other occasions in Horace, either presenting, as here, a deliberately implausible threat, or representing remote victims of Rome's fated world-conquest.

Wisely has **the god** shrouded the events
of future time in mist and darkness; 30
he laughs if a mortal frets beyond
his limits. Present things you should be sure

calmly to set in order; all the rest
is sped along as by a river, which now
slips peacefully along its bed 35
to the Tuscan sea, now snaps up stones,

rips tree trunks out, whirls cattle, houses
all together, while the mountains
bellow with the woods alongside,
when the wild flood provokes 40

quiet streams. He is **master of himself**
and will live happy, who can say each day
'**I've lived**.' Tomorrow let the Father claim
the heavens for his black clouds

or for undimmed sun; yet what is past 45
he will not make null and void, nor will he
reshape or undo quite
what once the flying hour has brought.

Fortune, delighting in her cruel work
and resolute in playing the callous game, 50
swaps honours unpredictably;
kind now to me, now to another.

I praise her if she stays; but at the flap
of her swift wings, I surrender what she gave,
and wrap myself in my own virtue 55
seeking, without dowry, honest Poverty.

---

the god   unnamed, the god appears more a philosophical idea than one of the Olympians. The point – the uselessness of prophecy – is Epicurean, though the presence of an undefined presiding god is Stoic.

master of himself   the virtue is self-control. This is usually control of the appetites and emotions, but here it is the mastery over hope and fear, enabling one to be happy in the present day, an Epicurean recipe.

I've lived   the Latin *vixi* can carry both a positive meaning ('I've had a good life') and a negative one ('my life is over'). Compare Seneca: 'Anyone who sets the seal on his life every day is in no need of time' (*Epistles* 101.8).

It's not my way, if the mast groans
at storms from Africa, to sink
to praying piteously and bargaining
to save my Cyprian and Tyrian goods   60

from adding riches to the greedy sea.
That's when I'll be rescued by my two-oared boat
and brought safe over the furious Aegean
by the breeze and by **Pollux** with his twin.

---

1   How effective is Horace's use of imagery in this poem?
2   When he reads this poem through, what message will Maecenas receive? Is
    Horace saying something about himself, or about Maecenas, or about the
    world?
3   Consider how Horace presents philosophical and moral ideas in pictorial form.
4   Compare this poem with *Epistles* **1.7**, pp. 152–8, as a communication from a
    client to his patron.
5   Does patronage have any place in modern literature or culture? Should it?

The poet on politics: *Odes* 1.12, 1.37; *Epode* 9; *Odes* 2.1, 3.2, 3.5; *Carmen Saeculare* excerpts; *Odes* 4.5

Horace was indebted to Maecenas for wealth and social standing (*Epistles*
1.7.14, p. 153; *Satires* **2.6.40–9**, pp. 153, 44–5). Augustus had a high regard
for him (see Introduction, p. 2) and gave him material support on more than
one occasion: 'and made him well-to-do by more than one act of generosity'
(Suetonius, *Life of Horace*). Readers have reacted to this in different ways.
Distaste for the autocratic regime created by Augustus (often inspired though
not wholly supported by Ronald Syme's great history *The Roman Revolution*)
has prompted some readers to regard Horace as a mere toady, one who went
over to the winning side for his own material advantage; others to see him
as treading a difficult path, being ostensibly supportive of the regime while
expressing covert doubts. Others have been inclined to take his opinions at
face value, as the expression of a man who had lived through a period of
chaos and was profoundly grateful for re-established order and confidence.

Pollux   his twin was Castor. Between them they make sea-journeys safe (p. 77).

Odes 1.12

In discussing the Greek authors who have inspired him, Horace is readiest to recognize Alcaeus (see *Odes* **1.32**, p. 62). Here he turns to the Theban poet Pindar (?518–*c*.440 BC), composer of a huge corpus of lyric poetry of which only the four books of poems in honour of victors at the great Games have reached us complete. In the second of his Olympian odes, Pindar is addressing Theron, ruler of the Sicilian city of Acragas, victor of the chariot race in 476. He begins, 'My hymns, commanders of the lyre, which god, which hero, which man shall we celebrate?' (trans. Verity), and proceeds to answer his own questions in quick succession: 'Zeus indeed is lord of Pisa [the venue of the Olympics], and Heracles founded the Olympic Games, the first-fruits of war; but the man we must proclaim is Theron, for his victory with the four-horsed chariot.'

Odes 1.12 is dated by the reference to Marcellus, who came to prominence only when he married Augustus' daughter in 25 BC, and died in 23.

A long passage in Virgil, *Aeneid* 6.756–886 shows striking similarity to this ode and is likely to have been influenced by it (Nisbet and Hubbard, p. 146). It is worth reading the Virgil passage and making the comparison.

What man or hero on your lyre or shrill
pipe do you, **Clio**, mean to celebrate?
What god? Whose name shall the merry
echo sing back

on the shadowy slopes of **Helicon**   5
or over **Pindus** or on chill **Haemus**,
where the woods came **scampering after**
Orpheus as he sang,

staying by **his mother**'s skill the tumultuous
descent of rivers and the speeding winds,   10
pleasing the long-eared oaks, drawing them on
with his tuneful lyre?

What can I utter before the time-honoured praise
of the Father, who rules the heaven and earth,
who **regulates sea, land and sky**   15
with changing seasons?

From all this, nothing is born so great as he,
nor is there any living being like or near him.
The highest honours after him
are claimed by **Pallas**   20

Clio   one of the nine Muses, who perhaps because of her name ('the giver of glory') was becoming specifically the Muse of History.

Helicon, Pindus, Haemus   mountains in Greece. Helicon, not far from Thebes, has the clearest literary association, especially with Hesiod: the Muses appeared to him on its slopes (*Theogony* 22). Haemus as a mountain in Thrace had associations with Orpheus. Pindus is the very high ridge which is the spine of the northern Greek peninsula, distinguished for its remoteness more than for association with the Muses.

scampering after / Orpheus   Orpheus' ability to make things animate and inanimate follow him is a commonplace of Greek and Latin literature; think also of Shakespeare/Fletcher, *Henry VIII*, 3.1.3: 'Orpheus with his lute made hills and trees / And the mountain tops that freeze / Bow themselves when he did sing.' 'Scampering' and 'long-eared oaks' (line 11) introduce a note of comedy.

his mother   the Muse Calliope.

regulates sea, land and sky   'The idea of a universe in equilibrium was particularly Stoic' (Nisbet and Hubbard, p. 151).

Pallas   Athena, or Minerva. She is recognizable in art by her helmet, shield, spear and the aegis (a tasselled goatskin with a Gorgon's head).

'Pallas the bold in battle' (Odes 1.12.20–1). Amphora from Athens, fifth century BC.

the bold in battle. Of you too I will tell,
Liber, and the **Virgin**, enemy
of savage beasts; you also, Phoebus, a terror
with your unerring arrow.

Alcides then I'll name, and **Leda's children**,   25
one known for victory with horses, one
with fists. Once their bright star
shines over men at sea,

the wild waters flow back from the rocks,
the winds drop, the clouds hurry away,   30
and the threatening wave, at their desire,
falls back to the sea.

Liber Bacchus. The divinities in this stanza are all conspicuous for their fighting qualities. For Bacchus as fighter, see *Odes* **2.19.21–8**, p. 65.

Virgin Diana, as huntress.

Alcides 'descendant of Alcaeus' refers to Hercules. (Alcaeus is not the poet here but a son of the mythical hero, Perseus.)

Leda's children Castor and Pollux. Under the name Dioscuri ('sons of Zeus'), they are the constellation Gemini ('the Twins'), and have the special function of protecting sailors at sea. Castor was by tradition the horseman, Pollux the boxer.

Romulus shall I sing first after these,
or **Numa**'s peaceful reign, or the **proud
insignia of Tarquin**, I wonder, or **Cato**   35
dying gloriously?

My words, made sweet by **Italy's glorious Muse**,
shall be of **Regulus, the Scauri, Paulus**
flinging his mighty spirit away as Carthage triumphed,
and of **Fabricius**.   40

This man, and **Curius** of the unkempt hair,
Camillus too, were made good men for war
by cruel poverty, **ancestral lands**
and fitting homes.

Romulus, Numa   first and second kings of Rome. Romulus has a special status as son of Mars. (One definition of 'hero' is 'having one human and one divine parent'.) Numa's traditional part was to establish Roman religion. (In the Latin he is given his other name, Pompilius.)

proud / insignia of Tarquin   'proud' is a transferred epithet. The reference is to Tarquin the Proud, last king of Rome. His deposition for tyrannical behaviour in 510 BC marked the beginning of the republican period in Roman history. The insignia are the *fasces*, for which see note on *Odes* **3.2.19**, p. 91. They are symbols of the autocratic power of the kings, but they then become symbols of republican authority. In *Aeneid* 6.818, Virgil speaks of the foundation of the republic as 'the recovery of the *fasces*'.

Cato   Marcus Porcius Cato, the most resolute opponent of Julius Caesar. In 46 BC as the commander of the African city of Utica, he committed suicide rather than surrender to Caesar's troops. He became a republican martyr. It is remarkable that Horace felt free to single him out for praise, and to do so in a striking and curious context, as he jumps from the deposition of Tarquin (510 BC) to the death of Cato (46 BC – still within the memory of most of the adults in Rome) and then back to Regulus (256 BC).

Italy's glorious Muse   at the beginning of the poem Horace addressed the Greek Muse Clio; here, talking of Romans, he uses the Latin word *Camena*.

Regulus, the Scauri, Paulus, Fabricius, Curius, Camillus   heroes of the republican era. For Regulus, see *Odes* **3.5**, pp. 93–8. Various members of the family Aemilius Scaurus achieved distinction: Horace's audience would probably think of two consuls of the end of the second century, one of whom died bravely while held captive by Gauls. Paulus was consul of 216 BC, one of the commanders at the disastrous battle against Hannibal at Cannae. Wounded, he refused the offer of a horse on which to escape. Curius and Fabricius were both famous for their incorruptibility, frugality and military success, especially at the time of the wars against the Greek invader Pyrrhus in 280–275 BC. Camillus was best known for re-establishing the Roman state after Rome was captured by the Gauls in 390 BC.

ancestral lands / and fitting homes   this compressed expression suggests that their lands brought no wealth and the houses on them were no grander than the estates justified. Augustus himself made moral capital out of the fact that he lived in a relatively unpretentious house on the Palatine hill.

On the left, a wreathed head of 'Caesar Augustus'; on the right, a comet with seven rays and a tail. 'Divus Iulius' ('the god Julius') recalls the appearance of a comet in 44 BC which was hailed as Julius Caesar's spirit going to heaven (Odes 1.12.46).

As a tree grows unperceived in time, so grows   45
Marcellus' glory; while the **star of Julius**
outshines them all, as does the moon
among the lesser fires.

Father and guardian of the human race,
O **son of Saturn**, to you by fate   50
the care of **Caesar** falls: may you, with Caesar
beneath you, reign supreme.

He – whether he has in rightful triumph
forced back the **Parthians threatening Latium**,

Marcellus   the great Marcellus (d. 208 BC) was consul five times, won the award called *spolia opima* for killing an enemy commander in single combat and played a great part in the war against Hannibal. Horace's audience would inevitably also think of Marcus Marcellus, Augustus' nephew, who married his daughter Julia in 25 BC and died of illness within two years.

star of Julius   in July 44 BC, four months after the murder of Julius Caesar, and during the celebration by Octavian of Caesar's victory games, a comet appeared which was identified as the spirit of Caesar passing into heaven. The star was used by Octavian to promote himself as *divi filius* – 'son of god' – and is seen very frequently in Augustan art.

son of Saturn   Jupiter.

Caesar   here refers to Augustus.

Parthians threatening Latium   Parthia was the Middle Eastern kingdom which had been established as the influence of the successors of Alexander the Great waned in the region. When the Roman empire came to have a common frontier with Parthia, there were frequent disputes. For recent Roman defeats see on *Odes* **3.5**, pp. 93–8. It is something of an exaggeration to suggest that the Parthians were threatening Latium.

or at the Eastern edges of the world   55
the men of **India and China** –

shall, under you, direct the world with justice.
You with the weight of your chariot shall shake Olympus,
you shall hurl down your thunderbolts of wrath
upon unhallowed groves.   60

---

1   Compare Horace's way of asking and answering his own questions with
    Pindar's in *Olympian Odes* 2 (see p. 75).

2   What ideology of empire is Horace presenting here? What values does
    Augustus seem to be promoting and how is he presenting them? How do they
    compare with your own attitude to government? Is it possible in the twenty-
    first century to inspire people in a similar way?

3   Some ten years after this, Horace began a poem (*Odes* 4.2) with the words:
    'Whoever is eager to rival Pindar is relying on wings treated, like Daedalus',
    with wax, and is destined to give his name to a glassy sea.' The reference is
    to Daedalus' unfortunate son Icarus, who flew too near the sun. Nisbet and
    Hubbard take the view that Horace has suffered the fate he predicted: 'We
    can accept the encomia [praise-poems] of Pindar, but Horace's exclamations
    evoke [a] derisive response' (p. 146). Do you agree?

Odes 1.37

This poem is written as a celebration for victory in the two campaigns of
Actium (31 BC) and Alexandria (30 BC) (see Introduction, p. 3). In it there
are references to the battle itself (line 13) which took place on 2 September
31 BC, to Cleopatra's flight (line 16), to her plan to flee from Egypt (line 24)
and to her suicide, which occurred shortly after Alexandria surrendered to
Octavian on 1 August 30 BC. The time is compressed. The poem seems to
evoke a moment after victory is complete and before, or at least not after, the
triumph celebrations of August 29 BC.

The first phrase is a direct translation of the first words of a **poem by Alcaeus**
commemorating the death of the tyrant Myrsilus. Thereafter Horace's poem
seems to take a different, Roman, tack, so that the Alcaeus reference serves as
what scholars have called a 'motto' – a brief reference indicating to the reader
a literary context within which to evaluate a poem.

India and China   Augustus records embassies from the Indians in *Res Gestae* 31.1;
Propertius speaks of possible conflicts with the Chinese (3.4.1).

poem by Alcaeus   see Denys Page, p. 238.

Now we must drink, now drum the ground
with free-footed dance, now dress, my friends,
as the Salii do, the couches of the gods.
It is time, at last, for feasting.

Till now it was wrong to bring the Caecuban   5
out from ancestral stores, while still for the Capitol
the queen set up a fury of destruction,
and death for the majesty of Rome

with vice-degraded men, a tainted rout,
she unrestrained, she limitless in hope   10
and with the sweetness of good fortune
inebriated. But it curbed her frenzy

when scarce one ship was rescued from the fires,
and her wits, maddened by Mareotic wine,
were brought to reality and fear by Caesar.   15
As she went flying from Italy,

Now we must drink   this is the famous tag *nunc est bibendum*.

the Salii   these were the dancing priests of Mars, an association founded, according to legend, by Numa Pompilius, second king of Rome. By Horace's time they had become an aristocratic club, and their dinners were gargantuan. (Livy 1.20.4; for a Saliar dinner, see Macrobius, *Saturnalia* 3.13.2.)

couches of the gods   at great festivals the images of the gods were placed on couches outside their temples, so that they joined the feasting with the gathered worshippers. The ceremony is called *lectisternium*.

the Caecuban   Caecuban wine came from just south of Rome and had a reputation for being the best.

for the Capitol   Horace may be referring to the story about Cleopatra, told probably by her enemies to blacken her name, that she used to take an oath 'by the day on which I shall deliver judgement on the Capitol' (Dio, *Roman History* 50.5.4).

vice-degraded men   certainly an allusion to the stories of excess which were current about the activities of Antony and Cleopatra in Alexandria. But the phrase may also be a periphrasis for 'eunuchs', a word apparently unacceptable in lyric poetry, which appears in *Epodes* 9.12 – iambics, the verse-form of personal abuse, being more tolerant.

scarce one ship was rescued from the fires   fire plays a significant part in the descriptions of the battle by Virgil (*Aeneid* 8.694–5) and Dio (*Roman History* 50.34.2–35.4), but Augustus himself apparently wrote in his despatches that he had captured 300 ships (Plutarch, *Antony* 68.1).

Mareotic wine   wine from the shores of Lake Mareotis, the lagoon which separates Alexandria from the mainland.

from Italy   strictly speaking, Cleopatra was fleeing not from Italy but from the Greek coast at Actium – but 'Italy' expresses where, according to Octavian's propaganda, she wished to be.

he pressed **upon her with his oars** as a hawk
on gentle doves, or a swift huntsman
on a hare in the plains of snowy
Thessaly, aiming to set his chains   20

on the god-sent bringer of doom. But she,
seeking a nobler death, unwomanlike,
did not tremble at the sword, nor **head
with speeding ships for hidden shores,**

daring to gaze upon **her ruined palace**   25
with countenance untroubled, bold too
to grasp **rough, cruel** serpents, to drain deep
into her body their black poison,

more headstrong in a voluntary death:
yes – she would spite **the cruel Liburnians;**   30
unthroned but never to be trailed along
(not humbled, she!) in **a parade of victory and pride.**

---

he pressed upon her with his oars   Cleopatra broke away from the battle in her 60
ships which had kept their sails on board when the battle started. (Dio, *Roman History*
50.33.2–5. It was standard practice to leave them ashore, to provide more room for action
on board.) Octavian, pursuing her, had to rely on oars.

head / with speeding ships for hidden shores   returning to Egypt, Cleopatra at first
planned to escape by ship down the Red Sea. She had ships hauled overland from the Nile
for this purpose. The plan was abandoned when the ships were burned by an Arabian
people (Dio, *Roman History* 51.7.1).

her ruined palace   in fact the palace was not destroyed. The ruins are figurative.

rough, cruel   this translates a single Latin word (*asperas*) which bears both meanings:
one referring to the touch of the snakes as Cleopatra handles them (though snakes are
not in fact rough to the touch), the other to the murderous deed for which they are
employed. The story of Cleopatra's death by snakebite became immediately accepted.
There was a placard illustrating two snakes carried behind Cleopatra's image in the
triumphal procession celebrated for the victory over her. However, the evidence for the
story (discussed by Plutarch in *Antony* 86) was even in antiquity recognized as slender.

the cruel Liburnians   *liburnae* was the name given to the small fast-sailing ships which
seem to have played a large part in the battle of Actium, especially on Octavian's side.
They stand for the attacking forces of Octavian.

a parade of victory and pride   this translates a phrase literally meaning 'a proud triumph'.
I have paraphrased 'triumph' because in English the word does not quite carry its Roman
suggestion, of a victory parade designed to provide maximum exaltation for the victors
and maximum humiliation for the losers. The humiliation was in many cases completed
when the enemy leader was executed (a cautious account of this in Beard, pp. 128–32).

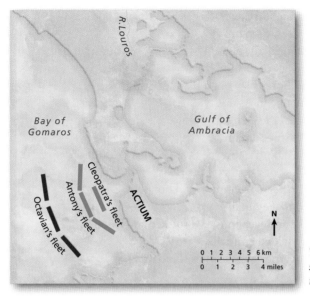

The position of the fleets at the start of the battle of Actium on the west coast of Greece.

1 What difference is there between the attitude to Cleopatra expressed at the beginning of the poem and that expressed at the end? At what stage of the poem does the change become apparent? Can you think of any reason why Horace should have expressed these two different attitudes?

2 Neither Antony nor Cleopatra is named either in this poem or in the following one (nor is Cleopatra ever named by any Augustan poet). Why not?

Epode 9

This poem has been placed here, separately from Epodes 3 and 7 (see pp. 10, 15), for comparison with *Odes* 1.37, the other Actium celebration poem.

There has been much argument over the poem. The dramatic setting is clearly in the immediate aftermath of the battle of Actium. It is either in Rome or on board ship. The answer to this hangs on the question (to which this poem itself contributes): 'Where was Maecenas during this time?' The historians Velleius Paterculus (2.88) and Dio (51.3) seem on the face of it to say that Maecenas was left in charge of Italy during Octavian's absence. But it is just possible to read them otherwise, and there are some suggestions that he was at the battle. The *Epodes* begin with a poem addressed to Maecenas: 'Are you going to venture in small galleys among the ships' high sterncastles, my friend Maecenas, ready to undergo all Caesar's peril at your own?' It is odd that Horace puts such urgent language into so conspicuously placed a poem if the events made to seem so probable never took place. Evidence has also been found in 'nausea' (line 35), which means literally 'sea-sickness', but can also mean sickness in general.

The **Caecuban** laid down for celebration
and joy at Caesar's victory
when shall I drink it, blessed Maecenas, in your high hall
with you, by grace of Jupiter,
as **lyres and flutes** play out a blended strain   5
one Dorian, one in Asian style,
as lately, when the **Captain, Neptune's son,**
fled with his ships aflame,
who said he'd bind on Rome those chains he'd **loosed**
from faithless slaves, their friend?   10
A Roman (in years to come you'll not believe it)
indentured to a woman
brings stake and weapons as a soldier and can be
a slave to wrinkled **eunuchs,**
and hideous among the army's standards   15

Caecuban   here and in line 36, a wine for a very special occasion (see also *Odes* **1.37.5**, p. 81).

lyres and flutes   the suggestion is of a distinctly wild party. There is a discussion of music in Plato, *Republic* 397–40: 'To mix styles or instruments is undesirable. Further, certain modes are in themselves conducive to fortitude and virtue, especially the Dorian; others to self-indulgence and immorality, particularly the Lydian and the Ionian.' These last fall under Horace's heading of 'Asian style'.

Captain, Neptune's son   the reference is to Sextus Pompeius, the son of Julius Caesar's enemy Pompey the Great. He controlled the sea and major islands between 40 and 36 BC and caused Octavian serious trouble by cutting off food supplies to Italy. His naval successes, according to Dio, 'caused him to believe that he was in truth the son of Neptune' (48.48.5). He was defeated in 36, largely owing to Agrippa's work in building and training a fleet.

loosed / from faithless slaves   Augustus refers to the victory over Sextus Pompeius in these self-glorifying terms: 'I pacified the sea from pirates, and in that war I captured about 30,000 slaves who had fled from their masters and had taken up arms against the republic, and I handed them over to their masters for punishment' (*Res Gestae* 25.1).

indentured   the Latin word is *emancipatus*, a legal term for 'handed over as property to another party', i.e. here, to Cleopatra. The reference is either to the Roman soldiers in Antony's forces or to Antony himself. If to the soldiers, they have been handed over by Antony; if to Antony, he has handed himself over.

brings stake and weapons as a soldier   the stake (used for building a stockade) stands for the huge load of equipment for building works which the legionary soldier normally carried in addition to his arms (Cicero, *Tusculan Disputations* 2.37; Josephus, *The Jewish War* 3.5.5); the whole burden indicates his strength and virility by contrast with the pampered eunuchs to whom he is enslaved.

eunuchs   conventional attendants on oriental royalty. For this instance, compare Plutarch, *Antony* 60.1: 'Caesar said that Antony had been drugged and was not even master of himself, and that the Romans were carrying on war with the eunuchs Mardion and Pothinus'.

the sun sees **a mosquito net**.
Two thousand now have turned their foaming mounts
to us – **Gauls, singing 'Caesar'** –
and there in port, the enemy ships' sterns,
hastening leftward, hide.   20
Hail, **Triumph**! are you holding back the cars
of gold and spotless oxen?
Hail, Triumph, you have brought to Rome **no leader**
to match Jugurtha's war,
no **Africanus**, he whose valour made   25
Carthage a sepulchre.
Subdued on land and sea, the foe has changed
his purple cloak for **sackcloth**.
Now towards lordly hundred-citied **Crete**
he sails with **alien winds**,   30
or seeks the **Syrtes**, swept by the Sirocco,
or drifts **where Ocean wills**.

---

a mosquito net a symbol of shameful enfeeblement. Propertius writes of Cleopatra wishing 'to spread the Tarpeian rock [the summit of the Capitol] with disgusting mosquito nets' (*Elegies* 3.11.45).

Gauls, singing 'Caesar' the 'Gauls' are Galatian cavalry from Asia Minor who, under their leader Amyntas, abandoned Antony during the battle and joined Octavian.

hastening leftward this indicates in some way that the ships have abandoned the struggle; there is no agreement on precisely how it indicates that. For the topography see the map on p. 83.

Triumph a triumph is the characteristic Roman victory parade (see *Odes* **1.37.32**, p. 82 and note). Here Triumph is personified as the god who is promoting the triumph.

no leader / to match Jugurtha's war Jugurtha usurped the kingdom of Numidia in North Africa in 118 BC. He held it, defeating several Roman generals, till he was himself defeated by C. Marius in 105. Caesar does not merely 'match' Marius, he far outstrips him, as he also outstrips Africanus.

Africanus the title of two members of the Scipio family, of whom one defeated Hannibal and ended the second Punic war in 202 BC, the other destroyed Carthage and ended the third war in 146. If the reference is to the elder Scipio, 'sepulchre' (line 26) means merely 'monument'; if to the second, the point is the death and destruction which attended the ruin of Carthage.

sackcloth Antony abandons his commander's uniform for the common soldier's cloak – 'fatigues' – in distress at his defeat.

Crete, Syrtes, where Ocean wills Antony's three possible destinations become increasingly vague and random. Crete is a possible stopping-place on the way back to Egypt; it is made more vivid by the Homeric description 'hundred-citied'. Syrtes is the name for the Gulf of Libya with its shallow and extremely dangerous waters.

alien winds winds which will carry him in a direction he does not want to go.

Bring larger tankards here, my boy, and wine
from **Lesbos** or from **Chios**:
or as a cure for nausea unchecked   35
a measure of Caecuban.
From care and fear for Caesar we rejoice
that the **God who Frees** will free us.

---

1   An important element is the idea in line 37: 'fear and care for Caesar'. Does it suggest that hostilities are not yet concluded?

2   What, if any particular, dramatic setting seems to you to suit the poem?

3   Compare the approach to Actium and the war against Antony and Cleopatra which is taken by this poem with that taken by *Odes* **1.37** (pp. 81–2).

4   Is it possible to make any judgements on the basis of these two poems about what is suitable style for odes and what for epodes?

5   Augustan propaganda represented the war of Actium as having been against a foreign rather than a Roman enemy, and therefore not carrying the odium associated with a civil war. Do these two poems support this propaganda?

Odes 2.1

This poem is dedicated to Gaius Asinius Pollio. Pollio came from north-eastern Italy. His grandfather had joined the anti-Roman alliance in the Italian war of 91–88 BC. He himself supported Julius Caesar in 45 and was consul in 40. Virgil dedicated to him two of the poems in his first published work, the *Eclogues*. Pollio was a military figure, winning a triumph for a Balkan war in 39, a writer of tragedies which earned the respect of his contemporaries, and the founder of the first public library in Rome, financed by the spoils of the Balkan war. When the final split came between Antony and Octavian, Pollio refused to join either side, saying 'Whichever of you wins may regard me as part of the spoils.' (Velleius, 2.86.4) In this poem Horace refers to him as being engaged in writing his history of the last 30 years.

Telling the truth about recent civil conflict is difficult, as is proved by twentieth-century experience in, for example, Spain, South Africa and Northern Ireland. There are many damaging secrets to be told, and many people have made compromises which they would prefer not to be brought out into the open.

Lesbos, Chios   first-rate Greek wines. It may be relevant that they are from roughly the same area of the Aegean as Samos, where Octavian spent some of the winter of 31–30 BC, the point being that eastern products are now once more available in Rome; the split in the empire is healed.

God who Frees   this represents the Latin *Lyaeus*, itself a Greek word meaning 'the Releaser', a name for Dionysus.

The Troubles, from Metellus' year, the war,
its causes, evils, and the way it was,
the game of Fortune, great men's
damaging friendships, and their arms

smeared with blood still unabsolved: 5
you're taking up a task risky as
the cast of a die, and walking over fire
where ash lies treacherous above.

Let the stern Muse of Tragedy awhile
desert the theatres. Later, when you've set   10
the state's affairs in order, you'll resume
your solemn duty, wearing the Attic buskin,

being for the wretched, the accused, a mighty tower,
and for the Senate, Pollio, who seek your counsel.
For you the bay tree bore eternal glory   15
at your triumph over Dalmatia.

The Troubles Horace's phrase, 'the civil disturbance', sounds in English like an understatement, which it is not. I choose 'The Troubles', borrowing the phrase with which the Irish refer to their civil war and its long aftermath.

from Metellus' year in Roman official dating, each year was referred to by the names of one or both of those who were consul in it. Metellus was consul in 60 BC, and Pollio has chosen this year as his starting point because it was then that Pompey, Crassus and Julius Caesar came together under the informal agreement ('friendships' in the text) which we know as the First Triumvirate, and parcelled out the rewards and offices of the Roman state between them. The agreement is seen as having led to the civil war of Caesar and Pompey which broke out in 49.

the cast of a die there may be a reference here to the phrase with which Caesar is said, as he crossed the river Rubicon in January 49 BC, to have launched the civil war: 'The die is cast' (*alea iacta est*) (Suetonius, *Caesar* 32). The war was a perilous undertaking, and so is telling its story.

Attic buskin a long boot which could fit onto either foot and was characteristic of the tragic actor. Tragic drama is Athenian ('Attic') in origin.

the bay tree triumphing generals wore a wreath of bay or laurel leaves.

Dalmatia a district in the Balkans. The exact name of the tribe over which Pollio gained his victory was 'Parthini'. There is some discussion as to why Horace uses the different name, but for our purposes it will do to say that Horace is being loose, as poets tend to be, in his use of geographical terms.

Fear in the faces (Odes 2.1.19–20) of the Persian king Darius and his men as they encounter Alexander the Great. Mosaic from Pompeii, c. 100 BC, based on a painting of about 300.

Now with the threatening blast of horns
you thrill my ear; now the trumpets bray,
now the glint of arms brings terror
to fleeing horses and **their riders' faces.**   20

I seem to hear of mighty leaders
grimy with honourable dust,
and all the world brought low
save **Cato** with his **shocking pride.**

---

their riders' faces   Pollio may here be recalling Pharsalus, the decisive battle of the first civil war, between Caesar and Pompey. Of this battle one of the vital moments was the defeat of Pompey's cavalry. Ancient sources (e.g. Plutarch, *Caesar* 45.2) have Caesar telling his soldiers to aim especially for the cavalrymen's faces.

Cato   one of Caesar's most determined opponents both in politics and on the battlefield, he led the opposition to him in Africa, and committed suicide at Utica in 46 when defeat became inevitable. Compare *Odes* **1.12.35** and note, p. 78.

shocking pride   of the Latin adjective, Nisbet and Hubbard say 'it is derived from [a word meaning] "black" and is complimentary only by way of paradox' (p. 24). It was Cato's pride not to admit defeat (Plutarch, *Cato Minor* 64). He cultivated an austere and uncompromising manner, and the circumstances of his suicide were grim in the extreme (Plutarch, 70).

Juno with any god who, well-disposed to Africa   25
but ineffectual, had left the country unavenged,
has brought the victor's grandsons
as offerings to dead **Jugurtha**.

Where is the battlefield not rich with Latin blood,
its graves witnesses to a wicked war   30
and to that sound they hear in Persia
of the **Western land** as it falls to ruin?

Where is the stream, where the ocean depth
that knows no dismal war? Where is the sea
unstained by **Daunian** slaughter?   35
What shore is there unbloodied by our blood?

But come, my cheeky Muse, stick to your games:
Why write the dirge of **Ceos** yet again?
With me down in **Dione**'s cave
go for a tune on a lighter instrument.   40

Juno, Jugurtha   Juno was the patron goddess of Carthage, the great city of North Africa which had been Rome's rival for 150 years until destroyed in 146 BC. Jugurtha was king of Numidia (part of modern Algeria), defeated by Rome and executed at the commander Marius' triumph in 104. Roman deaths in Africa during the civil war are seen as expiation of the violence employed long ago against Carthage and Jugurtha ('Latin blood' – line 29). The hostility between Rome and Carthage plays a significant part in Virgil's *Aeneid*, especially Book 4, the story of Dido.

Western land   Italy, as seen in contrast with Parthia. Virgil uses the name ('Hesperia') in the context of prophecies given to Aeneas when he is searching for the land which will one day contain Rome (*Aeneid* 1.530, etc.).

Daunian   Daunians lived in south-eastern Italy, in the vicinity of Horace's own home country. Here they represent Italians fighting on the Roman side, reminding us that the unity of Rome and Italy was one of Augustus' cherished ideals.

Ceos   home of Simonides, a Greek poet of the sixth–fifth centuries BC, who wrote poems commemorating the glorious defeat of the Spartan forces by the Persians at Thermopylae in 480.

Dione   the mother of Aphrodite (Venus) according to Homer; the name is used by later poets simply to refer to Aphrodite/Venus herself.

---

1 Why does Horace wait for so long before naming Pollio, to whom the ode is dedicated?

2 What qualities has Horace ascribed to Pollio in the first four stanzas?

3 In stanza 3, does Horace mean that the Muse of Tragedy will be temporarily unemployed, or that she will be cooperating with Pollio in his history-writing? (Aristotle, *Poetics* 1451b: 'Poetry is something more scientific and serious than history, because poetry tends to give general truths while history gives particular facts.')

4 Pollio is likely to have presented his history to the public in the form of a public reading. How far does Horace's poem acknowledge this as a scene?

5 Judging from Horace's presentation, what do you think the general tone of Pollio's history was? (It has, sadly, been entirely lost.) Can one say whether Horace was in sympathy with him?

6 What do you make of Horace's sudden switch in the last stanza to an apparently frivolous subject? Does it undermine the seriousness of the poem as a whole? (Richard Rutherford regards it as a matter of genre: 'the lyric poet has paid tribute to the tragic historian' (*CCH*, p. 253).)

Odes 3.2

The following two poems come from the six poems at the beginning of *Odes* 3 which are traditionally called 'Roman Odes'. All in the same 'Alcaic' metre, they recall the most politically active of Horace's models (see *Odes* 1.32, p. 62) and are his most concentrated expression of the Augustan ideology.

Poverty and privation: gladly to bear them
as he grows strong with the trials of a soldier's life,
let a boy learn, harassing the fierce **Parthians**,
riding to terrify them with his spear,

and living a life of high adventure   5
under the open sky. From the enemy's walls
the mother of a warrior king
should see him afar, and a girl full-grown

should sigh: ah, let not the prince,
her intended, new to war, provoke the lion   10
– bloody the hand that touches him – as he rampages
furiously through the battle's murderous centre.

Sweet and seemly it is to die for your homeland.
Death follows hard on him too who runs away,
unmerciful to the hamstrings and the backs   15
of unwarlike, frightened children.

Parthians   see *Odes* **1.12.53n**, p. 79.

Virtue, knowing nothing of sordid rejection,
glitters with honours uncontaminated.
She does not take or set aside the **Axes**
at the weathervane choice of the people.   20

Virtue to those who merit immortality
unlocks the heavens, seeks passage by forbidden ways.
The **assembled populace** and the **watery earth**
she spurns on wings fleeing aloft.

For **good faith** too which holds its peace, reward   25
is sure. I shall say no, if one has spread abroad

Axes   symbols of high office in the Roman republic. Executive government was the responsibility of two *consuls* annually elected by a vote of the whole citizen body. Consuls were escorted in public by 12 *lictors*, each carrying a bundle of rods wrapped round two axes, indicating the power (much circumscribed in later years) to flog and execute. The bundles were called *fasces*; they were used as a symbol by Mussolini's Fascist party in Italy, 1919–45.

Virtue … unlocks the heavens   the idea that individual humans can achieve divine status by heroic achievements was not unfamiliar. Hercules after his many labours was accepted on Olympus. Both Horace and Virgil make the comparison between Hercules and Augustus (*Aeneid* 6.801–4; *Odes* 3.14). In Cicero's work *On the Republic*, written in the late 50s BC when the Roman world was on the brink of civil war, the image of the hero Scipio Africanus the elder, conqueror of Hannibal, speaks in a dream to his grandson the younger Africanus, about to become the destroyer of Carthage: 'That you should be the swifter, Africanus, to protect the nation, I tell you this: for all those who have saved, aided or extended their countries, a sure place in heaven has been prescribed, where they shall enjoy eternal life in happiness' (6.13).

assembled populace   continuing the idea of fickle and unreliable popular opinion from line 20. More precisely, this sounds like a disparaging reference to the electoral assemblies of the Roman people, to which consuls and others owed their office.

watery earth / she spurns   that is, leaves what is lower – the material elements of water and earth – for the heavenly elements of air and fire (the components of the immortal soul in *Aeneid* 6.747).

good faith   just as, in Augustus' case, Virtue takes her course without reference to the mob, so Augustus can rely on those close to him to maintain his confidences. Augustus was determined that no more should be publicly known of his thinking than was necessary. He chose for his seal ring a sphinx, the creature whose utterances only the wise could understand (compare the story of Oedipus). He was drastic in punishing a breach of confidence (Suetonius, *Augustus* 50 and 67).

the **mysteries of secret Ceres** and seeks to go
on board with me or **launch in my company**

a fragile ketch. Often the **Father God**,
neglected, treats both bad and good alike.   30
The sinner walks ahead, but seldom escapes
the **Avenger, following on limping foot**.

---

1   How does the focus of attention shift in the first three
    stanzas?

2   How do the themes of lines 1–16 relate to the themes of
    lines 17–32? If there is an Augustan theme to this poem, is
    it clearly expressed?

3   Line 13 is the famous *dulce et decorum est pro patria mori*,
    appearing in Wilfred Owen's First World War poem as 'the
    old lie' told 'to children ardent for some desperate glory'. Is
    this the spirit in which Horace uses the words?

4   'It is a common characteristic of the *gnomē* (moralizing
    generalization) in Greek poetry … to be sudden,
    portentous, and oracular. Horace told us at the beginning
    of these Roman Odes that he spoke as *vates*: priest,
    prophet, poet. The tone of this ending exactly hits that
    mark' (West, 2002, p. 29). Is this a satisfactory explanation
    for the obscurity of the last two stanzas?

A lictor with *fasces (Odes 3.2.19). Augustan period. Notice also the
axe-head half-way down.*

---

mysteries of secret Ceres   Ceres is the Latin name for the Greek goddess Demeter, in
whose shrine at Eleusis near Athens Athenians and others were initiated into a cult whose
secrets were never to be (and never were) published. The cult acquired importance from
the fact that to the Romans Athens seemed the cradle of civilization. Augustus himself
took part in the celebration in 31 BC.

launch in my company / a fragile ketch   for the idea that it might be dangerous to be
on board ship with an offender, compare the story of Jonah in the Old Testament (Jonah
1.4–7).

Father God   Jupiter, for whom Horace here uses an archaic name (Diespiter).

Avenger, following on limping foot   surely the starting point for M. R. James's terrifying
ghost story, *Oh, Whistle and I'll Come to You, My Lad.*

During the 20s BC, confidence returned to Rome, and with it renewed thoughts of conquest. Augustus was absent from Italy from 26 to 24, but his military actions were largely devoted to consolidating Roman rule in Gaul and Spain, where it had been undermined by 20 years of civil war. He allowed it to be believed that he had plans for expansion in Britain and Parthia. In the case of Parthia, there was unfinished business. Roman armies had suffered serious defeats on at least two occasions, in 53 when Marcus Crassus had been attempting to secure his own military reputation by exploits which, he intended, would be comparable with those of his rivals Julius Caesar and Pompey, and in 36 when Antony's attempted invasion had gone seriously wrong. On both of these occasions, many prisoners had been taken and legionary standards captured. That legionary standards should be in enemy possession could be felt as a national disgrace. This ode captures that spirit by referring back two centuries to the time of the first war against Carthage.

In this war, the Roman commander Marcus Atilius Regulus conducted several effective actions against the Carthaginians in 256, including the capture of Tunis. At this stage the Carthaginians sued for peace. Regulus would only agree to this on terms which the Carthaginians found unacceptable. The war continued, and in 255 Regulus was defeated and taken prisoner along with his army.

This is the story of what follows as it appears in Cicero, *On Duties*:

> *When Marcus Regulus, twice consul, was captured in an ambush by a force under Xanthippus of Sparta, whose supreme commander was Hannibal's father Hamilcar, he was sent to the Senate having sworn an oath that unless certain noble captives were handed back by the Romans, he would return to Carthage. [In an earlier passage Cicero speaks of 'an exchange of captives' (On Duties 1.39).] Coming to Rome, he saw what seemed to be to his advantage, but, as events showed, he decided otherwise. That 'advantage' was to stay in Rome, to be at home with his wife and children, to think of the disaster which had befallen him as all part of the fortune of war, and to hold on to his status as an ex-consul. Who can deny that this was to his advantage? But courage and greatness of spirit say 'no'. What weightier authorities could you ask for? It is characteristic of these qualities to fear nothing, to despise human considerations, to be ready to suffer anything to which human nature is liable. What then did he do? He came to the Senate, he explained the terms as he had been instructed. He refused to make any formal recommendation, saying that so long as he was under oath to the enemy, he was no senator. But he made this point ('a foolish betrayal of his own interests' it may be said), that the return of prisoners was no advantage: they were young men and good leaders, while he was old and*

worn out. His authority prevailed. The prisoners were retained. Regulus returned to Carthage. Neither love of country nor of family restrained him. And even then he knew that he was going to a cruel enemy and to the most refined torture – but he held that an oath was to be kept. (3.99–100)

Regulus never returned to Rome. There are various accounts of his death in Carthage.

It has been suggested that there is no truth in any of this story, because there is no mention of it in the main and earliest source for the history of the first war against Carthage, the Greek historian Polybius. Whatever the truth, Horace has taken his own liberties with the story. In the tradition, the issue is the exchange of prisoners. In the poem the issue is ransom. The effect of this change is to bring the situation closer to contemporary affairs.

In the event, Augustus secured the return of the standards in 20 BC by means of pressure which was largely diplomatic. Augustan propaganda treats this almost like conquest, and the standards remain a part of imperial iconography for the rest of Augustus' reign. Little is said about the prisoners, except for a single reference in Dio (*Roman History* 54.8.1).

From his thunder we are made confident
that Jupiter reigns in heaven. **Augustus will be accepted**
as god among us when he adds the **Britons**
to the empire with the **threatening Persians**.

Augustus will be accepted / as god among us   the contrast is between Jupiter who (as thunder shows) is god *in heaven*, and Augustus who (as conquest of the Britons and Persians will show) is going to be god *among us*. In fact Augustus' divine status was a subject which required delicate treatment. Julius Caesar was enrolled among the Roman gods in 42 BC, since when Octavian/Augustus, his adopted son, had called himself 'Son of a God'. In the aftermath of his victory at Actium, he had been asked by the Greeks of Asia Minor for permission to worship him. He had conceded that he could be worshipped together with the goddess Roma. In *Odes* 1.2 Horace played with the idea that Augustus might be identifiable with the god Mercury. However, he did not achieve fully divine status until after his death. It is therefore convenient for Horace to put the idea into the future.

Britons, threatening Persians   see the introduction to this poem. 'Persians' is used for Parthians because of the ancient tradition of the Persian invasions of the fifth century, which the Greeks had repelled. They symbolized the eternal opposition of East and West, of civilization and barbarism. In Horace's day the Parthians had taken advantage of Roman civil wars to cause serious trouble during the 30s BC, though by the time this poem is published the description 'threatening' appears to have more to do with Roman than with Parthian politics.

And have **Crassus' soldiers** lived on,   5
in shameful marriage to alien wives, and reached old age
(shame to the **Curia**! shame for wrong now turned to right!)
wearing the arms of their brides' fathers, the enemy,

Marsians, Apulians accepting a Persian king,
the **Shields**, the name of Rome, the **toga**,   10
undying Vesta – all forgotten
while Jupiter and the city of Rome still stand?

Far-sighted **Regulus**, he saw to this,
casting his vote against the shameful terms,
knowing that this would be the beginning   15
of ruin on an age to come,

were not the captive youths to die
unpitied. '**Standards**,' he said,
'I've seen set high in shrines at Carthage,
weapons stripped from our soldiers   20

Crassus' soldiers for Crassus, see the introduction to this poem. Many of his soldiers were settled on the frontiers of the Parthian empire, beyond the Caspian Sea. It is even said that some of them fell into the hands of the Chinese. To judge by Dio's account, not all of them wanted in the end to come back to Rome, perhaps not surprisingly, if they had been away for more than 30 years.

Curia the Senate House in the Roman Forum. If this is what Horace wrote (there is some doubt), the Curia is being treated as a symbol of Roman values.

Marsians, Apulians two Italian peoples (Marsians from the central Apennines, Apulians from the south-east) who should represent martial valour. The fact that they are clearly being treated as part of the *Roman* community is a major element of the Augustan ideal. Much of the history of Italy, even of the recent past, was the story of the *hostility* between Romans and non-Romans. Coinage of the period has *Tota Italia* ('All Italy') as one of Octavian's slogans.

Shields, toga, undying Vesta all symbols of Roman-ness. In the reign of Numa Pompilius, second king of Rome, a shield of remarkable shape was said to have fallen from heaven. It was revealed that upon its preservation depended the survival of the Roman state. Numa therefore had 11 identical shields made, so that there was no means of knowing which was the original. The story is in Ovid, *Fasti* 3. They remained part of Roman ritual practice. The toga was the traditional formal wear for a male Roman citizen. Augustus was particularly keen that it should be worn (Suetonius, *Augustus* 40.5). Vesta was the goddess of the hearth, and her temple in the Forum housed the sacred hearth of the Roman state. It was the duty of the *pontifex maximus* to ensure that the fire never went out.

Regulus, Standards see the introduction to this poem.

Breastplate from a statue of Augustus found at his wife Livia's villa at Prima Porta just north of Rome. In the centre a Parthian hands a legionary standard to a Roman in military uniform but unarmed. Around them are symbols of peace, prosperity, victory and the blessing of the gods (Zanker, pp. 188–92).

with no blood shed; hands I've seen
pinioned to the free backs of citizens,
gates unclosed, and fields now tilled
which once our own war-god ravaged.

No doubt, a soldier, once bought back with gold,   25
will come home keener. To shame you are adding
cost. Treat wool with dye, and it will never
retrieve the shade it's lost;

true manliness, when once let go,
cares not to be restored to poorer spirits.   30
**If, freed from a close-meshed net, a doe
does battle**, then will he be bold

---

gates unclosed, and fields now tilled   these are the gates and fields of Carthage enjoying the peace consequent on victory over the Romans.

No doubt   the Latin expression conveys the sarcasm more clearly.

If … a doe / does battle   but of course it doesn't. One thing is just as impossible as the other. A familiar rhetorical form of expression with the name *adynaton* ('impossible' in Greek).

who gave himself to **faithless enemies**,
and Carthage will, in a second war, be crushed
by one who unresisting felt his arms   35
strapped back, faced death, and feared it.

Such men, not knowing **their true source of life**,
confounded peace and war. For shame!
O mighty Carthage, **raised to greater heights
on the disgrace and ruin of Italy**.'   40

He put aside, they say, his chaste wife's kiss,
his little children too. **'A citizen' he thought
'I am no more'**. He set his manly gaze
fiercely upon the ground,

strengthening the wavering senators   45
by counsel never until then proposed,
then passed between his grieving friends
in haste, **exile extraordinary**.

And yet he knew **what the barbarian torturer
had ready for him**; but, still resolute,   50
he moved aside those kinsmen blocking his way,
and the People holding him from his return

---

faithless enemies   the phrase perhaps recalls the Roman traditional tag 'Punic trustworthiness', meaning no good faith at all. Regulus is about to demonstrate that the opposite is true of Romans. (Of course one would like to know what was the comparable phrase in the Punic language about the Romans!)

their true source of life   that is, membership of the Roman community.

confounded peace and war   the idea seems to be that they acted in war in a way which only made sense in peace, i.e. attempting to make a bargain. Horace uses an archaic word for 'war', suggesting a solemn legal distinction between it and peace.

raised to greater heights / on the disgrace and ruin of Italy   'ruin' in Latin definitely suggests the rubble of a collapsed building; we should take 'raised to greater heights' literally. But in fact during the first Punic war Italy was not invaded; there were no ruins. The phrase applies much better to the second Punic war, when Hannibal was in Italy for 15 years, 218–203 BC. It perhaps also invites a Roman to think of the obliteration of Carthage in 146: did it raise Rome higher?

'A citizen … I am no more'   as indeed was true in law (see the introduction to this poem).

exile extraordinary   this is an attempt to render the striking Latin phrase *egregius exul*.

what the barbarian torturer / had ready for him   there were different accounts of his death: that he was rendered sleepless by the removal of his eyelids, or that he was put inside a wheel with spikes pointing inwards. It was also said that he had died of natural causes and that, even while acknowledging this, his wife and sons had tortured Carthaginian prisoners in revenge (Diodorus 24.12).

---

as if he had settled for some client
a lengthy action, case at last decided,
and now was making for his lands – **Venafrum**   55
or **Lacedaemonian Tarentum**.

---

1   What ideal of Roman conduct is Horace setting before his audience? What is
    your own view of it?

2   What attitude does Horace seem to take to Crassus' soldiers? Do you
    sympathize with it?

3   What are the similarities and what are the differences between Cicero's
    account and Horace's? Consider content, manner of treatment, and emphasis.
    Is there reason for thinking that Horace based his version on Cicero?

4   Where in your view does the climax of the poem come?

5   What liberties has Horace taken with history? Does it matter?

6   Augustus, and with him Horace, thought history could and should be used to
    inspire the present generation. Are you inspired by history in any way? Has the
    appeal to history in general had a good effect or a bad one?

From the *Carmen Saeculare* – 'Hymn for a New Age'

Augustus had a view about Rome's place in the world, and he had a view about
the sort of society Rome should be. With his success over Parthia in 20–19 BC
(see Introduction, p. 5 and introduction to *Odes* **3.5**, p. 93), he established the
former; with the **social legislation** of 18 he set about establishing the latter.
The two together formed the start of a new age. There was a traditional, formal
definition of an 'age', and also a tradition that the end or beginning of an age
should be publicly celebrated. Religious authorities were prepared to agree
with Augustus that the year 17 did in fact mark a new age, and a celebration
was suitably arranged to cover the three days starting from the evening of 31
May. Nocturnal sacrifices were offered on successive evenings to the Fates,
the Ilithyiae (goddesses of childbirth) and the Earth; daytime sacrifices to
Jupiter, Juno and (on 3 June) to Apollo and Diana. This last ceremony was

---

Venafrum, Lacedaemonian Tarentum   Venafrum is on the borders of Latium and
Campania (for this area, see map on p. 29). Tarentum is a city on the south coast. Regulus
is imagined as behaving like a Roman aristocrat not of the third century BC, but of
Horace's own time: he has estates to which he can travel in peace in distant parts of
Italy. The idea ties up with 'Marsians, Apulians' (line 9): the unification of Italy under
Augustus. Tarentum was founded by the Greek city of Sparta (also called Lacedaemon)
in the eighth century BC. The adjective 'Lacedaemonian' is relevant because the Spartans
were famous for their dour fortitude, which is the quality claimed for Regulus by Horace
here. Tarentum is also an idyllic rural retreat in *Odes* **2.6.9–12** (p. 114).

social legislation   see Introduction, p. 5, and Wallace-Hadrill, pp. 66–9.

Horace's name, 'Q. Horatius Flaccus', in the Ludi Saeculares *inscription. It is the only surviving mention of a poet's name in the government proceedings of the Roman empire.*

performed at Augustus' temple to Apollo on the Palatine. An inscription survives, recording the event, and continuing: 'And when the sacrifice was complete, 27 previously designated boys and the same number of girls, with both parents living, sang a hymn, and in the same manner on the Capitol. The hymn was composed by Quintus Horatius Flaccus.'

In text and summary, enough is here presented to indicate how the hymn brings together the themes of all three days of celebration.

1–8   Phoebus and Queen Diana of the woods,
heaven's bright glory, whom to worship
is duty and custom, answer now our prayers
made at this holy time,

when **the Sibyl's verses** have given the word   5
that chosen maidens and sound-hearted boys
to the gods who delight in **the seven hills**
should tell out the song.

9–48   The prayers continue: to the Sun, to find nothing greater than Rome to look on; to the goddess of childbirth, to make Rome populous and to ensure that the **new laws** may renew the people so that in due time they celebrate yet another new age; to the Fates, that the future age may be as prosperous as the past; to the Earth, that it may be fertile; to Apollo and Diana again, to listen to the song. Now the second half of the hymn begins: that the gods who brought Aeneas from the ruins of Troy should maintain their goodwill by granting prosperity to his descendants.

---

the Sibyl's verses Sibyl is the title given to certain prophetic priestesses of Apollo, especially the priestess at Cumae near Naples. There was a vast collection of prophecies known as 'Sibylline books' which were regularly consulted if divine backing were needed for Roman public acts. There was an official board, the Fifteen Men, who were responsible for this. Since Augustus' temple to Apollo was dedicated in 28 BC, the Sibylline books had been stored in a special location at the foot of the cult statue of Apollo.

the seven hills the city of Rome.

new laws see the introduction to this poem and also p. 5.

49–76   And all that with **sacrifice of white oxen to you**
the glorious **offspring of Anchises and Venus** requests,   50
may he obtain, sooner than in war,
gentle to the fallen enemy.

Now by land and sea the **Mede**
quakes at our mighty hands and at **the axes**
of Alba; now, once proud, **to the source of wisdom**   55
Scythians come, and Indians.

Now Truth, and Peace, and Dignity and Honour
and ancient Virtue **dare to return,**
and blessed Plenty with full horn
comes before our eyes.   60

And **Phoebus**, fair with gleaming bow,
prophet, whom the nine Muses love,
who with his healing skill relieves
weary limbs,

---

sacrifice of white oxen to you   the sacrifice to Apollo and Diana was made with various forms of cake. In writing of oxen Horace must be referring to the sacrifices on earlier days, to Jupiter and Juno. Horace's hymn is clearly not part of the ritual but a summary of it.

offspring of Anchises and Venus, gentle to the fallen enemy   respectful references to the recently published *Aeneid*. Virgil had made much of Augustus' ancestry. Julius Caesar, who had adopted him, claimed descent from Iulus, son of Aeneas, grandson of Anchises and the goddess Venus. Virgil had also described the duty of the Roman 'to spare those brought low and to humble the arrogant by war' (*Aeneid* 6.853).

Mede   i.e. Parthian. See *Odes* **3.5.4n**, p. 94.

the axes / of Alba   Alba Longa, on the mountain 15 miles south of Rome, was the city whose kings were descended from Iulus son of Aeneas and were ancestors of the Iulii. Romulus was a member of this family. The axes are those to be found in the *fasces* (see *Odes* **3.2.19** and note, p. 91), symbols of the coercive power of kings and consuls.

to the source of wisdom / Scythians come, and Indians   in section 31 of Augustus' *Res Gestae* ('Record of Achievements') he claims to have received embassies from India and Scythia (modern Ukraine). Horace's Latin 'they seek responses' is appropriate to petitioners at an oracle, hence 'the source of wisdom'.

dare to return   in days of old gods lived with humans on the earth; when humanity became corrupt they left. The last of the immortals to leave the earth was Justice. In Virgil, *Eclogue* 4.6 the return of the Golden Age is signalled by the return of the Virgin (Justice) to earth. Horace here hints at his friend's poem and also suggests that the return of these other virtues is the confirmation of Virgil's statement.

Phoebus   five of Apollo's traditional attributes are briefly referred to: his prophetic function, his beauty, his silver bow, his patronage of the arts, and his healing skill.

'Phoebus [Apollo], fair with gleaming bow' (Carmen Saeculare 61). The bow itself and both hands were lost; the hands have been restored. The god has just released his arrow, and his eye follows it. This famous statue ('Apollo Belvedere') is based on an original of the fourth century BC.

if he looks kindly on **the altars of the Palatine**   65
preserving the Roman commonwealth and Latium
for one more **stage** of blessedness
and to an **era** growing ever better,

and if Diana who rules the **Aventine and Algidus**,
attends to the prayers of **the Fifteen Men**,   70

---

the altars of the Palatine i.e. the altar outside his own temple.

stage, era the Latin words are *lustrum,* strictly a period of five years, and *aevum,* a lifetime or a longer period. Horace seems to be thinking in the sequence 'now … a finite period in the future … an infinite period'.

Aventine and Algidus Diana had a very ancient temple on the Aventine hill, which will have been clearly visible across the Circus Maximus from Palatine Apollo. Algidus is a summit in the Alban hills, also visible on a clear day in the same direction. The two embraced a good deal of Latium in the space between them (line 66).

the Fifteen Men see on 'the Sibyl's verses' (line 5).

and to the vows of **boys**
turns a friendly ear,

homeward I bear the sure and certain hope
that this is the will of Jupiter and all the gods,
I the choir skilful in speaking the praises
of Phoebus and Diana.

75

---

1   In his 1883 edition of the *Odes*, T. E. Page observed that the *Carmen Saeculare* is designed for a large public occasion, and understandably sacrifices subtlety for clarity and fine shading for resounding rhetoric. Does this seem to you a fair judgement, and, if it does, is the poem the worse for it?

2   What sort of themes are likely to succeed in an uplifting patriotic song? Do the themes dealt with by Horace above fit into this category? Consider, for example, Kipling's 'Recessional'.

Odes 4.5

In 16 BC Augustus left for Gaul to deal with what was presented as a military crisis. This poem is ostensibly written in expectation of his return. When he did return, on 4 July 13, the Senate decreed the construction of the Altar of Augustan Peace (*Ara Pacis Augustae*). This took more than three years to build, and was finally dedicated on 30 January 9 BC. With its sculptured representation of peace and prosperity under an imperial family blessed by the gods, it creates an impression very similar to this poem and to *Odes* 4.15, the last of Horace's odes.

Descendant of kindly gods, best protector
of Romulus' race, too long now is your absence.
To **the Fathers' sacred assembly** you promised
a speedy return. Come then,

---

boys   the word Horace uses here is regularly used to refer to children of either sex. But up to now he has mentioned girls separately. Ellen Oliensis sees this change as not merely shorthand, avoiding repetitiveness, but as implying that 'the girls are to efface themselves behind or within the … masculine community' (*CCH*, p. 228).

I the choir   this expression is paradoxical in the Latin too.

Descendant of kindly gods   Julius Caesar, and therefore also Augustus, claimed descent from Iulus son of Aeneas, whose mother was Venus and whose grandfather Jupiter. Mars may also be included, as father of Romulus. The Latin of this phrase could equally well mean 'Born with the favour of the gods'. Undoubtedly Horace was aware of both ideas. I have chosen the former because it recalls the language in which, according to the poet Ennius (third to second century) (Annals 117–21, Warmington), the Romans mourned Romulus.

the Fathers' sacred assembly   the Senate.

Panel from the Altar of Augustan Peace (Ara Pacis Augustae) decreed in 13 BC and dedicated in 9. Italy (or Mother Earth, or Peace herself) is surrounded by symbols of fertility and prosperity (Carmen Saeculare 65–8).

shine once more, good leader, on your country.   5
For when your countenance beams out like spring
upon your people, time runs past more sweetly
and days are brighter.

As a mother calls her youngster (whom with jealous blast
the south wind keeps in year-long idleness and more   10
beyond the waters of **the Carpathian sea**
far from his sweet home)

observing omens, making vows and prayers,
not shifting her gaze from the curving shore:
so, stricken with longing for the one she trusts,   15
the nation looks for Caesar.

---

the Carpathian sea   Carpathus is an island between Crete and Rhodes at the southern limit of the Aegean. It is precisely in this area of sea that St Paul was travelling (Acts of the Apostles 27) when the wise decision would have been to put in for the winter, and what actually followed was storm and shipwreck.

The ox walks in safety round his fields.
Ceres and kindly **Blessedness** nourish those fields.
Sailors skim the sea now pacified.
Truth fears reproach. 20

The spotless home is sullied by no vileness.
Custom and law have overcome the stain of sin.
Mothers win praise for children like themselves.
Guilt faces present retribution.

Who'd fear the **Parthian**, who the cold **Scythian**, 25
or those spawned by the horrid brood
of **Germany**, while Caesar's safe? Who'd worry
at wars in savage **Spain**?

Each lays the day to rest in his own hills,
marries the vine to his **unpartnered trees**, 30
comes happy home to his wine, begins his meal afresh
invoking you as god.

With many prayers to you, and much wine poured
from the dish, **he joins your sacred power**
to the Lar, as Greece in memory 35
of Castor and great Hercules.

Ceres   the Roman goddess of arable crops, hence 'cereal'.

Blessedness   this, as an abstract idea made into an active divinity, appears to be invented by Horace, but very much in the tradition of Roman deities such as 'Honour' and 'Virtue', to whom a temple was dedicated by Marcus Marcellus in 205 BC.

Sailors skim the sea now pacified   in the last few days of Augustus' life, as he was sailing across the Bay of Naples, he crossed the path of an Alexandrian trading ship. Seeing him, 'the passengers and crew, clad in white and crowned with garlands and burning incense, lavished upon him good wishes and the highest praise, saying that it was through him that they lived, through him that they sailed the seas, and through him that they enjoyed their liberty and good fortunes' (Suetonius, *Augustus* 98.2).

Parthian, Scythian, Germany, Spain   the conquest of Spain was completed by Augustus' chief associate Marcus Agrippa in 19 BC. Hostilities with Parthia reached a conclusion in 19 (pp. 93–4). For Scythians see *Carmen Saeculare* **55n**, p. 100. A campaign in southern Germany had been successfully concluded in 15.

unpartnered trees   ancient wine growers trailed their vines over pollarded trees. 'Marriage' is a regular image for the process of attaching the vine to its tree. Page quotes Shakespeare, *Comedy of Errors* 2.2: 'Come, I will fasten on this sleeve of thine. / Thou art an elm, my husband, I a vine.'

invoking you as god, he joins your sacred power / to the Lar   Augustus was only recognized as one of the gods of the Roman state after his death. But the process began in 30–29 when it was decided that libations at public and private banquets should be poured in his name, and he allowed himself to be worshipped along with the goddess Roma in the provinces (Dio, *Roman History* 51.19–20; compare *Odes* **3.5.2–3n**, p. 94).

'Good Leader, may you give **the Western Land**
long holidays!' we say when dry, at dawn
with the day before us, and when merry, as
the Sun sinks towards Ocean.   40

---

1   Lines 17–24 are unique in Horace: nowhere else do we find eight lines of verse each consisting of a single separate sentence. Compare the points made in these lines with the Augustan Inventory, p. 75. What is the effect of making points in this way?

2   Whose point of view does Horace on the whole adopt in offering his praise of Augustus?

3   Do you detect, and can you explain, differences of approach from earlier poems (*Odes* **1.12**, **3.2**, **3.5**, pp. 75, 90, 93)?

4   With what phrase does Horace twice address Augustus? What is the single word in the poem which sums up the Augustan age as seen from the poet's point of view?

5   Is Horace being sincere? Do you sympathize with him?

6   'But they shall sit every man under his vine and under his fig tree; and none shall make them afraid: for the mouth of the Lord of Hosts hath spoken it' (Micah 4.4). Does this make a good point of comparison for Horace's approach to Augustus here? What image would you choose to represent a state of perfect civil peace?

7   In the introduction to this section (p. 74), three different assessments of Horace are expressed. Which of them corresponds most nearly to yours?

Gods: *Odes* 1.31, 1.34, 3.13, 3.18

Odes 1.31

In 36 BC Octavian bought properties on the Palatine with a view to creating public space around his own house. When lightning struck a part of this space, the priests gave their opinion that Apollo was demanding that a temple be built to himself there. The structure was dedicated on 9 October 28. Its magnificence is described by Virgil (*Aeneid* 8.720) and Propertius (*Elegies* 2.31). If Virgil is to be taken literally (West, 1995, p. 148) it had also been made the setting for a great review as part of the celebrations in the previous year of Octavian's victories at Actium and Alexandria and in Dalmatia (the Adriatic coast: he had been campaigning here in 34 and 33). With this in our minds, Horace creates the expectation of a solemn prayer of national significance. The expectation is immediately undermined in line 3 by the mention of new wine, which carries us on to 11 October, the festival of the

---

the Western Land   see *Odes* **2.1.32n**, p. 89.

Meditrinalia. On this day the ritual words were: 'I drink the old wine and the new; I heal diseases old and new.' The connection with Apollo lies in the healing aspect: Apollo is Paean, the healer. Making a libation, the poet is standing outside the temple, in the presence (as seems likely) of a statue of Apollo the Lyre-Player.

What is the **seer** asking of Apollo
now consecrated? What is his prayer as he pours
new wine from the bowl? Not for the fertile
crops of prosperous **Sardinia**,

not for the lovely herds of sweltering   5
Calabria, not for Indian ivory or gold,
not for the fields which **Liris**' silent stream
gnaws away with its unhurrying water.

Let those to whom Luck has given the vines of **Cales**
check them with sickle; let the wealthy trader   10
drain dry from golden goblets
the wine he's earned from Syrian merchandise,

dear to the very gods, when thrice each year
and four times he sails to the Atlantic sea
undamaged. I eat **olives, chicory**   15
and mallows which lie light upon the stomach.

---

seer   Horace uses a word which can mean 'poet' or 'prophet'. Apollo delivered his oracles through speakers who were both. Horace here puts himself in a special relationship with the god.

Sardinia   the island was a very important source of grain for the Roman state from the third century BC until the fifth century AD.

Calabria   the name given to the 'toe' of Italy in modern times and to the 'heel' in antiquity. The geographer Strabo (6.3.5) observed it as an oddity that the region had little water, but nonetheless was thickly forested and offered good pasture.

Liris, Cales   the river Liris flows through the great wine-growing area of northern Campania, quiet in its lower if not in its upper course. The vines of Cales grow a little further south and more inland.

olives, chicory / and mallows   Horace talks of simple diet in *Satires* **2.6.63** (p. 45). It may be relevant that in poem 9 of the *Catalepton*, a collection traditionally attributed to Virgil, the writer aspires to be a new Callimachus (on whom see Introduction, p. 6) and ends with the words 'with plump people I have nothing to do'. Horace himself is plump when he is an Epicurean (*Epistles* **1.4.16**, p. 152).

Grant me the use of what I now possess
O Son of **Leto**, and, I pray, still healthy
and sound of mind, to live in my old age
not squalidly, and not without the lyre.   20

---

1   Identify similarities between this poem and *Odes* **1.1**, p. 58. In what way are
the conclusions they come to different?

2   Octavian regarded Apollo with especial reverence, particularly after the battle
at Actium, a place whose presiding god was Apollo. Would Octavian think that
Horace was doing the god justice here?

Odes 1.34

This poem comes nearest in form to a *palinode* ('recantation'), the legendary
origin of which was the sixth-century BC poem by Stesichorus, in which he
took back the unkind things he had said about Helen of Troy as having been
responsible for the Trojan war. Helen, by now a minor goddess, had struck
the poet blind, but restored his sight once he had recanted.

In lines 1–3 Horace represents himself as a paid-up Epicurean. Not believing
in gods active in the world, he does not court them. More than that, he has
committed himself to the fine detail of Epicurean philosophy, something
which in *Epistles* **1.1.14** (p. 150) he says he does not do. This failure of his
own to understand or respect the gods he sums up in two engaging oxymora:
'an expert all adrift' (experts are there to guide others, but who can a drifter
guide?) and 'wisdom which is lunacy'. All of a sudden, he is shaken out of his
Epicureanism, which is absurd, by a miracle which is impossible – thunder
in a clear sky (lines 3–12: 'now … were shaken'). But the conclusion which
follows – acceptance of a capricious and mocking Fortune – does not seem
quite consistent either with the Epicureanism from which he is coming nor
with the acknowledgement of the power of Jupiter to which he claims to
have moved.

Mean in my worship and irregular,
an expert all adrift
in wisdom which is lunacy, now full astern
I'm forced to spread my sails and travel back

Leto   (Latona in Latin) mother of Apollo and Diana; 'the kindest in all Olympus' says the
poet Hesiod (*Theogony* 408).

Mean   i.e. his offerings are not substantial.

---

on an abandoned course. For Jupiter 5
who splits the clouds with coruscating fire
routinely, drove across a cloudless sky
his thundering horses and his flying chariot,

at which the dull earth and the wandering rivers,
the **Styx**, and **Taenarum**, that hateful place, 10
and **the world's boundary which Atlas keeps**
were shaken. High and low – the god has power

to exchange them, and to make the glorious small,
bringing the unseen to the fore. Rapacious Fortune
takes this man's crown with piercing shriek 15
and puts it merrily upon another.

- Consider the following views of this poem (the first two quoted by West, 1995, p. 165). How many of them do you find valuable?

  - Dr Samuel Johnson: 'Sir, he was not in earnest: this was merely poetical.'

  - H. P. Syndikus: 'It is an allegorical statement of Horace's poetical intentions: that lyric poetry must be about gods.'

  - R. G. M. Nisbet and M. Hubbard: 'The serious point of the ode only emerges in the last stanza. It is the inexplicability, the violence, and the suddenness of Fortune's action on human life that have been symbolised by the lightning in a clear sky.' 'The poem is by no means trivial. Horace has the rare gift of being amusing and serious at once' (1970, p. 377).

  - West: 'We find it difficult to arrive at a clear and convincing understanding of this ode, because the argument is not meant to be clear' (1995, p. 167).

---

routinely   Horace deliberately chooses an unpoetic word, one which is a favourite of Lucretius. Lucretius, an Epicurean, held that thunder was a product of natural forces within clouds. If this is so, clouds will *always* have to be present. If they are only present *routinely*, Lucretius' argument collapses. Horace uses Lucretius' word to undermine Lucretius' argument.

Styx, Taenarum   both were actual places in Greece associated with the Underworld – the Styx a waterfall in Arcadia whose name was transferred to a river of Hades, Taenarum the middle cape of the three at the south of the Peloponnese, where a cave was thought of as an entrance to Hades.

the world's boundary which Atlas keeps   i.e. the western boundary of the known world, perhaps the southern Pillar of Hercules at the Straits of Gibraltar.

takes this man's crown with piercing shriek   the reference seems to be to the story of Tarquinius Priscus, fifth king of Rome, whose imminent kingship was indicated by an eagle which swooped down screaming and placed a crown on his head. (This is a combination of Livy 1.34.8 with Cicero *On Laws* 1.4.)

Odes 3.13

> This short hymn is one of Horace's best-known poems. Because of the animal sacrifice on which it dwells, it has aroused strong and different responses.

Spring of **Bandusia**, gleaming brighter than **glass**,
worthy of strong sweet wine and flowers too,
tomorrow you'll be gifted with a kid
whose brow, swelling with horns

just growing, promises love and battles –   5
in vain. In your cool springs will be
the stain of crimson blood,
from the frisky herd's child.

You are never touched by the blazing **Dog-star**'s
cruel season; you give a pleasant chill   10
to bulls weary from ploughing
and to the straying flock.

You shall be one of the **famous springs**,
when I tell of the ilex-tree which leans over your hollow
rock, where they come leaping down,   15
those chattering **waters** of yours.

Bandusia   the spring is most likely to be the one referred to in a papal bull of AD 1103. It is ten miles east of Venusia on the Appian Way, and therefore in the heart of Horace's childhood home country. The name is thought to be a corruption of the Greek *Pandosia* – 'she who gives everything'.

glass   see *Odes* **1.17.20n**, p. 135. Glass suggests a glittering reflective surface.

the stain of crimson blood   the kid's blood in the bright water has repelled many readers. For Horace too it appears to be more than a casual detail, to judge by the fact that on at least two other occasions (for one of them, see *Odes* **1.4.12**, p. 123) Horace speaks of the sacrifice of a kid, but with no descriptive embellishment of the killing or of the animal's lost future.

Dog-star   Sirius, the brightest star in the constellation Canis Major (the Great Dog). The Dog-star's season starts in late July, when Sirius rises just before dawn, and is the hottest time of the year. The ice-cold mountain spring is impervious to the summer heat.

famous springs   e.g. Dirce at Thebes, which inspired Pindar, and Arethusa at Syracuse, which inspired Theocritus. Bandusia 'the all-giver' is going to be Horace's Italian inspiration (compare *Odes* **3.30**, pp. 67–8).

waters   the Latin word Horace uses is *lymphae,* which is historically the same word as *nymphae*: water nymphs, divinities attendant on Bandusia just as Muses attend as sources of inspiration on other 'famous springs'.

Sacrifice is a thank-offering for favours or a means of securing future favours. If nothing else does, the reference to 'famous springs' makes it clear that Horace is speaking of his own poetic inspiration, hence that the sacrifice is being made in gratitude for that inspiration.

The general view of scholars up to now has been that the spring is on Horace's Sabine estate, given its name by Horace as a memento of the spring in his home country. In a recent article Llewelyn Morgan argues that there is no good reason for inventing a second Bandusia when we know about the one in the south already. He connects the sacrifice at Bandusia of the not-quite-adult kid with Horace's own departure thence for Rome as a not-quite-adult boy (see Introduction, p. 2). He left to go to school in Rome and then to a life of 'love and battles' (line 5) in the true manner of his poetic model Alcaeus, on whom see *Odes* **1.32.6–10**, p. 62.

---

1   Does the proposed association of the fulfilled life of Horace with the unfulfilled life of the kid make sense of the sacrifice to you?

2   Does the following quotation from Walter Burkert, the great historian of religion, affect your judgement?

> *The shock of the terrors of death present in the warm flowing blood strikes home directly, not as some painful adjunct, but as the very centre to which all eyes are directed. And yet in the subsequent feast the encounter with death is turned into a life-affirming enjoyment.*
>
> Homo Necans 55–6

Odes 3.18

The Fauns were spirits of the Italian countryside, a nuisance (Lucretius, *De Rerum Natura* 4.582) for their noisy nocturnal rampagings. Later, it seems, they coalesced into the single god Faunus, whose rustic festival was celebrated on 5 December (given its formal Roman name 'Nones' in line 10). In literature Faunus acquired some of the characteristics of the Greek Pan, including his erotic tendency (line 1). Here he gives his blessing to what the reader surely understands as Horace's Sabine estate.

Faunus, lover of the fleeing Nymphs,
over my lands and sunny fields
walk gently, and, as you leave, be kind
to the little ones, the young,

if at the year's end a tender kid falls,   5
and wine in plenty fills the mixing bowl,
companion of Venus, and the ancient altar
smokes thick with incense.

The whole flock's at play on the grassy plain,
when your December Nones come round again;   10
on holiday, the **village** takes its ease
in the pastures with the idle ox.

The wolf goes straying among fearless lambs;
the woods scatter for you their leaves from the wild;
the ditcher's glad **to strike the earth he hates**   15
with his foot, a three-fold blow.

---

1   Is Horace's picture of the rustic scene realistic?
2   What does Horace seem to believe about the gods? (Consider, as well as the
    poems in this section, *Odes* **1.12**, **3.5**, pp. 75, 93, *Carmen Saeculare* p.98, *Odes*
    4.5, p. 102 and any others which seem relevant.) Does he actually believe in
    them? Do any of the attitudes he expresses strike a chord with you?

Friends: *Odes* 1.29, 2.6, 2.7, 2.11, 3.21

Odes 1.29

Iccius is planning to join the expedition to Arabia led by Aelius Gallus in
25 BC and recorded by Augustus in *Res Gestae* 26.5. In spite of Augustus'
extravagant claims, it was not a success (Dio 53.29.3–8); there were many
casualties and nothing permanent was achieved.

One of the standard genres was the 'farewell' poem: the term is *propemptikon*.
(Compare *Odes* 1.3 and 1.35, where standard elements of the *propemptikon*
are worked into the hymn to Fortune.)

---

companion of Venus   for Venus as companion of Bacchus (wine) see *Odes* **3.21.21**, p. 121.

village   Horace's word is *pagus*, of a country district, but one with the sense of community
which 'village' gives. Horace's *pagus* included at least two villages, Mandela and Varia.
Some good manuscripts read *pardus* ('leopard'). The loitering leopard is charming, but
not convincing as a feature of Horace's landscape. The great eighteenth-century scholar
Richard Bentley (quoted in Nisbet and Rudd, p. 225) pointed out that medieval scribes,
carried away by Horace's idyllic landscape, had been thinking of Isaiah 11.6: 'The wolf
also shall dwell with the lamb, and the leopard shall lie down with the kid.'

to strike the earth he hates   the ancient commentator Porphyrio observes that 'it is
natural for everyone to loathe the things at which they have to work hard' (Nisbet and
Rudd, p. 226). The ditch-digger's opportunity to express his hatred is the dance, whose
rhythm is illustrated by the hard consonants of Horace's last line *ter pede terram* (literally
'thrice with his foot the earth').

Iccius, are you now envying the wealthy Arabs
their treasures, planning a sharp test of strength
for the hitherto undefeated **Sabaean**
kings? and **for the dreaded Mede**

are you weaving chains? What exotic maiden,   5
her bridegroom slain, will be your servant?
What royal stripling will be set
over your cups, his hair perfumed,

though trained to draw arrows from China on his father's bow?
Who can be sure that streams flowing down sheer mountains   10
headlong, cannot flow uphill,
that Tiber cannot turn back,

if you, who have bought up fine books everywhere
– **Panaetius**, the whole **school of Socrates** –
now look like changing them for **Spanish corslets**.   15
You had us thinking better of you.

Iccius   some years later Horace wrote a verse letter to Iccius, *Epistles* **1.12**, which appears in this collection on p. 151.

Sabaean   the Sabaeans lived in what is now Yemen, in the south-western corner of Arabia. They controlled the trade route to India, which seems to have been a major reason for the invasion. Hence Iccius' alleged covetousness (line 1).

for the dreaded Mede   as in the Latin, the phrase could go with the preceding words, and it only becomes clear as you read that it goes with 'are you weaving chains?' This brings the phrase 'are you weaving chains?' forcibly to our attention. 'Medes' can be equivalent to Parthians, i.e. occupiers of Mesopotamia and Iran and nowhere near Arabia. The suggestion seems to be that Iccius has been captivated by the romance of the Orient, and has no clear idea about the location of the peoples against whom he is marching – or that Horace is teasing him by pretending to be so ignorant.

that Tiber cannot turn back   an impossibility (*adynaton*) – a conventional means of indicating surprise.

Panaetius   Panaetius of Rhodes was head of the Stoic school of philosophy at the end of the second century BC. He was influential in Rome, having spent some time there; he wrote an important ethical work, *On Seemliness*.

school of Socrates   another major philosophical group, the Academics, who inherited their name from the Academy in Athens, where Socrates' pupil Plato taught. By labelling the school as belonging to Socrates, Horace indicates that here too Iccius' interest is mainly in ethics.

Spanish corslets   because of the superior quality of Spanish metalwork.

1   It is relatively unusual for the name of the addressee of Horace's poems to appear as the first word of the poem, unless the addressee is a god; when it does, it seems to indicate some urgency on the part of the poet. What urgent message does Horace seem to have for Iccius?

2   Judging from the content of the poem, how serious is Horace being? How far is his message consistent with what he says in *Odes* **3.2** (p. 90)?

Odes 2.6

In about 20 BC Horace wrote a reference for Septimius in the form of a letter to Augustus' stepson, the young Tiberius Caesar (*Epistles* 1.9). This poem probably dates from about five years earlier, with its reference to unfinished wars against the Cantabrians in northern Spain. Augustus returned to Rome in early 24 after campaigning against them.

Horace wished to remind his reader of Catullus 11, a poem in the same (Sapphic) metre. For a translation of it, see below. By inviting the comparison he evidently wished to make a contrast between himself and the earlier poet.

Septimius, with me you would visit **Gades**, and
the Cantabrians untaught to bear our yoke, and
the savage **Syrtes**, where the Moorish sea
rolls for ever.

Tibur, established by its Argive founder,   5
should be – I pray – the home of my old age,
should mark the end **of weary travels by land and sea**,
of warfare too.

Gades   modern Cadiz, in western Spain, a symbol of the western edge of the world.

Syrtes   the shallow seas of the Gulf of Libya and its desert coasts, regularly a symbol of the inhospitable south.

Tibur   modern Tivoli, in the hills 18 miles east of Rome. A tradition said the town was founded by the brothers Tiburnus and Catillus, grandsons of the hero-prophet Amphiaraus of Argos. Horace's Sabine estate was further on up the valley of the Licenza, but at some stage he acquired a property in Tibur too – Suetonius was shown it by a guide. By putting the word 'Tibur' at the beginning of the stanza, Horace is setting it in strong contrast with the places mentioned previously, the contrast stronger in Latin for the absence of any word for 'but'.

of weary travels by land and sea, / of warfare too   Horace's land journeys had taken him to Athens and to Turkey and back with Brutus on campaign. From *Odes* 3.4.28 it seems that he took part in the naval campaigns of 36 BC; from *Epodes* 1 that he was present at the battle of Actium. These combine sea-travel and warfare, and of course he fought at Philippi too (*Odes* **2.7**, p. 116).

But if an unkind Fate bars me from Tibur,
I shall seek the river, sweet to **coated sheep,**   10
the Galaesus, and the countryside once ruled
by Spartan **Phalanthus.**

That patch of country smiles on me
beyond all others, where **Hymettus'** honey must
accept an equal, and the olive   15
rivals green **Venafrum;**

where Jupiter makes spring long
and winter mild, and **Aulon,** loved
by fertile Bacchus, feels no twinge of envy
for the **Falernian** grape.   20

That place, those blessed towers are calling you
and me as well; there with due tears
you'll wet the still-warm ashes of
your poet friend.

---

1 How does the second stanza provide specific responses to the various
suggestions of the first?

2 Why is Horace so content with second best (line 9)? On Tarentum, see the last
stanza of *Odes* **3.5**, p. 98, and *Epistles* **1.7.45**, p. 155.

---

coated sheep   by a series of references Horace makes it plain that he is referring to
Tarentum on the south coast of Italy. The wool of Tarentum was famous; herdsmen
protected the fleeces of their sheep by covering them with leather jackets, the heat of
which must have made the water of the river Galaesus attractive.

Phalanthus   leader of the Spartan colonists who founded Tarentum in about 700 BC.
Given that not long after this time Horace was complaining about his receding hairline
(*Epistles* **1.7.26**, p. 154), it may be relevant that the name Phalanthus means 'going bald'.

Hymettus   a mountain just north of Athens, particularly famous for its honey.

Venafrum   in the hills south-east of Rome. It is coupled with Tarentum also in *Odes* **3.5**.

Aulon   evidently a valley near Tarentum, unidentified.

Falernian   these grapes, grown in Campania between Rome and Naples, produced some
of the most sought-after wine in Italy.

> **Catullus 11**
>
> *Furius and Aurelius, you will be with Catullus*
> *whether he intends to visit the remotest Indians*
> *where the shore is pounded by the far-echoing*
> *Eastern wave;*
>
> *or the Hyrcanians or the soft Arabians*
> *or the Sagae or the arrow-bearing Parthians*
> *or the waters coloured*
> *by the sevenfold Nile,*
>
> *or if he will march across the lofty Alps*
> *to visit the mighty works of great Caesar,*
> *the Gaulish Rhine, that dreadful stream,*
> *and the farthest Britons.*
>
> *All these things, whatever is the will*
> *of the gods, you are ready to attempt with him.*
> *Just go and pass on to my girl a few*
> *remarks, not kind ones.*
>
> *Let her live and prosper with her lovers,*
> *whom she keeps, three hundred at once, in her embrace,*
> *loving none of them genuinely, but time and again*
> *busting all their groins.*
>
> *And let her not heed my love, as once she did;*
> *it has, because of her, collapsed like a flower*
> *at the edge of a meadow, when once by a passing*
> *plough it has been grazed.*
>
> - How has Horace built on Catullus' ideas in this poem?

Odes 2.7

Julius Caesar was murdered in 44 BC, and in 44–42 Horace was fighting for the Republican leaders Brutus and Cassius in the war which ended at Philippi in 42 with the victory of Mark Antony and Octavian, the later Augustus. The Pompeius to whom this poem is dedicated is otherwise unknown. It is clear that he continued to fight against Octavian, and perhaps did so until the last moments, when Antony killed himself in Egypt rather than surrender. If so, this poem was written shortly afterwards, perhaps in 29, when Pompeius will have been permitted to return as part of the amnesty towards opponents which was an important part of Octavian/Augustus' plan.

The 'welcome home' speech is another genre, to which the name *prosphonetikon* is given. Other examples are *Odes* 1.36, 3.14 and Catullus 9.

How often you and I were in deadly danger
serving with Brutus in command!
Who brought you home, **citizen at peace** once more,
a gift to your country's gods, to Italian skies,

Pompeius, first of my companions?   5
With you I often broke the day's resistance
as we drank our wine unmixed, our heads in garlands
and hair agleam with **Syrian cassia**.

I saw **Philippi and that hasty flight**
with you, **my little shield shamefully dropped**,   10
when **Virtue** broke, and **they**, so full of threats,
felt the vile earth beneath their chin.

But I was rescued: **through the enemy**
swift **Mercury took me**, trembling, in thick mist,

---

citizen at peace   Horace uses the single word *Quiritem*, a particularly Roman word for 'Roman', which suggests both 'citizen as opposed to alien' and 'civilian as opposed to soldier'.

Syrian cassia   Horace uses the exotic word *malobathrum,* itself derived from Sanskrit, to suggest the good times which he and Pompeius enjoyed out east on their military exercises. Brutus took his army to Syria in 43, chiefly in order to raise or extort money for the Philippi campaign.

Philippi and that hasty flight   in September 42 there were two battles in the vicinity of Philippi near the Aegean coast in northern Greece. The first was a stalemate, the second a rout in which Antony defeated Brutus.

my little shield shamefully dropped   Horace here sets himself alongside the lyric poets of sixth-century Greece, Archilochus and Anacreon, both of whom boasted, no doubt ironically, of having saved their own lives by doing that most disgraceful thing, abandoning their shields. He uses the diminutive form of a word which in any case means 'a small shield', in ironic self-defence. The literary precedents make one wonder, indeed, whether Horace did throw his shield away.

Virtue   the supreme good for the Stoics, of whom Brutus was one. It was said that, defeated and just before committing suicide, he quoted a couplet from tragedy: 'O wretched Virtue, were you but a word? I followed you, but you were Fortune's slave' (Dio 47.49.2 cf. Introduction, p. 7).

they   Horace is vague as to who 'they' are, but the historian Appian (*Civil Wars* 4.124) refers to Brutus' army at this stage as being impatient and aggressive.

through the enemy / swift Mercury took me   in Homer's *Iliad*, Aeneas is rescued 'in a dark cloud' (5.345) and Hector 'in a thick mist' (20.444) by Apollo. Horace ironically associates himself with such heroes. Compare *Satires* **1.9.78**, p. 41, though here he employs Mercury, to whom he dedicates two odes (1.10, 3.11) and whose special protection he acknowledges in 2.17.29.

while waves of war swallowed you up again   15
and **carried you off over the seething waters**.

So pay to Jupiter **the feast you vowed**,
and lay beneath my laurel tree your limbs
weary with long campaigning, and **show**
no mercy to the **casks** marked with your name.   20

Fill the bright **chalices** with **Massic** wine
that brings forgetfulness. Pour out the perfume
from well-filled **shells**. Someone hurry, please,
fetch the moist **celery**; make a wreath of it,

or one of myrtle. Who will Venus declare   25
as **drinking master**? I will be revelling
with **Thracian self-restraint**. It's sweet
to go crazy, having lost and found a friend.

---

carried you off over the seething waters   the sea is a metaphor for the troubled times of war. But there is also the suggestion that Pompeius went to fight with Sextus Pompeius (no relation, it seems), who kept up a naval campaign against Octavian until finally defeated in 36.

the feast you vowed   it was standard practice to promise Jupiter a feast if a prayer for safe return was answered. Here it is Horace who seems to be fulfilling Pompeius' vow on his behalf.

show / no mercy   at last Pompeius can prove himself the ruthless warrior, at the expense of the wine-casks.

casks   large wine jars, holding (according to Lewis and Short's Dictionary) nine gallons.

chalices   the word Horace uses is *ciborium*, found nowhere else in Latin. It is said to be a drinking-vessel 'shaped like the flower of the Egyptian bean'. Perhaps one can link this with 'Syrian cassia' in line 8, and connect it with time spent by Pompeius with Antony in Egypt.

Massic   a very reputable wine from northern Campania.

shells   either real shells or shell-shaped vessels.

celery   'celery was often used at symposia for garlands' (Nisbet and Hubbard on *Odes* 1.36.16).

or one of myrtle   it is only between the first two and the last two stanzas that the sense carries over without a break. It may represent Horace's strong feelings, on the first occasion of delight at seeing his friend again, on the second of the urgency of getting the party going. The Latin of 'Someone hurry, please' is the language of a master giving hasty and abrupt orders to his slaves.

drinking master   the responsibility of the drinking master was to decide for the company what proportion of water should be drunk with the wine. The matter was decided by the throw of four dice. If each one showed a different number, it was called 'Venus' throw'.

Thracian self-restraint   an oxymoron: Thracians were, traditionally, anything but self-restrained. (Horace's adjective is actually 'Edonian'. The Edonians were a Thracian tribe of especial ferocity: they tore Orpheus to pieces.)

1   What is the answer to Horace's question 'Who brought you ...?' (line 3)? How does knowledge of this affect your reading of the poem as a whole?

2   In talking of 'Virtue' (line 11), is Horace here lamenting the failure of an honourable cause or speaking satirically of ineffectual political slogans?

3   How successfully does Horace deal with the fact that he and Pompeius fought on the losing side at Philippi?

4   Does either of the following judgements reflect your own view of this poem?

> Horace's poem is a masterpiece of tact. ... Yet in spite of all its charm the poem to some extent offends. ... Horace treats Brutus, who had raised him up, with disrespectful irony (line 12). ... The whimsicality of his treatment may be attributed not just to the frivolity that covers hurt but to political discretion. Yet after all, he could have said nothing.
>
> (Nisbet and Hubbard, 1978, p. 109)

> Horace has hunted with the hounds and run with the hare, producing a testament of loyalty not only to an old friend but also to current friends and benefactors. As Syndikus says, 'this freedom of speech does as much honour to Augustus as it does to the poet.'
>
> (West, 1998, p. 55)

Odes 2.11

This poem takes the form of an invitation (*vocatio*). Quinctius is troubled by the political questions of the day, perhaps 29 BC, when war with the Cantabrians became a serious issue (see the introduction to *Odes* **2.6**, p. 113). The Scythians are said to have sent a peace mission to Augustus in 25. Horace encourages him to give up his political anxieties, for sound Epicurean motives (lines 4–12), and spends the rest of the poem putting those principles into practice. For the treatment of the topic, compare the invitations to Maecenas in *Odes* **1.20** and **3.29**, pp. 69 and 71.

What is the warlike Cantabrian planning,
Hirpinian friend Quinctius, or the Scythian,
kept off by the Adriatic in between? Give up
that question, and do not fret at the needs

of a life which calls for little: away from us speeds   5
smooth-cheeked youth and beauty,
while dry grey hairs drive off
exciting love and easy sleeping.

Hirpinian friend Quinctius the Hirpini lived in the central Apennines, inland from Naples. Quinctius was the name of the brother-in-law of Pollio, to whom *Odes* **2.1** (p. 86) is dedicated; there is a possibility that this poem, in a conspicuous place at the beginning of the second half of the book, is dedicated to his kinsman.

The flowers of spring do not for ever keep
their splendour, nor does the bright moon always shine   10
with a single face: why weary your spirit with thoughts
of an eternity which is beyond it?

Here, under this tall plane tree or this pine
why do we not lie down just as we are,
scent our grey hairs with roses, while we can,   15
or anoint them with **Assyrian nard**,

and so drink deep? The **ecstatic god** dispels
gnawing anxiety. Quick now! Some boy
come quench the fiery **Falernian**
cups with water from the passing stream!   20

And someone must tease out from her house that skulking wench
Lyde! Tell her to come with her ivory lyre
and be quick about it, tying her hair
like a **Spartan** girl into a simple knot.

1	How consistent are the views expressed in lines 4–12 with Epicureanism as briefly described on p. 7?
2	In what way does the party take a different turn from line 13 onwards?
3	What does Horace seem to expect us to make of the change of tone?
4	How different would be the incentives which a modern verse invitation to a party might offer?

Odes 3.21

This is another invitation, to a special occasion, but expressed in the form of
a prayer summoning a god (*kletikon*), though this does not become apparent
until line 4. The guest is Marcus Valerius Messalla Corvinus, one of the great
men of the Augustan regime. He was a patrician, a member of the oldest

---

Assyrian nard   nard is properly the oil derived from the root of a Himalayan herb. It has
the name 'Assyrian' no doubt because of its point of entry into the Roman world. In *Odes*
4.12 Horace offers to exchange a cask of decidedly expensive wine for one flask of nard.

ecstatic god   Dionysus is in fact given here his title Euhius, 'the one associated with the
Bacchic cry *Euhoe*' (*Odes* **2.19.5**, p. 64).

Falernian   among the most highly prized Italian wines. It seems clear that the guests
begin by drinking it unmixed (see *Satires* **2.6.68n**, p. 46)!

Lyde, Spartan   her name 'the Lydian' may indicate a luxurious, extravagant disposition,
contrasting with her recommended hairstyle, 'Spartan', which will be plain and
practical.

aristocracy of the Roman republic. He was with Horace as a student at Athens (see Introduction, p. 2), and like Horace fought for the Republicans at Philippi. In 31 BC, the year of Actium, he was consul, having, like Horace, come over to Octavian's side. He was himself a literary figure, patron of the poet Tibullus, a poet and a distinguished orator. After Actium he was governor of Syria and then of Gaul, where he earned a triumph for the (re-) conquest of Aquitania. This triumph was held in 27 BC. We might think of this as a 'welcome-home' poem like *Odes* **2.7**, p. 115.

Horace is doing Messalla proud with a jar of some of the best wine which Italy has to offer. Its region of origin may itself be a compliment to Messalla, whose ancestor of some three centuries before seems to have played a part in subduing the area to Rome. As Horace's contemporary, the wine must now be about 40 years old. While 'older' does not necessarily mean 'better', there is some presumption that it will, as the exhibitionist millionaire Trimalchio in Petronius' novel *Satyrica* (34.6) shows by boasting of his (of course undrinkable) 100-year-old vintage.

Horace addresses this wine-jar as though it were a god, and would, if addressed correctly, be willing to dispense a holy blessing.

Born with me **when Manlius was consul,**
whether you have in you moans or merriment
or quarrelling **or** maddened love
or peaceful sleep, good wine-jar –

however named the Massic vintage in you,   5
you're worth **displaying** on a special day.
Come down now. I'm requested by Corvinus
to offer wines of restful character.

---

when Manlius was consul   Romans did not date their years numerically, but named them after the consuls (see Introduction, p. 5) who held office in them. Manlius' year was 65 BC.

whether, or, or, or   to suggest a range of possible names or functions as part of an address is a very frequent method of beginning a prayer to a god.

however named   in Latin 'name' can also mean 'heading' or 'function', so that the prayer-theme is here maintained. It was also regular practice to allow the god to choose what name he was to be addressed by – thus Catullus at the end of poem 34 says to Diana: 'may you be blessed under whatever name you choose'.

displaying   the Latin word is appropriate also to bringing images or cult objects into public view for a religious festival.

Come down now   gods would come down from heaven; wine-jars from the attic where, we are told, they were stored.

He's not the man, though soaked in Socrates'
discourse, to play the ascetic and ignore you.   10
Often, they say, even old Cato's rectitude
lost something of its chill in unmixed wine.

You work the gentle rack upon the spirit
which tends to stiffness; you, taken by the wise,
expose their troubles; secret thoughts you bring   15
to light by means of the merry Loosener.

You bring new hope to the tormented spirit;
you grant the poor man strength; you give him horns
and after you he'll fear no raging tyrant,
crowned though he be, nor soldier under arms.   20

Bacchus, and Venus if in joyful mood,
the Graces too, slow to untie their knot,
and living lamps will carry you along
till Phoebus comes and puts the stars to flight.

---

1   How successfully does Horace maintain the prayer
    parody?

2   Does Horace address this poem to Messalla in terms that
    are particularly appropriate to Messalla?

3   What is the wine-jar going to achieve in making the party
    go better? Does it seem better to you?

'Good wine-jar' (Odes 3.21.4). An amphora of a type specially used for
superior wines.

---

soaked   in Latin as in English with a hint of 'intoxicated'.

Socrates' / discourse   if in Athens Messalla was engaged in the same studies as Horace
(see *Epistles* **2.2.43–5**, p. 166), he will have studied at the Academy and read Plato's
work, almost all of which took the form of dialogues between Socrates and friends or
opponents. The style of these conversations is described by Cicero as 'easy' and 'not in the
least aggressive' (*On Duties* 1.134). This will have appealed to Messalla.

Cato   a great man of the first half of the previous century. He was appointed to the
censorship in 184 BC and used the office to express his hostility to the 'corrupting'
influences of Greek civilization and increasing wealth. He was the father-figure of
traditional Roman-ness.

You   for the hymn-like effect of the repeated 'you', see *Odes* **2.19.17–33**, pp. 65–6.

Loosener   a translation of *Lyaeus*, a cult-title of Bacchus.

horns   'The bull's horns, indicating courage and pugnacity, are often attributed to
Bacchus' (Nisbet and Rudd, p. 252 on this line).

the Graces   see *Odes* **1.4.6n**, p. 123–4.

Carpe diem: Odes 1.4, 1.9, 1.11, 4.7

Odes 1.4

Lucius Sestius, to whom this poem is addressed, served in Brutus' army in the campaign leading up to Philippi in 42 BC. After the battle he was proscribed (i.e. declared an outlaw, with all his property forfeited) but was subsequently pardoned. He maintained his loyalty to Brutus and Cassius, whose statues he kept in his houses and even showed them off to Augustus when he visited him once. When Augustus gave up the consulship on 1 July 23 BC, he appointed Sestius to succeed him, advertising, no doubt, his clemency and the return of the state to normality after the civil wars. It is Sestius' consulship which qualifies him to have a poem dedicated to him at this stage in the collection: *Odes* 1.1–4 are dedicated respectively to Maecenas, Augustus, Virgil and Sestius. This dedication is used as evidence that *Odes* 1–3 were published in this year, 23 BC.

David West (1995, p. 21) points out that the Sestius family owned a substantial pottery in Etruria, much of whose production was exported by sea. When the pottery produced bricks they were sometimes stamped with the abbreviation for 'workshop'. In addition there was a splendid fortified villa in the neighbourhood, built with Sestius bricks. These points fit neatly with the ships in line 2, the workshops in line 8, and the castles in line 14 ('king' being a standard epithet for a rich man) to suggest that the poem is carefully composed to suit its dedicatee.

The topic of spring and the prospect of renewed activity, especially navigation, was familiar from Greek poetry, such as this short piece from the *Palatine Anthology* (10.1):

> *Now is the season for sailing. The twittering swallow / is here already with the pleasant westerlies. / The meadows are in flower, the sea has fallen quiet, / churned up before by violent waves and wind. / Weigh anchor, sailor; cast off the mooring ropes; / stand under full sail out to sea. / It is I, Priapus of the harbour, who give you this command, / mortal, for you to sail in quest of every sort of commerce.*

The themes of winter and spring and of renewed activity are present here. The activity is particularly nautical, but the poem takes an epigrammatic turn in the last couplet. Priapus is a god of sexuality; his presence suggests that it is the sea of love on which the mariner is to set sail. (Compare *Odes* **1.5.5–10**, p. 132.)

In this poem and in *Odes* 4.7 (below, p. 128), Horace returns to the verse forms he had used in the *Epodes*: couplets of alternately long and short lines, with no separation into four-line stanzas. This fact and their similar subject-matter make it clear that Horace, writing the second poem some ten years after the first, is inviting us to consider them together.

Biting winter melts, pleasantly changing with spring's west winds.
　　　Winches are hauling dry ships to the water,
Nor are cattle still happy in the stall, nor the ploughman by his fire,
　　　nor are pastures white with hoar frost.
Now **Cytherea** is leading her dances as the moon hangs close above,　　　5
　　　and with the nymphs together the comely **Graces**
make the ground quiver as they tread, now left, now right, while blazing Vulcan
　　　inspects the **massive workshops of the Cyclopes**.
Now is the time to bind the gleaming hair with myrtle
　　　or with the flowers which the loosened earth brings out;　　　10
now too to sacrifice to **Faunus** in shady groves,
　　　whether he asks a lamb of us or a kid.
Pale Death kicks with impartial foot at the hovels of the poor
　　　and the turrets of kings. Sestius, you happy man,
life's short span says 'Form no hopes for the distant future.'　　　15
　　　Soon upon you will press night and the spirits of legend
and Pluto's **narrow** house. Once you go down there,
　　　you will not **throw the dice to be King of Wine**,
nor will you **gaze with delight at tender Lycidas**, for whom all young men
　　　are burning now, and girls will soon grow warm.　　　20

Winches are hauling dry ships to the water　ancient ships were usually light enough to be hauled up onto the beach whenever they were to be moored for a substantial period of time.

Cytherea　the goddess Aphrodite/Venus was so called because she was born of the sea-foam (*aphros* (Greek) = foam). One of the places where she was said first to have come to land was the island of Cythera in southern Greece.

Graces　the three Graces have a place in the canon of Greek divinities and are called Splendour, Good Cheer, and Festivity. They are appropriate spirits to celebrate the arrival of spring.

massive workshops of the Cyclopes　there were three Cyclopes, brothers of Jupiter's predecessor Cronus (Saturn to the Romans). In their forge, traditionally placed beneath Mount Etna in Sicily, they made for Jupiter the thunderbolts with which he overthrew Cronus. They seem to have no connection with the Cyclops with whom Odysseus had an unpleasant encounter in *Odyssey* 9.

Faunus　a god of the Italian woodlands, identified with Pan (*Odes* **3.18**, p. 110).

narrow　the space required by the urn containing his ashes, as opposed to his present spacious residence.

throw the dice to be King of Wine　see *Odes* **2.7.25n**, p. 117.

gaze with delight at tender Lycidas　in Horace, as in other Latin and Greek poets, it is taken for granted that boys are sexually attractive. On this see especially Jasper Griffin (pp. 25–6).

The comely Graces (Odes 1.4.6). In this painting of 1478, 'Primavera' ('Spring'), Botticelli picks up Horace's idea of the goddesses as representing the joys of the season. Mercury stands to the left.

1 Which of the following judgements do you find the more satisfactory?

  – The poet Walter Savage Landor: 'Pale Death [line 13] has nothing to do with the above [i.e. with what precedes it in the poem].'

  – R. G. M. Nisbet and M. Hubbard: 'In line 13 Death kicks at the door with thrilling suddenness' (1978, p. 60).

2 Is this a gloomy poem?

Odes 1.9

Of the few surviving fragments of Alcaeus, one reads: 'Rain's falling from Zeus, and from the heaven a mighty storm, and the streams of water are frozen … Defy that storm, setting up a fire and mixing sweet wine unstintingly, while you wind a scarf round your head' (Fr. Z14, quoted in Denys Page, p. 309). The similarities between this and the first two stanzas of *Odes* 1.9 are quite enough to suggest that Horace wished to acknowledge his debt. Unfortunately we cannot know how Alcaeus' poem went on. But the scenes from city life – specifically from Roman life (the Campus), and the structure of the poem around the advice to the young Thaliarchus – sound contemporary with Horace rather than with Alcaeus. The likelihood is therefore that here is another poem (compare *Odes* **1.37**, p. 80) whose germ Horace has taken from a predecessor but which he wishes to present in a new way, his own.

You see how **Mount Soracte** stands gleaming
white with deep snow, and how the straining woods
can carry the burden no longer, how in the keen
frost the river waters are stilled.

Make the cold thaw right through! Heap up   5
logs on the fire! Pour generous cups
of the **four-year wine**, Thaliarchus,
from its **two-eared Sabine cask**.

Mount Soracte   'Among the gentle and green hills of Tuscia Romana, suddenly a unique and lonely mountain stands out: Mt Soratte' (regional tourist pamphlet). It is a high hill for its immediate surroundings, but not much more than half the height of the summits of the Sabine hills not far away to the east. Snow on it suggests an especially cold winter snap. It is visible from Rome, but the setting of the poem seems rural.

four-year wine, two-eared Sabine cask   four years is no great age, and Sabine is only mid-quality wine. It is a homely rather than an especially festive scene. The setting is rustic, the wine from somewhere near Horace's own estate. But for 'two-eared', Horace has adapted a Greek word which appears nowhere else in surviving Latin literature. Taken along with the obvious debt to Alcaeus, this combination of Italian and Greek ideas seems to reflect what Horace claims in *Odes* **3.30.12–14** (pp. 67–8) as his achievement: 'I … first found for Aeolic song a home in Italian melodies'. The boy has a Greek name (Thaliarchos = 'leader of the festivities'). He is pouring the wine and setting the fire, which might perhaps suggest that he is a slave, and that the scene is a Greek-style drinking party (*symposium*). Just before he died, the emperor Augustus spent some time in Capri ('Donothingville', as he called it – *Apragopolis*) 'encouraging Romans to use the Greek dress and language, and the Greeks the Roman' (Suetonius, *Augustus* 98.3). We seem to have here just that fusion of Greek and Roman at both the literary and social level.

Let the gods take care of the rest. Once they
have lulled the winds which fight their battle   10
over the boiling seas, the **cypresses**
stand motionless, the ancient ashes too.

What will tomorrow bring? – avoid that question!
Whatever new day Fortune offers,
call it profit. Do not disregard love   15
or **dances** while still you're young,

still growing, green, not grey of head,
not set in your ways. For now make these your aim:
the **Campus**, the piazza, those soft whispers
in the twilight at an appointed hour,   20

the sweet laughter (which tells you where
she's hiding, deep in some corner)
of a girl whose token you pluck from her arm
or from her scarcely resisting finger.

- • To which of the following judgements does yours come closest?
  - – Eduard Fraenkel: 'The heterogeneous elements [location, weather,
    particular/general] have not really merged into a harmonious unit' (p. 177).
  - – R. G. M. Nisbet and M. Hubbard: 'The Soracte Ode has been censured for its
    inconsistency … This view is mistaken. Horace is not professing to describe
    something that really happened … Rather he is weaving together various
    strands from reading and experience, and … gives hints of sensitive and
    convincing attitudes' (1970, pp. 117–18).
  - – David West: 'As we read *Odes* 1.9 we enter a world known by Horace and
    adjusted for his poem. There is nothing impossible or even implausible
    about it. The fact that it features in earlier poetry does not mean it could
    not have occurred in Horace's Rome' (2002, p. 44).

---

cypresses   tall and slender trees, so especially noticeable when tossed about by a high
wind.

dances   stern Romans professed disapproval of dancing (Cicero, *Pro Murena* 13: 'dancing
is the symptom of luxury and extravagance carried to extremes'; Nepos 15.1.2: 'Roman
custom dictates that for a senior statesman it is not quite the thing to be a musician, and
positively disgraceful to be a dancer'). But Cicero at least was speaking tongue in cheek,
and Thaliarchus was surely not expecting to be a senior statesman.

Campus   that is, the Campus Martius, the floodplain in the bend of the Tiber which was
used for military parades, election meetings and outdoor recreation.

the sweet laughter … deep in some corner   these are two of the most untranslatable
lines in Horace. His order of words is 'now, hiding, betrayer, deep inside, pleasant, girl,
laughter, corner'.

Odes 1.11

The 'message' of this poem – 'harvest the day, and don't be sure you'll see tomorrow' – is very similar to that of *Odes* **1.9** (p. 125) – 'What will tomorrow bring? – avoid that question!' Yet they are very different poems.

The poem starts in Latin with an abrupt 'You', described by R. G. M. Nisbet and M. Hubbard as giving 'a tone of serious admonition' (1970, p. 136). It is as if Horace has come across Leuconoe's astrological researches, or has just been shamefacedly told by her about them. If this is right, we have from the beginning a dramatic confrontation between two individuals, and it is reasonable to ask about their motivation and how the scene develops. (West, 1995, pp. 50–3, has vivid observations on this theme.)

For this poem Horace uses a metre of long lines and breathless speed. The translation does not use Horace's exact metre but attempts to convey something of its spirit.

Leucónoë, you should not ask – **we must not know** – what end to me
or you the gods have given; never test the **Babylonian**
arithmetic. It will be better (come what may) to bear with it,
if Jupiter permits you further winters or none after this,
which now is **wearing out the sea that falls upon the pumice rocks**   5
of Tuscany. Be canny! **Strain the wine**! and to a little space

we must not know   see the following note. Astrologers were periodically expelled from Rome, most recently in 33 BC.

Babylonian / arithmetic   astrological calculations. Astrology began in Babylonia, and the astronomical calculations of the Babylonians are famous. At Rome you could find people who were deeply suspicious of astrology and others who were devoted to it. Here Leuconoe seems to have been trying to find out when she and Horace were doomed to die. Augustus (Dio 56.25.5) forbade one-to-one consultations with astrologers on the subject of death. But he also published in detail his own horoscope.

wearing out the sea that falls upon the pumice rocks   we expect the sea to be wearing out the land, but here it is the land which winter is using to wear out the sea.

of Tuscany   a clear geographical location, left nearly to the end of the poem, not, as in *Odes* **1.9** (p. 125), at the beginning. The sea of Tuscany is the Mar Tirreno, the triangle of sea bounded by the Italian coast, Sicily, and the islands of Sardinia and Corsica. David West points out that beaches of pumice stones are particularly to be found in the volcanic area of the bay of Naples, where Horace might well spend the winter (*Epistles* 1.15.1–10).

Strain the wine   when being encouraged to take advantage of the present time, one expects to be told to 'drink' the wine rather than 'strain' it. In *Satires* 2.4, a pretentious gourmet enunciates a whole string of rules, among which is 'Massic wine is best left to stand overnight' (to allow the sediment to sink). 'If you strain it, it loses its flavour.' If Leuconoe strains her wine, though it may not be quite so good, she won't have to worry about not being here tomorrow to drink it.

cut back long hopes – for greedy time will, **as we talk**, have come and gone.
Harvest the day and don't be over-trusting in a coming one.

---

1 Why has Leuconoe been consulting astrologers both for herself and for Horace? How does Horace discourage her, other than by simply saying 'don't'?

2 How is this poem different from **1.9**:
   – in setting?
   – in the content of the advice?
   – in the characters concerned?
   – in the tone?

Odes 4.7

The poem is, like *Odes* **1.4** (p. 122), addressed to a person of some consequence. There, it was the consul Sestius, whose family had risen from relative obscurity in the last generation. Here it is Torquatus, member of an ancient family which had been giving conspicuous service to the state for 350 years, but which from now on disappears altogether.

The snows have gone, grass returns to the fields
        and leaves to the trees;
the earth turns and changes, and the rivers, **diminished**,
        flow between their banks.
With the nymphs **the Grace and her two sisters** dare   5
        to tread the dance unclothed.
'Hope not for immortality,' so says the year, and the season
        which hurries the kindly day along.
The cold softens with the zephyrs, summer treads down the spring,
        doomed herself to perish   10
when fruit-bearing Autumn has squandered her bounty, and then
        lifeless winter comes hurrying back.

---

cut back   the image is of the vine-dresser pruning his vines, and prepares for the next line.

as we talk   Horace and Leuconoe are clearly enjoying a tête-à-tête, of which the only disadvantage, as Horace sees it, is that the wine is not ready. Leuconoe, being told to strain it, is evidently a slave, as was Thaliarchus in *Odes* **1.9.7**, p. 125. When she has done so, the party proper can begin.

Harvest the day   this is the famous tag *carpe diem*, often translated as 'seize the day'.

diminished   a hint of what is to follow: spring is the season of growth, but the rivers grow smaller.

the Grace and her two sisters   see *Odes* **1.4.6n**, p. 124.

But moons can repair their heaven-inflicted losses.
>   When once *we* have gone down
where **Father Aeneas**, where **Tullus and wealthy Ancus** have gone,   15
>   we are dust and shadow.
Who knows if the gods above are adding tomorrow's
>   time to today's total?
Your successor's greedy clutches will lose whatever
>   you give to your own good self.   20
When once you die and **Minos** passes
>   on you his solemn judgment,
no lineage, no eloquence, Torquatus,
>   no goodness will bring you back.
Diana does not free from nether darkness   25
>   her **chaste Hippolytus**,
nor has **Theseus** strength to break the **chains of Lethe**
>   and free his dear **Pirithous**.

But moons can repair their heaven-inflicted losses i.e. when the moon has waned, it will wax again.

Father Aeneas, Tullus and wealthy Ancus Aeneas was forefather of the Roman race; Tullus and Ancus the third and fourth kings of Rome. These three are perhaps chosen in acknowledgement of two great works on Roman origins: Virgil's *Aeneid,* presented to the public after Virgil's death in 19 BC, and Livy's histories still in progress (for Tullus and Ancus, see Livy 1.22–35).

Your successor's greedy clutches the heir who has a greedy eye on the wealth which death will bring him is a character out of satire (*Satires* 2.5).

Minos the legendary king of Crete. After death he became one of the judges of the Underworld. He appears as such in Virgil, *Aeneid* 6.432.

chaste Hippolytus Theseus' son by the Amazon queen. He was a hunter, a follower of Diana, and, like Diana, devoted to virginity. His stepmother Phaedra fell in love with him and, when rejected, killed herself, leaving a letter for Theseus to discover in which she accused Hippolytus of attempting to rape her. Theseus cursed Hippolytus, who was destroyed by a bull from the sea. In Euripides' play *Hippolytus*, Diana (Artemis) appears at the end in order to commiserate with the dying Hippolytus but not to help him.

Theseus, Pirithous Pirithous wished to take Hades' wife Persephone for himself. Theseus accompanied him on the descent to the Underworld. Both were welcomed by Hades and invited to sit. Having done so, they were unable to stand up. Hercules later came to the Underworld and rescued Theseus but not Pirithous. Horace imagines Theseus returning to the Underworld after his own death, still wishing to rescue Pirithous and still being unable (hence the present tense '*has* strength') to do so.

chains of Lethe Lethe is the river of forgetfulness. Pirithous cannot remember Theseus.

> 1 Compare this poem with *Odes* **1.4**, p. 122. How is the idea of spring treated in each poem? How does Horace manage the transition from the thought of spring to the philosophical considerations which follow?
>
> 2 How are the ideas of death and of 'Enjoy the present time' treated in themselves? What is the different tone of the conclusion of each?
>
> 3 With these two poems compare Shelley's treatment of the seasons in 'Ode to the West Wind'.
>
> 4 The seventeenth-century English bishop Thomas Ken wrote a famous hymn one of whose lines is: 'And live this day as if thy last'. Is he likely to have meant the same as Horace? And are you prepared to accept the advice of either of them?

Love poetry: *Odes* 1.5, 1.13, 1.17, 1.22, 1.25, 1.27, 3.9, 3.10, 3.26, 4.11

Odes 1.5

As we have seen, the first four poems of Book 1 are dedicated, in order, to Maecenas, Augustus, Virgil and Sestius (on whom see p. 122), each with his own special significance. Poems 6 and 7 are also dedicated to men of importance in the regime, Agrippa and Plancus. Poem 5, with its erotic subject, seems to intrude. Just as surprisingly the poet, here at the beginning of his collection, is not celebrating himself being in love, but having escaped from love. (The type has been given a name: *renuntiatio amoris*, the renunciation of love.) Elegiac poets were full of obsession with love: Gallus, Propertius, Tibullus. And elegiac poetry is a genre for which Horace seems, from **all he says and does not say**, to have had very little time. David West (1995) suggests that Horace is here setting out a programme for himself: his lyric verse will include erotic elements, but it will be very different from the writings of the elegists. His method of doing so, a poem on the escape from love, is itself a traditional theme of Greek poetry.

What **slender boy**, bathed in liquid perfumes,
is pressing himself on you, lying, **Pyrrha**,
on heaped-up rose-petals in a lovely cave?
For whom do you tie back your yellow hair,

---

all he says and does not say in *Odes* 1.33 he is distinctly dismissive about the elegiacs being written by Albius, probably Tibullus. The only other writers of elegiacs he names are Calvus and Catullus, disparagingly (*Satires* 1.10.19). Gallus and Propertius are ignored.

slender boy he is deliberately presented as very young.

Pyrrha her name means 'fair-haired girl'.

'Pressing himself on you' (Odes 1.5.2). Terracotta from a tomb at Myrina in Asia Minor.

simple and elegant? Oh how often he will weep   5
at promises broken and gods turned against him,
while at the sea made rough by **blackening** winds,
new to it all, he will stare amazed,

though now he enjoys you, trusts you, golden you,
hopes you will always be there, always loving,   10
knowing nothing of the treacherous breeze!
Unhappy are they for whom

---

blackening   because they darken the surface of the sea and also bring dark storm-
clouds.

your brightness is untested. For me, **a plaque**
set as an offering on a temple wall
shows how I hung up my soaking clothes 15
to **the mighty god of the sea.**

---

1   What emotions is the poet experiencing and why? ('It is the rhetorical
    instability of the Pyrrha ode, its indeterminate temperature (warm or cool?)
    that generates its erotic appeal' (Ellen Oliensis, *CCH*, p. 229).)

2   How successful is Horace in combining the literal and the metaphorical aspects
    of this poem?

3   Compare with this poem any poem from Ovid's *Amores* (accessible online) or
    Propertius, *Elegies* 1. In what ways does Horace in this poem treat the subject
    of love differently?

Odes 1.13

In one of the very few poems of Sappho which have come to us anything like
complete, she (Fragment 31) speaks of herself watching the girl she loves talking
delightfully to a man and laughing sweetly. Lines 7–15 run: 'When I so much
as glance at you, my voice fails altogether, my tongue falls quite silent, a subtle
flame has instantly slipped under my skin, with my eyes I see nothing, my ears
hum, a cold sweat covers me, I shiver all over, and I am paler than grass.'

Catullus (51) too has Lesbia 'laughing sweetly, a thing which steals all my
senses from me, for the moment I look at you, Lesbia, I have nothing left [to
say], but my tongue is paralysed, a subtle flame flows down my limbs, my ears
buzz with their own noise, night shrouds my two eyes'. We do not know how
Sappho's poem ends. If the text of Catullus is to be trusted, he concludes with
a stanza in which he tells himself, 'Pull yourself together, Catullus, and find
something to do.'

Horace seems to have taken from Sappho and Catullus the idea of using
detailed physical symptoms to express strong emotion. In the last stanza he
seems to have used an idea from another poem by Catullus (109) in which the
poet prays 'that we may be permitted to maintain throughout our lives this
everlasting treaty of blessed love'.

---

a plaque / set as an offering on a temple wall   Horace combines two different sorts
of temple-offering: the trade-equipment offered by a retiring worker and the thank-
offering to the god who has saved one from disaster.

the mighty god of the sea   Neptune, who rescues Aeneas from shipwreck in a famous
passage of *Aeneid* 1 (124–55). But he does not normally have anything to do with the
perilous ocean of love, over which Venus presides. Venus is also a goddess of the sea
(*Odes* **3.26.5**, p. 145). Some scholars (including Nisbet and Hubbard, 1970, p. 79) have
wanted to change the Latin word *deo*, 'god' to *deae*, 'goddess'.

When you, Lydia, praise Telephus
for his rosy neck, Telephus
for his waxen arms, then – yes – my
liver boils and swells with indigestible bile.

Then neither mind nor colour   5
stay in a single place, and moisture down my cheeks
slips stealthily, revealing
how slow the fires that stew me deep inside.

I burn, if your white shoulders
are marred by brawls made violent with wine,   10
or if the maddened boy has marked
your lips with his teeth, to say 'remember this'.

If you take in what I'm now saying,
you won't expect he'll stay for ever, bruising
those sweet lips which Venus   15
has dipped in **the fifth part of her own nectar**.

Thrice happy and happier still
are those joined by an unbroken bond, whose love,
not torn apart by spite and rancour,
is parted no sooner than their final day.   20

> 1   How successfully has Horace connected the ideas of the two Catullus poems?
> 2   Treating the poem as a small drama with three participants, what part does
>   the poet play?

Odes 1.17

This is another invitation poem which, like *Odes* **3.29** (p. 71), develops into
something rather different.

---

liver   very often treated as the seat of strong emotion.

the fifth part of her own nectar   Latin has no article, so it is up to us to translate (a)
'a fifth part' or (b) 'the fifth part'. With (a), we think that Venus' nectar is divine, and
therefore as mortals we would be entirely content with something only one-fifth as
strong. With (b) we are possibly directed to a doctrine of Aristotle: in addition to the four
elements earth, air, fire and water, there is a fifth one (the 'quintessence'), more perfect,
which explains how the heavens can move themselves. So we get not merely nectar at 20
per cent strength, but super-nectar.

'The stinking husband's wives go wandering' (Odes 1.17.6).

Swift **Faunus** often for pleasant **Lucretilis**
gives up **Lycaeus**, careful to keep
blazing summer and the gales
of winter rain from my kids.

Untouched in these protected woods   5
the stinking husband's wives go wandering
in search of hidden arbutus and thyme,
nor do they fear green snakes

Faunus, Lucretilis, Lycaeus Faunus is the Italian country-god, equated with Pan (*Odes* **3.18**, p. 110). Pan's Greek home is Arcadia and its wild countryside, where one of the conspicuous mountains is Lycaeus. Like Pan, Faunus characteristically plays on the pipes, which spread an enchantment on the places and the people that hear them. Lucretilis is a name which appears only here in Latin literature: it evidently refers to a hill near Horace's Sabine estate.

the stinking husband's wives nanny-goats. The personification, engaging, down to earth and mildly erotic, prepares for the appearance of Tyndaris in this protected landscape.

nor do their kids fear the **wolves of Mars**,
whenever the valleys, **Tyndaris**,   10
and the smooth rock slopes of **Ustica**
ring to the sweet sound of his pipe.

The gods protect me. To the gods **my faithfulness**
and my muse are welcome. Here
will the glories of the country flow for you   15
in wealth and plenty from a generous **horn**.

Here deep in a long valley you'll keep off
the **Dog-star**'s sultry heat, and **with the lyre**
of Teos you'll describe how one man troubled
the two, **Penelope and glass-green Circe**.   20

---

wolves of Mars   in Roman eyes, wolves are closely associated with Mars by means of the she-wolf who looked after Mars' children Romulus and Remus. They are also, of course, fierce and warlike.

Tyndaris   not a name frequently found in Latin love poetry. It can mean 'daughter of Tyndareus', so it may be relevant that both Tyndareus' daughters, Helen and Clytemnestra, were competed for, as Tyndaris seems to be, by more than one man. Competition for Helen led to the Trojan War; competition for Clytemnestra led to the murder of Agamemnon, of Clytemnestra herself and of her lover Aegisthus.

Ustica   evidently another hill-feature of Horace's landscape. The area around the villa which is said to have been Horace's has remarkable acoustic qualities: R. G. M. Nisbet and M. Hubbard (1970, p. 221) have a story that the excavators working on the site would call for their lunch to their wives at home half a mile away in the village of Licenza (see photo on p. 42).

my faithfulness   as so often, Horace assumes a belief or an attitude to suit the poem he is writing. In *Odes* **1.34** (p. 107) he represents himself as having his theological scepticism or at least his indolent tendencies sharply corrected by a surprising clap of thunder.

horn   this is the Horn of Plenty which also appears in *Epistles* **1.12.27** (p. 161).

Dog-star   see *Odes* **3.13.9**, p. 109.

with the lyre / of Teos   i.e. in the manner of Anacreon, the sixth-century BC lyric poet whose home was the island of Teos. Fragments of Anacreon survive, along with a collection called *Anacreontea* attributed to him but almost certainly by later writers. Some of these describe pastoral summer scenes, and it is these, no doubt, which Tyndaris will be imitating.

Penelope and glass-green Circe   Penelope was Odysseus' faithful wife, who waited for him for the 20 years while he was fighting at Troy and making his long journey home. One year of his return journey was spent in the company of the enchantress-goddess Circe, daughter of the Sun God. 'Glass-green' has given readers trouble. But in *Odes* **3.13.1** (p. 109) the spring of Bandusia is 'gleaming brighter than glass'; the gleam may relate to Circe's connection with the Sun, and glass as Horace knew it was opaque, distorting and iridescent, as might be appropriate in Circe as a sorceress.

Here in the shade you'll drink slow cups
of harmless **Lesbian**, and **Semele's Thyonian son**,
won't join with Mars, won't bring wild fighting on,
nor will you fear the shameless

jealousy of Cyrus, that, violent and unrestrained,   25
he may lay hands on you, no match for him,
tearing the wreath close-fitting on your hair
and your clothes which do no harm.

> 1 The theme of this poem seems to be 'protection'. Who (or what) is protected
>   at various stages of the poem, and against whom (or what)?
>
> 2 Why do you think Horace chooses this particular story (lines 19–20) for
>   Tyndaris to tell? If we think of the poem as a dramatic monologue, does it cast
>   any light on the character which Horace has given himself?
>
> 3 Is any progress in Horace's relationship with Tyndaris suggested by the last
>   three stanzas? If so, how does Horace suggest it?

Odes 1.22

This is a poem whose noble opening sentiments caught the attention of
educationists in **Scotland** and **Germany** and prompted them to set it to
music as an uplifting song for the edification of students.

If his life is pure, unstained by vice,
a man will need no Moorish spears, no bow,

Lesbian 'I hate the things that tend to madness. Bind my head with narcissus ... wet
my gullet with wine from Lesbos and join me with a home-loving virgin' (Horace's
near-contemporary Philodemus in the *Palatine Anthology* 11.34). One may dispute the
translation 'home-loving', but the emollient quality of Lesbian wine is clear.

Semele's Thyonian son Semele was Dionysus/Bacchus' mother. Thyone was another name
for her, but the name is given to Bacchus here probably because it was thought to be
connected with a Greek noun 'Thyiades' which refers to Bacchus' maenads as they race over
the hillsides.

Scotland, Germany see *The Scottish Students' Song Book*. For Germany, Fraenkel p. 184
(even at funerals!).

If his life is pure the idea of the first two stanzas is: the truly good man will need no
weapons to defend him, because he will be defended by his own moral excellence. Greek
and Roman philosophy put the pursuit of happiness at the centre. Stoics took the line that
only the virtuous man can be happy, and that therefore happiness consisted in the single-
minded pursuit of virtue, which is identical with wisdom. True wisdom will make one proof
against the assaults of Fortune, i.e. indifferent to grief, pain and danger. Epicureans came to
a similar conclusion by a different route. The greater the happiness, the greater the fear of
its removal. Therefore the only true happiness is that which cannot be removed. Therefore
the wise man will take care not to be in need of any of the things which he might lose.

no poisoned arrows, **Fuscus**,
in a bursting quiver,

go as he may by the sultry **Syrtes**   5
or through the unwelcoming **Caucasus**
or those lands washed by the **Hydaspes**,
river of legend.

Me now: in the Sabine woods a wolf,
as I was strolling carefree past the bounds   10
of my land singing of Lalage, saw me
unarmed, and fled –

a monster such as neither **martial Daunia**
bore in her wide forests of winter oak,
nor did the land of **Juba**, parched   15
foster-mother of lions.

Fuscus   see *Satires* **1.9.61n**, p. 40. There he failed to rescue Horace. It would be nice to think that Horace is pointedly addressing this ode to him: 'Now I don't need rescuing'.

Syrtes   strictly the shallow waters of the Gulf of Libya, but also the land around them. A very famous journey had been made through this scorching landscape in 47 BC by Marcus Cato, leading the remains of the forces with which Pompey had opposed Julius Caesar. The hardships of this journey were vividly described by Cicero in the pamphlet *Cato*, with which he made Cato into a martyr for the cause of those who opposed Julius Caesar and his successors. See also *Odes* **2.1.24n**, p. 88 and **1.2.35n**, p. 78. Cato made much of his Stoic philosophy, which is perhaps a reason for thinking that Horace wants us at this stage to think of his philosophical armour as Stoic.

Caucasus   the mountain range which separates the Black Sea from the Caspian. The Black Sea had the name 'Welcoming' (*Euxinus*) as a name designed to avert its dangerous qualities. Horace uses 'unwelcoming' here in emphatic, and ironic, contrast.

Hydaspes   the Sutlej, easternmost of the five rivers of the Punjab. It was the scene, in 326 BC, of the greatest victory of Alexander's Indian campaign, hence its place in legend.

martial Daunia   Horace's home-territory in northern Apulia, 'martial' either from its mythological association with the Greek hero Diomedes, or from its historical connection with the Samnites, with whom the Romans had fought hotly contested wars in the third century BC.

Juba   king of Numidia, roughly the north of modern Algeria. His father had fought against Caesar and, like Cato, committed suicide when defeated. He himself fought for Octavian at Actium (see *Odes* 1.37 and *Epodes* **9**, pp. 80–86) and was restored to his kingdom. Among many other achievements, he wrote a book on African matters, including material about lions (Nisbet and Hubbard, 1970, p. 270). Horace may well have known him during his time in Rome.

Set me where, in the **torpid plains**,
no summer breeze revives a tree,
that part of Earth oppressed by mists
and a malign Jupiter.   20

Set me **where the sun's wheels pass too near**
in a land closed to human habitation:
I will love **Lalage**: her sweet laugh
and her sweet words.

---

1   A simpler translation of lines 9–12 might be: 'For while I was strolling in
    the Sabine woods, singing of my Lalage in carefree spirit, well outside the
    boundaries (of my farm), a wolf fled from me though I was unarmed.' As they
    are, the lines nearly preserve Horace's word-order. Why does Horace present
    the ideas in the order he does?

2   Where is the hyperbole in this poem?

3   What is the connection between the last stanza of the poem and the first?
    Does the poem seem uplifting and edifying?

4   On this poem, Eduard Fraenkel comments that 'this ode is one of Horace's
    most charming and most perfect ... Horace may have glimpsed a wolf
    shambling off in the middle distance, but the incident was a trivial one at best.
    Yet the ode is not just a conventional exercise devoid of personality. Only a
    poet could have expressed so agreeable a blend of self-mockery and self-
    satisfaction' (p. 263). Does this seem a satisfactory judgement of the poem?

Odes 1.25

> Mockery of old women is a convention of Hellenistic poetry. There is a
> group of such poems in the huge collection known as the *Palatine Anthology*
> (11.66–74).

Less often now do your closed windows shake
as **impudent young men** throw stone after stone.
Your sleep is undisturbed. The door
is fond of its frame,

---

torpid plains   a Mediterranean view of the far north.

where the sun's wheels pass too near   i.e. the deserts of the south. The Sahara, in legend,
owed its origin to Phaëthon, son of the Sun-God, who took the reins of the solar chariot
for a day and lost control, causing the horses to run too close to the earth and scorch it.

Lalage   her name means 'the chatterer'. 'Her sweet laugh' is a direct quotation from
Catullus 51, which is itself a direct translation from Sappho (see the introduction to *Odes*
1.13, p. 132). In Sappho's poem, the girl 'talks delightfully' too. Catullus omits this; Horace,
'correcting' him, goes back to the original.

impudent young men   they traditionally used such methods to attract the attention of
their lovers. Compare *Odes* **3.10**, p. 144 and **3.26**, p. 145.

where once it made the hinges move 5
so smoothly; now you hear this less and less:
'The long nights pass. I die, though I am your own,
and, Lydia, are you sleeping?'

Your turn will come. When old, you'll be ignored
by insolent lovers, and in your alleyway 10
you'll weep alone, while the wind from **Thrace**
howls louder in the moonless night;

while blazing love and passion,
the maddener of mares,
rages around your ulcerated liver, 15
and you complain

that vigorous youth delights in green ivy
and dark myrtle; dry foliage
it consigns to winter's follower,
the Eastern wind. 20

Statuette of an old woman (Odes 1.25). She wears a wreath of vine-leaves as if for celebration, but has become careless of her dress, which has slipped from her shoulder. First-century AD copy of a Greek work of the second century BC.

---

1   Is there any suggestion that the poet thinks of himself as subject to the same laws of decay as those which affect Lydia?

2   Do any of the following judgements come close to yours?
   – 'This poem has no merit and may be omitted with advantage' (T. E. Page).
   – 'In spite of its conventionalism and inhumanity this is a good poem' (Nisbet and Hubbard, 1970, p. 292).
   – 'Our very revulsion at his cruelty is testimony to the power of what he writes' (West, 1995, p. 119).

Odes 1.27

Horace has taken two separate themes from a number of Greek poems – a party out of control, and a lover obliged to reveal a secret – and made a dramatic monologue out of them.

Thrace   roughly, modern Bulgaria; traditionally (seen from a Greek point of view) the north-eastern source of freezing winter winds.

the maddener of mares   Aristotle refers to mares as proverbially oversexed (*History of Animals* 572a8).

Wine cups were made for joy. To use them
as weapons is a savage, **Thracian** thing.
Away with it! Bacchus is a modest god:
Keep him from bloody brawls.

Lamps and wine are one thing, **Persian scimitars**   5
another altogether. This shouting, friends,
is a disgrace. Tone it down,
and **keep your elbows firmly on your couches.**

You want me too to take my share
of **strict** Falernian? **Megylla from Opus – her brother**   10
must tell us: what's the wound making him
happy? What's the arrow killing him?

Not quite so keen then? On those terms I'll drink –
no others. Whoever your **Love**, your conqueror,
it's not a flame you need to blush for,   15
it's always an honest passion

sends you astray. Come now: whatever it is,
drop it in trusty ears. What? You poor boy!
Why, that's a **monstrous sea** you're floundering in,
my lad: that girl's not good enough for you.   20

Thracian   Thracians had had a bad reputation for over-drinking at least since Plato's day
(*Laws* 627 d–e). Compare *Odes* **2.7.27**, p. 117.

Lamps   symbols of a party. It is going well when the guests start seeing more of them
(*Satires* 2.1.26).

Persian scimitars   perhaps the party-goers have started taking down the trophies
hanging on the wall. The further point is that *any* violence is taking this party out of its
proper, civilized, Graeco-Roman context into a world of savagery.

keep your elbows firmly on your couches   if elbows are placed thus, Horace can be
absolutely sure that their owners are not misbehaving.

strict   the Greek word for 'dry' (of wine) is 'austere'. The word also carries its moral
meaning. Horace chooses to give us the moral version of the word, which suggests, in a
deliberately self-contradictory way, 'abstemious'.

Megylla from Opus – her brother   to refer to a man by the name of his sister is unusual.
Opus is an obscure place in Greece. Horace evidently knows family details about the
company, and is perhaps suggesting that he could reveal information about other guests
too, if they don't behave.

Love   Horace says 'whatever Venus is conquering you': he turns the unnamed boy's
passion into a god.

monstrous sea   Horace's word is *Charybdis*, the whirlpool-monster which caused
Odysseus trouble in *Odyssey* 12.

The Chimera (Odes 1.27.24), a bronze statuette from Etruria.

What witch, what **mage from Thessaly** can set you free
with dreadful potions? What god, indeed?
Scarcely will **Pegasus** extricate you
bound to that triple horror, the **Chimera**.

> • The poem presents an eventful and dramatic scene. Has the poet been at
> the party all the time, or does he arrive at the beginning of the poem? How
> do the other guests respond to him? What role does he seem to be playing
> (a) in lines 1–8, (b) in lines 9–18, (c) in lines 18–24? Is there any inconsistency
> between these roles? With what image of the poet are we left at the end?

Odes 3.9

This poem takes the form of a dialogue between Lydia and an unnamed man.
But the poem is symmetrical: the stanzas balance against each other, and we are
told the names of the currently preferred rivals. Some readers have therefore
given the name 'Horace' to the male speaker. The characteristics he ascribes
to himself here (lines 22–3) are not unlike Horace's description of himself in
Epistles **1.20.25** (p. 163). There is perhaps even a contrast between the rival's
age ('the boy', line 16) and Horace's rueful admission of middle age in *Odes*
2.4.23. However, to say that Horace presents a consistent characterization of
himself is not to say that he is referring to things which actually happened.

---

mage from Thessaly   mages in Roman literature (they appear as *magi* – Wise Men – in
the Christmas story) are traditional sorcerers from the East. Thessaly is a traditional home
of Greek witchcraft. The poet is so horror-struck that he confuses the two.

Pegasus, Chimera   the hero Bellerophon was set the task of killing the Chimera (a fire-
breathing monster with a lion's head, a snake for a tail and a goat between). He only
succeeded because he was riding on the winged horse Pegasus.

So long as I gave you pleasure,
and no other young man was putting his arms
around your fair neck before me,
I was in my prime, more fortunate than the King of Persia.

'So long as you were not on fire for another girl,   5
and Lydia was not put second to Chloe,
but 'Lydia' was everywhere,
I was in my prime, more glorious than Roman Ilia.'

Now I am ruled by Thracian Chloe
whose genius is in music and she plays the lyre with skill.   10
For her I shall not fear to die,
if the Fates spare her soul and let her live.

'Myself, I am burned with a fire which burns him too –
Calaïs, son of Ornytus of Thurii.
For him I shall be content to die a double death,   15
if the Fates spare the boy and let him live.'

What if Venus returns in her former guise,
and under her yoke of bronze forces parted souls together;
if fair-haired Chloe is cast off
and the door opened for rejected Lydia?   20

'Though he is lovelier than a star,
while you change course more than a floating cork
and rage worse than the Adriatic sea,
it would be my love to live with you, my pleasure to die with you.'

| • | If this is the story of a quarrel resolved, who makes the first accusation, and who makes the first concession? Is the quarrel in fact resolved? |

'Lydia' was everywhere   i.e. Horace's poetry was full of the name of his beloved.

Roman Ilia   daughter of King Numitor of Alba Longa and mother of Romulus by Mars, so not strictly a Roman (Rome did not yet exist), but glorious in the history of Rome.

Thracian   compare *Odes* 1.27, p. 140.

Calaïs, son of Ornytus of Thurii   he has a distinguished ancestry – Calaïs and Ornytus are names from the legend of the Argonauts; and a distinguished provenance – Thurii is the ancient Greek city on the south coast of Italy which was the home of Augustus' grandfather.

yoke of bronze   in *Odes* 1.33.11 Venus uses the yoke of bronze to force incompatible couples together as a joke.

Catullus 45

> Septimius, holding his sweetheart Acme
> upon his lap, said to her, 'Acme my sweet,
> if I don't love you and if I'm not ready
> to go on loving you year in, year out,
> dying with love as dead as dead can be,
> alone in Africa or scorching India
> may I go out and meet a green-eyed lion.'
> When he said this, Love on the left as once
> upon the right gave blessing with a sneeze.
>
> But Acme, with her head bent gently back,
> and with those bright-red lips
> kissing the boy's intoxicated eyes,
> said to him, 'Septimius my own, my life,
> to this one master let us continue in service,
> as a much greater fire, one much more fierce
> burns in the tender marrow of my bones.'
> When she said this, Love on the left as once
> upon the right gave blessing with a sneeze.
>
> Beginning thus with blessings from the heavens,
> they love alike and know each other's love.
> Septimius desperately wants his Acme
> more than all your Syrias or Britains,
> while, loyal to Septimius alone,
> Acme has all her joy and passion in him.
> Who ever saw a pair so fortunate,
> or who a love more heaven-blessed?

R. G. M. Nisbet and Niall Rudd make a comparison with the Catullus poem printed above:

The poem, like Horace's, has a symmetrical structure [declarations of love by Septimius and Acme, refrain about Cupid's sneezes, concluding eight-line benediction by the poet in couplets arranged ABBA]. *Here, as in Horace, the attitudes of the man and the woman are differentiated: the forthright speech of Septimius ... is capped by Acme's more emotional response. But there is no parallel in the ode for the sensuous details that appeal to the eye ... Catullus' poem seems to reflect a genuine love-affair; it is perverse to look, as some have done, for cynical undercurrents.* (p. 134)

Such 'perversity' is perhaps to be found in David West, who writes that the two poems are

very similar in tone ... Two lovers have parted because of a lapse by the man, who now comes to beg for reconciliation. In each poem the woman agrees to take him back, but not without crushing the guilty party, detail by detail. (2002, p. 91)

- Which verdict appeals to you?

Odes 3.10

For lovers seeking to tempt their mistresses to open the door to them at night – or even the window – there was the *paraklausithyron*: a type of poem to be recited outside closed doors. Ovid, *Amores* 1.6 is one, very well worth comparing with this poem for common themes.

Were you a drinker of the distant river **Don**,
and married, Lycē, to **a brute**, still you'd be sad
to expose me, stretched before your cruel doors,
to the resident **Easterlies**.

Do you hear how the door rattles, how the **trees**   5
set between fine buildings groan
in answer to the winds, how Jupiter
freezes the snows with his **unclouded majesty**?

Put aside that arrogance, which Venus hates,
in case **the drum turns backwards** and the rope runs out.   10
You were not born to that **Tuscan** father
to be a **Penelope** and keep your suitors off.

Though swayed by neither gifts nor prayers
nor lovers' faces sallow-pale
nor husband's **Macedonian mistress** –   15
upon those who pray to you

Don one of the great rivers of Scythia (southern Russia). The inhabitants of a region are identified by the water they drink: 'Nile-drinker' would signify 'Egyptian'.

a brute Scythians are said elsewhere to be savage, also (in *Odes* 3.24.24) to have drastic penalties for moral offences.

Easterlies the winds are imagined as difficult neighbours.

trees we are back in Rome. Lycē ('she-wolf') evidently lives in a fine house with a well-planted peristyle garden.

freezes the snows in inviting Lycē to listen to the snow freezing, Horace is perhaps going deliberately over the top.

unclouded majesty Jupiter is god of the sky and the weather. The phrase refers to a clear sky.

the drum turns backwards the process of winning Lycē is like winding up a heavy bucket of water from a well. If the process is too much effort, the winder gives up and the bucket falls back down, perhaps carrying the rope off the drum with it.

Tuscan the Etruscans were traditionally free-and-easy in moral matters.

Penelope in the *Odyssey*, Odysseus' wife Penelope famously held out against a band of suitors until her husband returned from Troy after being missing for ten years.

Macedonian mistress possibly Lycē's husband is away in Macedonia and Horace, suggesting that he may be up to no good, is encouraging her to follow his example.

have pity! You are no softer than the unbending oak,
nor gentler-hearted than the snakes of Africa.
This body will not for ever bear
the hard threshold or the rain from heaven.   20

1	How many different tactics does Horace use to win Lyce over?
2	Is there any structure to the poem beyond the presentation of one persuasive ploy after another?

Odes 3.26

A traditional form for a short poem is that it should purport to be the prayer
with which a retiring craftsman dedicates the tools of his trade to the patron
god of his profession. Horace adapts this to the *renuntiatio amoris* (see on *Odes*
1.5, p. 130). The presence of the weapons hints also at the *paraklausithyron*
(*Odes* **3.10**, p. 144).

I have lived my life, fit for the girls until just now,
and my campaigning has not been inglorious.
My **arms** now, and my **battle-weary**
lyre will hang upon this wall,

which shelters Venus of the Sea   5
upon her left. Here, here set the gleaming
torches, crowbars, and the bows:
a threat to doors which stand against them.

---

arms, battle-weary / lyre   these items make one think of Alcaeus and the words of *Odes*
1.32, p. 62.

upon her left   possibly because the left side is a warrior's unguarded side, most in need
of sheltering. R. G. M. Nisbet (in Nisbet and Rudd, p. 313) thinks there may be a reference
to the Temple of Venus Erycina on the Capitol, upon whose left stood the Temple of
Sound Mind, a goddess to whom Propertius dedicated himself (3.24) when he reached
port after a perilous journey over the sea of love.

torches, crowbars, and the bows   now we discover what the arms are: the equipment
needed for serenading a mistress and then breaking into her house should she not open
the door herself. Readers are puzzled by the bows, not much use for house-breaking.
Alternative solutions are: (a) that scribes have omitted or mis-copied a word for a
different weapon (axe?); (b) Horace is presenting a deliberately incongruous scene, for
the purpose of self-mockery (West, 2002, pp. 215–16).

O goddess, dweller in blessed **Cyprus** and
Memphis untouched by snows of **Thrace**:   10
O queen, with whip raised up high
touch, just once, Chloe the scornful.

> • How clearly is the scene envisaged? Who else is present? Are they expected to
> hear everything the poet says? Is the poet retiring from his profession? This
> amounts largely to 'What does he hope the effect of Venus' whip will be?'
> Scholars differ (Nisbet and Rudd, pp. 310–11).

Odes 4.11

This is a last invitation. It may be relevant that this poem comes fifth from
the end of Horace's collection and that the Pyrrha ode (p. 130) comes fifth
from the beginning.

A cask I have now passing its ninth year
and full of **Alban**. In the garden, Phyllis,
I have celery for making wreaths;
of ivy I have

a mass, to tie your hair and make you lovely.   5
The house is bright with silver, the altar bound
with holy greenery: it longs to be
wet with a sacrificial lamb.

The company's all busy; a crowd goes running
here and there, slave-boys and girls together;   10
quivering flames send sooty wheels
of smoke from their tops.

And should you wish to know for what delights
you are invited, you must keep the **Ides**,
which split the month of Venus of the Sea –   15
the month of April,

Cyprus, Memphis, Thrace   Venus is at home especially in Paphos on Cyprus, but also
in Memphis, the ancient Cairo, according to the geographer Strabo (17.1.31). Thrace is
proverbially cold (*Odes* **1.25.11**, p. 139); Cairo is not. Horace implies a contrast between
warm Venus and chilly Chloe.

Alban   said to be the most sought-after wine after Caecuban and Falernian (Pliny,
Natural History 14.64).

Ides   the 13th day of most months, including April. Maecenas was born in about 70 BC.

a day I duly celebrate as holier
almost than my own birthday, since from it
my own **Maecenas** counts the stream
of passing years.   20

It's Telephus you're after. He's a lad
not of your standing, claimed too by a girl
rich and unprincipled: she has him bound
in chains he loves.

Burned **Phaëthon** fills greedy hopes with fear.   25
And there's an object lesson too
in **Pegasus** objecting to his earthling
rider **Bellerophon**:

always desire what you deserve; rule out
as wicked hopes which run too far; and so   30
shun an unequal match. Come now,
my loves' end –

for after now I'll not grow warm
for any other woman: study the songs
you'll render in that lovely voice: dark care   35
will mend with singing.

Maecenas   this is the only reference to Maecenas in Book 4. Eduard Fraenkel points out how it is given importance by being placed in the exact centre of the poem and at the climax of a long, complex sentence covering two stanzas when the next longest sentence covers only one.

Phaëthon   son of the Sun-God. Given by his father reluctant permission to drive the Sun's chariot for a day, he lost control. When the erratic course of the Sun threatened to destroy the earth, Jupiter sent a thunderbolt which killed Phaëthon.

Pegasus, Bellerophon   see *Odes* **1.27.24n**, p. 141.

my loves' end   this is a very literal translation of Horace's words, and any reasonable interpretation (I think) which you put on it will be consistent with the Latin.

---

1 Compare this poem with *Odes* **1.17**, p. 133.

2 What impression of the party is created by the preparations for it? Who is invited to it?

3 If Horace is hoping to persuade Phyllis to return his love, how does he seek to do it? How persuasive is he? Whose 'dark care' (line 35) would be mended?

4 Ellen Oliensis sees the last stanza as picking up in detail the ideas of the last stanza of the *Carmen Saeculare* (p. 102), and the presence of slave-girls (very rare, so described, in Horace) as recalling the double choir of the hymn. 'It is as if the whole stable world (of) the communal hymn were darkening and shifting before our eyes' (*CCH*, p. 233). How far do you concur with this judgement?

5 Considering Horace's love poetry as a whole, these are two of the criticisms which have been levelled at it. Do you feel they are fair?

   − 'It is too much like W. S. Gilbert's character Iolanthe, who says, of love, "On fire that glows with heat intense / I turn the hose of common-sense".'

   − '[The poems present] the (male) poet–lover whose drive for autonomy and control leads him to resist any form of desire that enforces immersion in temporality.'

   (Both judgements quoted from the American scholar Ronnie Ancona in a review of her book *Selected Odes and Satire 1.9*, American Journal of Philology (1996), 657.)

3 The philosopher poet: *Epistles* 1

Odes 3 ended with the proud boast of **3.30** (p. 67). But it seems that the poems were not received as well as Horace hoped. At the end of *Epistles* 1, his next published work, he writes to Maecenas in these terms:

> *You may wish to know why the ungrateful reader praises my little works and loves them when at home, but criticizes them unfairly in public. I am not one to hunt for the votes of the empty-headed crowd …*

> (Epistles *1.19.35–6)*

But he has more positive reasons for embarking on his new project.

Friendship has always mattered (see *Satires* **1.5**, **2.6** and the *Odes* whose subject is friendship and friends). Now Horace will concern himself with philosophy, i.e. moral improvement. In *Satires* **1.4.131–2** he gave the recipe for this: time, friends, and thought. All these points come together: he is older, philosophy interests him, and he has friends to address by the means of *sermo* – *sermo* thought of either as conversation or as the verse medium of the *Satires*. This makes sense. Moral philosophy delivered as a lecture is as likely to be offensive as effective (as Davus found in *Satires* **2.7**). But when it is conducted as part of a conversation by someone who acknowledges that he seeks to improve himself as much as his correspondent (*Epistles* **1.4.15–16**), perhaps it will work better.

From these considerations is born the philosophical verse letter written for publication. Verse letters had existed before. Lucilius writes to a friend who had failed to ask after him when he was ill. Lucilius' letter is effectively an apology for having recovered (5.186–93 Warmington). Lucius Mummius, who captured Corinth, wrote witty verse letters, says Cicero (*To Atticus* 13.6.4). Philosophical letters had been written by, among others, Plato and Epicurus. As for personal letters, Cicero considered publishing a collection of his own (*To Atticus* 16.5.5); even though this came to nothing, the efforts of his secretary Tiro to make a collection after his master's death must have been widely known. Putting all these three aspects together was Horace's own invention, and the *Epistles* have often been regarded as his best poetry.

There is something odd about writing letters to one's friends for the world to read (though it has been suggested that Facebook performs a similar role: the communication is private, but the words are there for all to see). Are these writings literary pieces, in which case to address someone is merely to dedicate a piece to them; or are they personal communications whose content is determined by the circumstances and character of the addressee? The tension between these two aspects is something Horace is able to exploit.

Epistles 1.1

1.1.1–19 My earliest Muse spoke of you, and so must my last.
But now I've proved myself and **earned my wooden staff**,
you want me back, Maecenas, locked up in the training school.
Youth's gone; will's gone. **Veianius, his arms attached**
to Hercules' door, hides far from town. He dreads   5
to fight all day, and every day **to coax the crowd**.
My ear's attentive to **a voice** which hourly says,
'Wise man, set free the ageing horse in good time, or
he'll stumble at the end, jeered at and gasping.'
Now verse and other foolishness I set aside.   10
What's true and proper: that's my quest, my care, my all.
I store, I settle things I'll put to use anon.
'Who is' you ask 'my leader? where am I at home?'
I'm bound to none, no Master has my plighted word.
Wherever the weather takes me, I put in as guest,   15
now active and awash in seas of politics,
Virtue's defender and unflinching bodyguard;
now, slipping slyly back to **Aristippus'** rule,
seeking to order things, not be **ordered by them**.

---

earned my wooden staff   gladiators received a wooden baton on retirement.

Veianius, his arms attached / to Hercules' door   Veianius is evidently just such a retired gladiator. He has hung up the tools of his trade (compare *Odes* **1.5**, p. 130 and **3.26**, p. 145), and gone to the country without leaving his address, for fear that he will be called back to the amphitheatre.

to coax the crowd   Veianius makes a suitable comparison with Horace, because he was clearly very successful as a gladiator. The wooden baton is awarded by popular acclaim. Veianius is so popular that he is kept fighting all day, and regularly, when he asks for his discharge, the members of the crowd refuse it because they cannot bear to part with him.

a voice   as Horace announces his conversion to philosophy, this reminds us of Socrates' 'divine voice', which always said 'Don't do this', never 'Do this' (Plato, *Apology* 40a).

Virtue's defender   i.e. a Stoic.

Aristippus   of Cyrene, a philosopher of the late fifth century BC, a believer in the principle that pleasure is the supreme good, and unrefined in his understanding of it.

ordered by them   the Stoic organizes his life according to Nature. The follower of Aristippus evidently organizes Nature to suit himself.

In an interesting paragraph John Moles (*CCH*, p. 175) finds some 15 references in these lines, hinting at different philosophical schools.

'The poetic mask donned by Horace is different. The poet no longer strolls about the city, seeking out occasions for laughter or censure at the expense of ridiculous maniacs, or even of himself; and the choice and treatment of a topic are conducted with a friend's wish or need in mind, not as points on the diatribic agenda.' (Ferri in *CCH*, p. 128).

Epistles 1.4

'Albius' is also the recipient of *Odes* 1.33. That Albius writes elegiac verse. It is very likely that the addressee of both poems is the poet Albius Tibullus.

Albius, **good-natured critic** of my '**Conversations**',
out there in the **Pedana** what shall I say you're doing?
Outdoing **Cassius of Parma** and his little books?
or strolling silently around those healthy woods,
concerned with what befits a man who's wise and good?   5
No, you were never body without mind. The gods

---

good-natured critic   unlike Quintilius in the *Art of Poetry* **438–44** (p. 187)!

Conversations   the Latin word is *sermones*, which Horace uses to cover both his satires and his epistles.

Pedana   a region east of Rome, in the curve between the Alban hills and the Sabine mountains. Albius evidently has a villa there.

Cassius of Parma   evidently Albius is writing poems similar to Cassius. Unfortunately, we have none of Cassius' writings, so we cannot know what Horace is suggesting about Albius. Cassius (not the same as Cassius Longinus, Brutus' fellow-leader in the conspiracy) was one of the assassins of Julius Caesar, and for this was in the end put to death by Octavian, probably not until after the battle of Actium, but even so some ten years before the publication of this poem (see *Epistles* **1.20.28n**, p. 163). There is no reason to think that surpassing this Cassius was a very lofty ambition on the part of Albius.

No, you were never body without mind   according to Eduard Fraenkel, this line gains point from being an adaptation of a line in the *Odyssey*, where Odysseus says to Antinous, the elegant chief of the villainous suitors, 'It seems that you never had the wits to go with your [fine] appearance.' Albius is revealed as the antithesis of Antinous.

gave you looks, wealth and skill to make the best of them.
What better could a little nursemaid pray for,
whose charge had sense, could speak his mind, who had
good name, good friends, good health in plenty too,   10
and lived with style and with a purse that's deep enough?
Amid anxiety and hope, anger and fear,
think of each day that dawns as if it were your last.
Each unexpected hour will be a gift of joy.
I shall be plump, kempt, glossy when you visit   15
to laugh at one from **Epicurus' herd**: a pig.

Epicurus, the philosopher of individual contentment.

---

1   'Skill to make the best of them' (line 7): Mayer (p. 134) describes this as 'the keynote' of the poem. Does it seem so to you?

2   What does the idea of the 'little nursemaid' (line 8) add to the spirit of the poem? (The diminutive is Horace's.)

3   Compare Horace's situation on his Sabine estate with Albius' in his property in the Pedana. Are they at all different?

Epistles 1.7

This epistle, with its three narrative passages (the Calabrian pears, the vixen and the weasel, and Volteius Mena) can be seen either as a theoretical discussion of the nature of generosity or as a statement by Horace of the terms of his relationship with Maecenas.

In his book *On Duties* (1.42) Cicero expressed three principles which the giver of a gift should observe: 'One must be sure first that a gift should not be harmful either to the very people for whom the kindness is designed or to anyone else, secondly that the gift should not exceed the giver's resources, thirdly that the gift should be proportional to the recipient's deserts, since this is the basic principle of justice, which is the standard by which all these matters should be judged.'

Epicurus' herd   on Epicureanism, see Introduction, p. 7.

If thought of as a particular discussion of Horace's friendship with Maecenas, the overall impression is of what he will *not* do for his patron rather than what he will. At least two things have changed since the early days of the Sabine farm. Horace is older (lines 25–8), and Maecenas seems to have lost something of his standing with Augustus. (The event with which this development is associated took place in 23 or 22 BC. Maecenas' brother-in-law, Terentius Varro Murena, had participated in a plot against Augustus. The plot had been discovered, and Maecenas had taken advantage of his inside information to pass a warning to Murena (Suetonius, *Augustus* 66).) But Maecenas is still the addressee of three of twenty letters of *Epistles* 1, the first, the seventh and the nineteenth, which occupies the same position of importance (last before the seal-poem) as did *Odes* **3.29** in its book.

For just five days, I promised, I'd be in the country.
It was a lie. You've missed me all of August. But,
if healthy, strong, alive is how you want me,
you'll be as kind, Maecenas, to my fear of illness
as when I'm really ill: when the first fig and the heat   5
call out the undertakers with their black-robed men,
while **fathers and mums** all tremble for their children,
while **legal chores and social obligations**
bring on the fever and unseal the wills.
When winter coats the Alban fields with snow,   10
your bard will go **to the coast**; he'll take things easy,
he'll wrap up warm and read: he'll visit you, dear friend,
with spring winds and the early swallows, by your leave.
You have made me rich – but not like the **Calabrian** host
feeding his guest on pears. 'Come, have some more.'   15

---

fathers and mums   Horace uses the standard word for 'father' and an affectionate diminutive for 'mother'.

legal chores and social obligations   very much the kind of urban commitment bemoaned by Horace in *Satires* **2.6.23–58** (pp. 43–5).

When winter coats the Alban fields with snow   Maecenas may well expect the second half of this sentence to be 'I'll come and visit you then'. He gets something rather different.

to the coast   perhaps to the villas of the bay of Naples, which is where his horse wants to take him in *Epistles* 1.15.10–13.

Calabrian   Calabrians occupy the 'heel' of Italy: near neighbours to Horace in his youth, but rustic in the extreme. (Modern Calabria is in the 'toe' of Italy.)

'That's plenty.' 'Take them, all you want.' 'Thank you, but no.'
'They'll make good presents for the little children.'
'I'd not be more grateful if I were leaving heaped with them.'
'Very well. Leave them, and I'll feed them to the pigs today.'
It's waste and folly, making gifts of what you loathe. 20
The fruits have been – will always be – ingratitude.
The good, the wise man says he's open to the worthy,
yet knows his coins: what's true, what's counterfeit.
My worth – I'll prove it – matches my benefactor's name.
But if you want me never to leave your side, give back 25
my healthy loins, **dark hair and narrow forehead,**
sweet conversation, charming laughter; give me back
laments for lively **Cinara**, fled from among the cups.
One day a skinny vixen crept through a narrow crack
into a chest of corn, then ate her fill, and tried, 30
now corpulent, to creep back out, in vain.
A nearby weasel said, 'If you want to get out of there,
slip thin through that small hole by which you entered thin.'
Held up against this image, I surrender all.
It's not dyspepsia makes me envy the poor their sleep. 35
Lose independence, and Arabian wealth's no gain.
'Modest' you've often called me. I call you '**king**'
and 'father' when you're present; if absent, just the same.
Look now! Can I hand back a gift without a qualm?

The good … what's counterfeit Horace's text is opaque, as is my translation. 'Worthy' seems to refer to one of the ideas expressed by Cicero: the good man will ensure that the recipients of his gifts are worthy people. The next idea seems to be that, ready as he may be to give gifts, he knows the difference between a cheap pretence of a present and the real thing, which will cost him something. Horace, evidently, is a worthy recipient and Maecenas a discriminating donor.

dark hair and narrow forehead one guarantee of male youth and beauty was hair which grew, or was brushed, so far forward as to make the forehead narrow.

Cinara the love of his distant youth, earning another nostalgic reference in *Odes* 4.1.4: 'I am not the man I once was, under the reign of kindly Cinara'.

Held up against this image, I surrender all if the vixen story is the correct analogy for Horace's behaviour, the corn-chest stands for Maecenas and his generosity. It would follow that Horace, the vixen, had gorged himself there for no reason except selfish satisfaction. If that is so, he is no worthy (line 22) recipient and he is morally obliged to give back what he has received.

king a standard word used by clients for the patron who looks after them.

Telemachus spoke well, hardy Ulysses' son: 40
'Ithaca's no place for horses: no flat ground
to gallop on, no good supply of grass.
Your gifts, **Atrides**, suit *you* well. Please keep them.'
Small folk, small things. For me now, not majestic Rome,
but quiet **Tibur and Tarentum** with its peace.   45

Philippus, bold, industrious, an orator
well known, returning one mid-afternoon from court,
fussed at the distance **from the Forum to the Keels**
(he was no longer young). Then, so they say, he saw
a close-shaved fellow in a barber's shady shop   50
cleaning his nails, all peaceful, with a knife.
'Demetrius,' (the **boy** was there, attentive to Philippus)
'off with you, ask him; tell me his name, address,
position: **who's his father, who's his patron?**'
He goes, returns, explains: 'He's called **Volteius Mena**,   55
an **auctioneer**, not well off, honest fellow, known
as active at need, or easy; makes his money, knows its use;
happy with friends (no grand ones), with a settled home,
with public shows, and with **the Campus** after work.'

Telemachus   in *Odyssey* 4, Telemachus came to Sparta searching for his father Odysseus. There he met King Menelaus, who entertained him kindly and offered him, as a parting gift, horses and a chariot. In refusing them with consummate tact, Telemachus earned Menelaus' respect and a different, equally splendid, gift.

Atrides   'son of Atreus', i.e. Menelaus.

Tibur and Tarentum   pleasant country resorts, Tivoli in the hills near Rome, Taranto on the south coast (see *Odes* **3.5.56**, p. 98 and **2.6.10–20**, p. 114).

Philippus   at least two distinguished men called Philippus are known, the younger of them Augustus' stepfather.

from the Forum to the Keels   'the Keels' was the name given to the area at the south-western slope of the Esquiline hill, after the pirate ships which Pompey used to adorn his residence there in the 60s BC. The area is no great way from the Forum, but Philippus is not young, and he has done a day's work. (See map, p. 4.)

boy   Philippus has a slave in personal attendance, as did Horace in *Satires* **1.9.10** (p. 38).

who's his father, who's his patron?   he may be (as in fact he turns out to be) a freedman, in which case, from the point of view of the law, he will have a patron, who has given him freedom, not a father. This will also answer the question about (social) position.

Volteius Mena   Volteius will be his patron's name; Mena is the Romanized version of a Greek name not uncommon for slaves. So he is evidently a freedman.

auctioneer   as, Horace tells us (*Satires* 1.6.86), he might well have been himself.

the Campus   the Campus Martius: the place for open-air exercise (see map, p. 4).

'I'd like to hear that from the man himself. Go back: 60
ask him to dinner.' Mena was sceptical:
'What's up?' he wondered. Finally, 'No, thanks,'
he answered. 'Him, refuse me?' 'Cheeky fellow, yes.
He's rude – or scared.' Philippus caught Volteius
selling cheap **oddments** to a **tunic-wearing** crowd   65
next day. **He didn't wait**, but greeted him. The other
contrived excuses – work, employers' calls –
for **having made no morning visit**, having failed
even to see him coming. 'You're forgiven, if
you dine with me this evening.' 'As you wish.' 'Well then,   70
come after **three**. Now go, work hard and make some profit.'
He dined; talked sense and nonsense; rather late
went off to bed. And now more frequently one saw
the fish come swimming to the hidden hook.
A morning client, frequent diner, he was asked,   75
'Come to the country for the Latin festival.'
There in the coach he praised non-stop the Sabine skies,
the Sabine scenery. Philippus noticed, smiled,
and, **wanting peace himself and laughs** (no matter how),

---

oddments   the Latin word is *scruta*. According to Lucilius 1170–1 (Warmington), it could cover things like a chipped strigil ('skin-scraper') and a sandal which has lost its pair.

tunic-wearing   that is, not wearing togas, and therefore not of any social standing.

He didn't wait   normal etiquette required the social inferior to take the initiative.

having made no morning visit   Volteius is thoroughly embarrassed. He is being treated by Philippus as if Philippus were already his patron. He feels he should have acknowledged this somehow by acting as a client and attending the morning *salutatio*, though he didn't know he was a client. Even his curt response to the dinner invitation 'As you wish' (line 70) reveals the gaucherie of embarrassment.

three   that is, three o'clock (the ninth hour), the appropriate time for dinner. (Martial, *Epigrams* 4.8 gives the schedule for the normal day.)

Come to the country for the Latin festival   a six-day festival held in the spring at a time dictated by the consuls each year. The relatively short time, and perhaps the lack of notice, mean that Philippus is only going to one of his nearby country estates, not to the more distant resorts such as those on the bay of Naples.

There in the coach   the conversation is rather like Horace's with Maecenas in *Satires* **2.6.42–6** (p. 44).

wanting peace himself and laughs   Philippus is not an unkindly person, but he has got rather more than he bargained for in this energetic chatterbox, and he has not thought through the responsibilities of generosity which are very much the subject of this poem.

'The Sabine skies, the Sabine scenery' (Epistles *1.7.77–8*).

he made a gift of **seven thousand,** and a loan   80
the same, persuading Mena thus to buy a farm.
He did. I won't by long digressions waste your time
more than I need. From townsman he turned scruffy, **and**
his talk was vines and furrows. He **stripped his elms, he worked**
himself to death; grew senile in his zest for gain.   85
But when his sheep were lost to thieves, his goats to plague,
his harvest hopes deceived, his ox dead at the plough,
fed up with loss, **at dead of night,** enraged, he took
a nag and went to find Philippus at his home.

---

seven thousand   that is, 7,000 sesterces. 'The sum apparently would have secured only a fairly small property' (Mayer, p. 171).

and   appears in Horace, as here, at the end of the line. Subverting his own verse-form, he creates a colloquial effect.

stripped his elms   it was standard practice to train vines over elm trees which had been heavily pruned so that their branches appeared in layers one above the other.

he worked / himself to death; grew senile   these two ideas are metaphors in Latin too. Horace turns them here into obvious clichés by putting them the wrong way round.

at dead of night   partly as an expression of despair, partly because he will thus be able to reach Rome in time for the morning *salutatio*.

Philippus said, on seeing him unshaven, scabbed, 90
'Volteius, you seem overworked and underfed
by far, to me.' 'Yes, patron, you could call me wretch,
were you to want to call me by a proper name!
Now by your Genius, your right hand, your household gods,
I humbly beg, restore that life I had before.' 95
He who would change, then finds what's changed is lost,
may unchange change and thus retrieve his cost.
If each man's measure is his own, the measure's true.

---

1 How relevant is each of the three anecdotes in this epistle to Horace's relationship with Maecenas? (Consider Peter White: 'Both [Philippus and Mena] behave badly, and Mena's life is ultimately ruined by Philippus' careless attentions. Horace leaves it to the reader to determine whether the pair are adduced as analogues or as antitypes of Maecenas and himself, or as something in between' (*CCH*, p. 205).)

2 Is the picture of life in the country consistent with the way Horace has presented it elsewhere, especially *Satires* **2.6.60–70** (pp. 45–6)?

3 Is it your impression after reading this epistle that Horace wishes his relationship with Maecenas to be less close?

4 'The portrayals of city and country life in Roman satire are not included for their simple descriptive or documentary value but serve a purpose, and in doing so reveal aspects of Roman ideology' (Braund, *Satire and Society*, p. 44). Based on the evidence of this poem, how did Romans perceive the city and the countryside?

Epistles 1.12

Iccius was the recipient of *Odes* **1.29** (p. 111). Compare what he was doing then, and what he seems to have been thinking then, with what he is doing and thinking now.

He who would change ... retrieve his cost   the moral of what has been effectively a fable. Horace's language offers us something of the sententiousness of a moralizing conclusion. This translation seeks to capture that, while departing substantially from Horace's own words: 'He who has once seen how much better is that which one has let go than that which one has sought, let him speedily return and seek back again that which he has left.'

If each man's measure is his own, the measure's true   each man has his own foot-ruler in the form of his own foot. That people should follow Nature as a universal principle is a Stoic rule. But each man has his own individual nature, and that must also be followed (Cicero, *On Duties* 1.110).

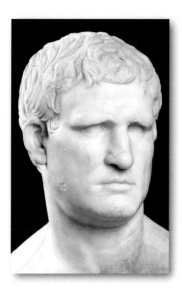

Profits in Sicily you're gathering for Agrippa, Iccius.
From them if you profit rightly, no gift more plentiful
could come to you from Jupiter. Complain no more:
no man is poor who has good things **by right of use**.
Digestion good? Feet? Heart and lungs? There's nothing   5
the wealth of kings could give you any better.
And if, abstaining from good things to hand, **you live
on herbs and nettles**, why, you'll live so that instantly
by a clear stream from Fortune **you'll be plated gold**,
perhaps since money cannot alter nature,   10
perhaps since you set Virtue above all things.
No wonder if **Democritus' flock ate up
fields, crops**, while that swift mind, unbodied, was on tour,

Marcus Agrippa (Epistles *1.12.1*).

Profits in Sicily you're gathering for Agrippa   Iccius is evidently serving in Sicily as Agrippa's *procurator*: the agent managing his estates. Marcus Agrippa was, with Maecenas, one of the two men most closely associated with Augustus. He was more than anyone responsible for Augustus' victory in the Sicilian War against Sextus Pompeius in 36 BC and at Actium in 31. His wealth was enormous. His *procurator* will have held considerable responsibility and earned a substantial reward. Iccius should be satisfied with his lot.

by right of use   Iccius' complaints seem related to the idea that the property he is managing is not his own. Horace cheers him up by referring to his right as *procurator*, which is not merely to have the use of Agrippa's property, but to have the use *and profit* from it – which is, philosophically speaking, the most anyone can expect even of the estates he owns in law (*Satires* 2.2.134).

you live / on herbs and nettles   a vegetarian diet of the most extreme sort! Compare the simple diet proposed for himself by Horace in *Satires* **2.6.63–4** (p. 45), or Ofellus' in *Satires* 2.2.116–17.

you'll be plated gold   in a letter to a lawyer friend serving with Caesar in Gaul, Cicero says 'I think you'd rather have Caesar ask your opinion than plate you with gold' (*Ad Familiares* 7.13.1) – i.e. the phrase is a conversational expression for 'to make super-rich'.

Democritus' flock ate up / fields, crops   Democritus of Abdera was a philosopher of the fifth century BC, to whom Aristotle attributed a major part in the development of an atomic theory of the universe. But here Horace seems to have in mind a passage of Cicero, *De Finibus* ('On the Ends of Good and Evil'):

> The importance of philosophy consists in its power to provide a life of happiness. … So we should ask ourselves: can philosophical thinking achieve this? It seems to offer the possibility. Why else would Plato have gone to Egypt to learn astronomy from foreign priests? … Why did Democritus do likewise? It is said that he put out his own eyes. We know that he neglected his estate and left his land uncultivated. All this so that his mind should not be distracted from speculation. And for what purpose? A life of happiness. (5.86–7)

when you, amidst the infectious rottenness of wealth
think no mean thoughts, still caring for higher things.   15
What stills the sea? – What makes the seasons turn? –
The planets: do they stray at will or at command? –
What dims the moon? – What brings her sphere to view?
What will, what power in **Nature's disunited unity**? –
On this **Empedocles, Stertinius the Sharp** may rant.   20
You may be **murdering** fish, or leek and onion:
but **use Pompeius Grosphus**; what he asks,
give him unasked. He'll only want what's just and true.
Where good men are in need, the price of friends is low.
But should you wish for news of how Rome stands,   25

Nature's disunited unity this striking phrase (*rerum concordia discors*) appears to represent an idea attributed to Empedocles (see below) that the universe is propelled by the complementary principles of Love and Strife.

Empedocles, Stertinius the Sharp more philosophers. Empedocles (also fifth century BC) is relevant to Iccius because he came from Sicily. So determined a vegetarian was he that he was said to have served up at a sacrificial dinner an ox made of honey and barley-meal (Diogenes Laertius, *Lives of the Philosophers* 8.53). Stertinius appears in *Satires* 2.3 as a Stoic fundamentalist preaching the doctrine that, if you are not wise, you are mad. 'The Sharp' is an ironic title.

murdering in Pythagorean doctrine onions, as well as living creatures, might be inhabited by a potentially human soul.

use Pompeius Grosphus the word 'use' is less striking of a person in Latin than in English, but it is still noteworthy, and stressed by its placing. It reminds us that 'right use' is an important theme of the poem. Use what? 'Use a person.' Quite suddenly the letter has turned into a letter of recommendation. Such letters must have been very common indeed. We have several examples. Cicero, for instance, writes to Caesar in Gaul in 54 BC suggesting that he take the young Trebatius onto his staff. (The letter, *Ad Familiares* 7.5, is itself evidently part of a sequence of such recommendations.) Horace writes *Epistles* 1.9 to the future emperor Tiberius, apologizing for his presumption in recommending one Septimius. Grosphus himself seems to be a Sicilian landowner (*Odes* 2.16 is dedicated to him).

Where good men are in need, the price of friends is low if a person needs something, one can make him a friend simply by the easy method of giving him it. Horace part-translates a sentence of Xenophon where Socrates is made to say, encouraging someone to make the first move towards friendship, 'In these bad times, one can acquire friends very cheaply' (*Memorabilia* 2.10.4). It may be relevant that Horace goes on immediately to indicate that the times are very good.

The Spaniard to Agrippa's strength has bowed,
the Armenian to Nero's. Caesar's power and rule
Phraätes, kneeling, owns. On Italy
Plenty pours golden wealth from her full **horn**.

---

1   In lines 1–11, why is Iccius adopting the lifestyle he evidently is adopting? Horace seems to suggest at least two possible reasons. What are they?

2   In lines 12–20, what attitude to these philosophers is Horace encouraging us to take? In particular, exactly what use does Horace make of the Cicero passage (note on 12–13)? What does he wish to convey to Iccius?

3   That cosmology could make thrilling poetry is suggested by Virgil, *Eclogues* 6.31–40 and *Aeneid* 1.740–7, where the bard Iopas holds a very late-night audience spellbound with such topics. Propertius too presents himself in 3.5.20–43 as faced with the same choice as Iccius in *Odes* **1.29**: he comes to the opposite conclusion.

4   Horace's own professed attitude is expressed in the following passage (*Epistles* 1.1.23–6): 'All time passes slowly and unpleasantly, if it holds back my hopes and my determination to work energetically at that which will be of equal advantage to rich and poor, and if neglected equally harmful to old men and children.' How does Horace develop the ideas of 'use' and 'profit' in this epistle?

5   Should Iccius be glad to have received this epistle and then seen it published?

Epistles **1.20**

This is the last poem in the first book of *Epistles*, and the first thing that strikes the reader is that it is not an epistle. This attracted attention in antiquity too. Horace was defended on the grounds that there might be greater freedom at the beginning and end of a collection. It does, however, have an addressee: Horace is talking to his book, the book of *Epistles*. The book is a slave-boy who is tired of living cooped up in his master Horace's house. He wants his freedom, to enjoy the wide world. Horace maintains the double identity book/boy throughout the poem.

The Spaniard … Phraätes, kneeling, owns a quick summary, deliberately compressed, of the prosperity the Roman state is currently enjoying. The date is 20 BC. Agrippa has finally managed to pacify Spain after nearly ten years of campaigns by himself and Augustus. Phraätes is king of Parthia and has handed to Augustus the standards won from Crassus and Antony (see *Odes* **3.5**, p. 93). Nero is Tiberius Claudius Nero, the future emperor Tiberius.

horn the Horn of Plenty is a common sight in classical art of the ancient or modern world, hence 'cornucopia'.

1.20.1–19	You're eyeing **Janus**, little book, **Vertumnus** too,
	it seems: you want to go and **sell yourself**,
	smoothed with the **pumice of the Sosii**.
	Keys and the seals which decency prefers, you hate.
	On show to few, you moan: you love publicity –	5
	not as I trained you. Go then, down where you long to be.
	Once gone, you can't come back. 'Not fair! **What did I do?**
	I meant no harm,' you'll say, when you get hurt. You know
	you're put in your place, as soon as the lover has had enough.
	You make me cross. **Unless that clouds my second sight**,	10
	in Rome they'll call you **dear** till youth abandons you.
	When, passed from hand to common hand, you lose your bloom,
	the philistine grubs will get you, or you'll run away
	to **Utica**, or be shipped to **Ilerda**, bound.
	He'll laugh, the mentor who you wouldn't listen to,	15
	like him who **pushed a stubborn donkey off a cliff**

Janus, Vertumnus there was a statue of the god Vertumnus in the Vicus Tuscus, a street which led from the Forum to the Tiber. It was full of expensive shops. (In *Satires* 2.3.228, a man who wants to spend a fortune quickly invites 'the shameless crowd from the Vicus Tuscus' to visit him.) There were several places described as 'Janus' in the city, and it is not clear to which this refers: perhaps Janus Medius in the Forum itself. There may be the point that Vertumnus was a god of changes (so, at least, Romans derived his name, even if wrongly) and Janus a god of beginnings, so that Horace is emphasizing the book's desire for a new start in life.

sell yourself the (book)/slave is a boy who intends to earn his living by prostitution.

pumice of the Sosii the Sosii were booksellers. Pumice stone was used to polish papyrus. For the slave, it would be useful to rub his legs and get rid of hair.

What did I do? / I meant no harm for the slave-boy, the classic excuses when faced with punishment: 'I haven't done anything, and, if I have, it was an accident.'

you're put in your place Horace speaks of being 'shut up in a narrow space'. For the book, this is clearly one of the compartments of a bookcase (*scrinium*). It is less clear what is happening to the boy. The translation is designed to give the idea of some humiliation.

Unless that clouds my second sight literally 'unless the augur has lost his touch'. Augurs were members of the official priesthood of Rome, with the technique and the responsibility of making predictions.

dear the Latin word too can be a term of affection or mean 'expensive'.

Utica, Ilerda Utica was a city of North Africa. Once important, it had lost power to the nearby Augustan colony of Carthage. Ilerda is a dead-end town in Spain. Evidently the book is exported to places where no one will read it. The boy either runs away (to Utica) or is punished by being sent to work in a chain-gang.

pushed a stubborn donkey off a cliff in Aesop's fable, a donkey driver punished his recalcitrant donkey thus. The fable shows up the folly of the driver, but here Horace tells it, on the face of it, at the expense of the donkey.

in anger. Who'd give help to one who won't accept it?
This is your future: **teaching children A, B, C**
at urban street-ends. Mumbling Age will grab you there.

> Here Horace begins a tiny autobiographical passage with which to conclude
> the book. It is a little like the passage at the end of the *Georgics* (4.559–566) in
> which Virgil puts his name to the whole collection of his published poetry so
> far, both *Eclogues* and *Georgics*. Such a passage has the technical name *sphragis*
> ('seal'), indicating a clear end and stating the poet's claim to authorship. But
> Horace does not mention his own name, and, typically, it is not 'Horace' who
> is giving the autobiography – it is the slave, the book.

1.20.20–29   When **the warm sun** brings in a larger audience   20
you'll tell them how I was not born to wealth –
a freedman's son, I spread my wings beyond the nest –
('The lower my birth, the greater were my merits,' say.)
welcome **in war** and peace to Rome's chief leaders –
puny in size, sun-loving, prematurely grey,   25
quick-tempered, but as quickly mollified.
If any chance to ask about my age,
forty Decembers say I had finished and four,
that year when Lollius named as colleague Lepidus.

---

1   The poem depends on the conflation of the two ideas, 'book' and 'boy'. How
    successfully has Horace managed this?

2   Compare the poem as a seal-poem (*sphragis*) with *Odes* **3.30**, p. 67.

3   Could anything like Horace's *Epistles* be written today?

---

teaching children A, B, C   in the absence of elementary textbooks, basic literacy was
likely to be learned by studying any scraps of writing available. To such a condition has
the book descended. The slave-boy, now old, is like Lenaeus, the old confidential slave
of Pompey the Great, who spent his old age running an elementary school by the Keels
(see *Epistles* **1.7.48n**, p. 155).

the warm sun   this is either early in the day (schoolmasters started very early: 'before
cockcrow' (Martial, *Epigrams* 9.68)) and it has just got warm enough for other people to be
about, or late in the day, when the excessive heat has gone out of the sun.

in war   compare *Epistles* **2.2.47–8**, p. 167. Horace is prepared to advertise his early
opposition to Octavian.

that year   Romans dated years with reference to the two consuls of the year. Lollius and
Lepidus were consuls in 21 BC. The idea is expressed like this because Lollius was originally
elected on his own, and only later, when it was accepted that Augustus was unwilling
to stand for the consulship, was Lepidus elected and installed by his colleague. It might
be thought that this line gave a date to the book. But the reference to the Parthians in
1.12.27–8 (p. 161) must come from a year later.

4 The poet critic: *Epistles* 2 and the *Art of Poetry*

Horace wrote three very long epistles which discuss poets and poetry. Two of them make up the second book of his *Epistles*, and one is a separate letter, just under 500 lines long, addressed to three members of the family Calpurnius Piso, father and two young sons. Selections from these three poems are presented in the order in which it is believed Horace wrote them: *Epistles* 2.2, *Epistles* 2.1, *Letter to the Pisos* (which is commonly called the *Art of Poetry*).

Horace's discussion of literature forms part of an immense tradition going back to Plato and Aristotle, or even to passages in the Homeric poems. In *Epistles* 2.2 the focus is not so much on poetry as on the poet. Horace presents an ironic picture of himself as subject to social pressures and also determinedly independent of them, rather as he did in the *Satires*. *Epistles* 2.1 is addressed to Augustus himself and focuses on the contribution which good poetry can make to society. The *Art of Poetry* is the closest to a formal consideration of the subject of poetic composition: see the introductory note on pp. 175–7.

Epistles 2.2

The letter is written to Julius Florus, to whom Horace wrote *Epistles* 1.3 when he was in the east on the staff of Augustus' stepson Tiberius, almost certainly in 20–19 BC. Since Florus is introduced to us in the first line of the present letter as 'good friend to valiant, noble [Tiberius] Nero', it is not unlikely that it was written not much later than the earlier one. The overall argument ('Horace is giving up writing poetry for the serious study of the ethical life') is also very similar to the argument of *Epistles* **1.1** (pp. 149–51).

Florus seems (like Augustus in *Epistles* 2.1) to have complained to Horace that he was failing to live up to a promise to write some lyric poetry for him. In one respect the letter is a series of excuses for failing to comply with Florus' request. Paradoxically, the longer Horace's excuses go on, the more substantial is, in fact, his compliance, even if in a different genre. In another respect the letter is an argument designed to make us see that writing is a serious business.

2.2.1–66
> Florus, good friend to valiant, noble **Nero**,
> if you were made the offer of a slave-boy, born
> at **Gabii or Tibur**, and the vendor's line was 'Here's
> a fair lad, handsome all the way from head to heel:
> he's yours to own for just **eight thousand down**.   5
> **Home-bred**, trained in his duties at the master's call,
> a smattering of Greek, ready for training in
> whatever skill: soft clay for moulding as you please.
> Yes: while you drink he'll sing – an untrained voice, but sweet.
> Promise too much, and one is disbelieved,   10
> puffing one's goods too loud, wanting to palm them off.
> I'm not under pressure, and my credit's good.
> No dealer would do this for you. It's a special offer
> for you alone. Once he slipped up, and, as they do,
> hid below stairs **in terror of the hanging strap**.   15
> Cash down then? – if you're not bothered by his escapade.'
> He'd take his price, I think, and fear no penalty.
> You bought a dud. You knew it, and you knew the rules.
> The law's against you, and you still pursue the man?
>
>   I said, **as you left**, 'I'm lazy.' I said too   20
> 'I'm useless at such duties', so that you'd not get cross
> and scold me, having had no letter from me.
> What good did I do myself? The law is on my side,
> and you contest it. Here's another charge you make:
> 'You said you'd send some poems. You sent none. You lied.'   25

Nero   one of the family names of the first husband of Augustus' wife Livia. Here it refers to her son Tiberius, the later emperor. The emperor Nero was so called because he was the great-grandson of Tiberius' brother.

Gabii or Tibur   were towns in the country close to Rome. It may be suggested that the slave-boy was born in the house of some grandee with an estate in one of these desirable locations.

eight thousand down   that is, 8,000 sesterces. 'The standard value of a slave often assumed for legal purposes is just 2,000 sesterces' (Brink, p. 271). Not cheap, then, except as the seller is trying to persuade his victim.

Home-bred   see *Satires* **2.6.66n**, p. 46, for 'home-bred' slaves. Knowing Greek would make him useful as a secretary.

in terror of the hanging strap   in detail obscure, even if the general gist is clear. Either the strap from which slaves were suspended for a flogging or the strap used on the boy.

as you left   to serve, evidently, with Tiberius in the east.

A soldier of **Lucullus**, weary, slept one night,
and all his painfully saved cash, to the last coin,
went missing. Then like a savage wolf, enraged alike
with self and enemy, teeth hunger-sharpened,
he stormed, they say, a royal garrison 30
solidly fortified and crammed with wealth.
Famous for this great deed and **decorated**,
he was awarded **twenty thousand sesterces**.
His colonel, not much later, keen to overthrow
some fortlet, came to the man and urged him on 35
in words which might make brave the faintest heart.
'Go, hero, go where courage calls! Go blessed by god!
Your deeds will earn a handsome payment. What? Still here?'
At this the fellow – peasant, but shrewd – said, '*He* will go,
yes, *he*'ll go anywhere who's lost his money-belt.' 40

Rome was my foster-mother. There **I learned**
how in his rage Achilles harmed the Greeks.
From kindly Athens I received some further skill:
the wish to tell the crooked from the straight
and seek truth in the woods at **the Academy**. 45

Lucullus   this story is attached to the campaigns of Lucius Lucullus, whose great achievement, in 73–68 BC, was to capture the capital city of Armenia and substantially to break the power of King Mithridates of Pontus, the greatest threat to Roman influence in the east.

decorated   Roman military decorations included various kinds of crown, a special spear and banner, neck-rings, armlets, badges, and horse-trappings (see Rudd, 1989, p. 126).

twenty thousand sesterces   a sizeable sum, but not a fortune. Fourteen thousand just bought Volteius his farm in *Epistles* **1.7.80–1** (p. 157).

Rome was my foster-mother   in *Satires* 1.6.71–8 Horace tells how his father, unsatisfied with the school at their home town Venusia, took him to school in Rome.

I learned / how in his rage Achilles   that is, Horace studied Homer's *Iliad*, the important words of whose first line are 'the rage of Achilles'. But of course the *Iliad* stands for the whole canon of Greek literature.

the Academy   the name of the gymnasium just outside Athens where Plato spent much of his time teaching. It was a precinct sacred to the Athenian hero Academus, and the trees were planted in his honour in the fifth century BC. In 'the crooked from the straight' (line 44), Horace refers to the ethical teaching of the Academy and probably also to its interest in mathematics. (Plato famously had the rule 'Let no one enter here without geometry' inscribed at the door.)

But hard times took me from that lovely place;
as **civil conflict** dragged me, raw recruit, to arms
unequal to the sinews of Augustus Caesar.
Then, when Philippi gave me my discharge,
brought low, wings clipped, deprived of father's house and farm,   50
the **impudence of poverty** reduced me
to making verses. Now that I have enough,
what **hemlock-dose** could purge me if I don't
think sleep seems more desirable than writing verse?
The passing years steal from us, one by one,   55
laughter, love, company, frivolity,
and soon they'll seize my verse. What would you have me do?
And then there's taste: not everyone's the same.
Your preference is lyric, he enjoys **lampoons**,
while he likes **Bion's satires** and their caustic wit.   60
Three guests I have and three conflicting views,
with different palates wanting incompatibles.
What should I give – or not give? What *you* spurn, *he* wants.
What one wants, two reject as nasty, sour.
And after all, can I, do you think, write poems here   65
in Rome, with cares and troubles all around?

---

civil conflict   Horace was in Athens when Brutus, one of Julius Caesar's assassins, visited in late 44 BC. He was recruited by Brutus into his army and fought at the battle of Philippi in 42, when Brutus was defeated and killed himself.

unequal to the sinews of Augustus Caesar   the battle of Philippi was won by the leadership of Mark Antony; Octavian, who did not become Augustus for another 14 years, took very little part. Horace is telescoping things in order to set up an absurd imaginary duel: (tiny) Horace *v.* (mighty) Augustus. (This is one of only two places in Horace where both names 'Caesar' and 'Augustus' are used together.)

impudence of poverty   if poor, you presume to do things which otherwise you wouldn't. In fact Horace at this time acquired the post of treasury clerk, perhaps because his skill at writing had brought him to the attention of men of patronage.

hemlock-dose   hemlock cures madness here and in line 137. If Horace is so mad as to write poems when he doesn't have to, he must be incurable.

lampoons   iambics, on which see the introduction to the *Epodes*, pp. 9–10.

Bion's satires   on these see the introduction to the *Satires*, p. 17.

Three guests I have   a more usual experience for a poet was to be the guest himself, expected to perform for his well-to-do host. Horace turns the tables here by imagining himself the host, offering literary delicacies.

---

1   After three separate narratives (1–25 slave and vendor, 26–40 Lucullus' soldier, 41–54 autobiography), Horace comes to the point. In what way is each of them a different type of narrative?

2   Which character in the first narrative, if any, represents Horace?

3   What does the choice of characters tell us about how Horace is presenting himself (what literary critics would call his *persona*)?

4   Why does Horace take so long to get to the point?

5   Do you know any poets? If so, what inspires them to write? What does Horace here claim as sources of his inspiration? Does his attitude surprise you, and does it tell us anything about his status as a poet in Rome?

2.2.67–216   Horace continues: the noise and chaos make Rome no place for the writer. Go to Athens for quiet study for seven years and you'll still come back dumb. What chance in Rome? Everyone's writing poetry and expecting you to praise their own, and if you don't they'll praise it themselves. Work hard, satisfy your own standards. Even if they aren't universal standards, delude yourself that they are. Don't worry what others think. And this applies to life too. Live by your own standards; don't trouble to acquire the things that other people account blessings. Accept your own limitations – which means, in the end, mortality.

Epistles 2.1

In his *Life of Horace*, Suetonius writes: 'After reading some of Horace's *sermones*, Augustus complained to the poet that there was no mention of himself. He wrote: "Let me tell you, I am cross with you. You should have presented yourself in several of those writings of yours as talking with me more than anyone. Are you worried that it will look badly for you with posterity if you seem to have been on good terms with me?" As a result, he got him to write the piece which begins "So great, so many are the tasks …"' (i.e. what we know as *Epistles* 2.1).

To judge by Suetonius' chronology, Augustus wrote this letter after the *Carmen Saeculare* and after the publication of *Odes* 4. In the epistle itself there also seem to be references to the performance of the *Carmen Saeculare* (lines 132–5) – 17 BC – and to the establishment of altars dedicated to the cult of the *Lares* (see note on p. 46) and the *Genius* of Augustus, likely to have taken place in 12 BC. The reference to 'talking with me' makes it sound as if Augustus was thinking of the first book of *Epistles*, though some of the *Satires* (1.1, 2.1, **2.6**) are also addressed to individuals in a somewhat similar way. Horace in fact uses the term *sermones* ('conversations') to cover both *Satires* and *Epistles*.

Could this be Augustus? He wears the lion-skin of Hercules (Epistles 2.1.10). Cameo from Naples attributed to the Augustan artist Gnaios.

2.1.1–22   So great, so many are the tasks you bear alone:
your arms safeguard, your ways ennoble Italy,
your laws correct her. I would do a public wrong
were I by long discourse to trespass, Caesar, on your time.
Romulus, Father Liber, Castor with Pollux,   5
enshrined in temples after doing mighty deeds

So great, so many … your laws correct her   in these lines Horace touches on three of the most important points of which Augustus was most proud: peace at home (the Altar of Peace had been dedicated in 13 BC, a year or so before this epistle was written), the reform of society through laws (the Julian Laws were passed in 18 BC) and by the Emperor's personal example ('your ways'), and the unification of Italy under the leadership of Rome.

Romulus   the founder of Rome, mentioned in the context of Augustus, the second founder. Before he took the name Augustus, Octavian is said to have considered taking that of Romulus.

Father Liber   the Roman god identified with Dionysus/Bacchus. The wine with which this god is associated is one aspect of his mission to create and preside over social harmony in all its forms. In his youth he had travelled from India to Greece, bringing civilization with him. This, at least, is the aspect of Liber which Horace wishes us to have in mind here.

Castor with Pollux   the brothers of Helen of Troy and of Agamemnon's wife Clytemnestra. They are especially the protectors of sailors, but have a particular association with Rome in that they were held to have fought for the Romans in the great battle of Lake Regillus in 493 BC, by which Rome established its supremacy in the region of Latium. The brothers brought the news to Rome and a temple was built for them in a very conspicuous place in the Forum.

---

in **taming earth** and humankind, in ending
fierce wars, assigning lands, and founding cities,
lamented still that for these deeds they did not win
the praise they looked for. **He who crushed the fearsome Hydra,**   10
subduing famous monsters by predestined labour,
found envy overcome by death, and death alone.
In overwhelming smaller talents, genius
sears them with its brilliance – yet will, once gone, be loved.
To you, still with us, we are quick in granting **honours.**   15
On altars now we swear by your divinity,
and say 'There never was one like you, nor will ever be.'
But yet your people, wise and just in setting you
alone above our leaders and above the Greeks,
in every other judgement go by rules   20
quite different. Everything but what they see
is finished, dead and buried, **they despise, they loathe.**

---

taming earth   this and the other activities in lines 7–8 can be loosely associated with the divinities mentioned and with Hercules (see below), but the only figure to whom they are all appropriate is Augustus himself – especially the business of 'assigning lands'. In *Res Gestae* 28 Augustus claims to have founded 28 colonies for his ex-soldiers to occupy in Italy alone.

lamented   Castor was killed in a family quarrel; Pollux survived him and negotiated immortality for them both. Dionysus was never to be thought of as mortal. It is the deaths of Hercules and Romulus about which Horace is thinking. Hercules was unintentionally killed by his wife Deianira, who gave him a robe soaked in poison which she believed was a love-charm. One story of the death of Romulus was that he was killed by a group of senators. It was only after their deaths that they received glory in the form of admission to heaven as gods.

He who crushed the fearsome Hydra   Hercules killed the Hydra, a nine-headed giant snake, as the second of his Twelve Labours.

honours   in January 27 BC, apart from the name Augustus, Octavian was awarded a Civic Crown (an award for saving the lives of citizens) and a Shield of Virtue, commemorating his courage, clemency, justice and piety. Many other honours are recorded in *Res Gestae* 9–12.

On altars now we swear by your divinity   from early in Augustus' reign there were temples built in the provinces dedicated to 'Rome and Augustus'; later on there developed the practice in Rome of worshipping the Genius of Augustus. He was not formally deified until after his death.

they despise, they loathe   excessive veneration for dead poets was not limited to Horace's generation. A hundred years later Martial wrote the epigram (8.69):

> Of poets, Vacerra, you say
> It's only the dead ones you cherish.
> Forgive me, Vacerra, I pray:
> To please you, it's too much to perish.

| 2.1.23–33 | Horace continues: they say that the oldest, most crabbed and dreary passages of primitive Latin are the direct inspiration of the Muses! The oldest Greek literature may be the best, but it is not so with Latin. |

2.1.34–49	If age improves a poem as it does a wine,
	tell me: what year gives paper added value?
	A writer who's been dead a century, should he
	be listed with the old and perfect, or among
	the new contemptibles? Let there be no dispute.
	'He's old and good who's lasted for a hundred years.'
	Suppose he missed it by a month, a year,
	which party should we put him with? The bards of old,
	or those despised by this age and by that to come?
	'Oh, *he* will fairly earn his place among the old,
	if he falls short by just a month, or just a year.'
	With your assent, I'm plucking (as it were)
	one hair and then another from a horse's tail,
	till he who looks at dates and reckons worth by age,
	admiring only what **the tomb** has sanctified,
	collapses at **the logic of the shrinking heap**.

Line numbers: 35 (at line 2), 40 (at line 7), 45 (at line 12)

| 2.1.50–9 | The Latin poets of previous ages, Ennius, Naevius, Pacuvius, Accius, Afranius, Plautus, Caecilius and Terence are all regarded as classics, Horace says. Criticism is limited to saying that each is supreme in a particular field. |

2.1.60–75	These are the works which mighty Rome peruses, and
	packed tight in theatres, watches. These she reckons her poets,
	to our times from the age of **author Livius**.
	Sometimes the crowd sees straight, sometimes it's wrong.
	In praise and admiration of the old, if it
	admits no better, even no equal, it's mistaken.
	If it believes and grants that those men's speech

Line numbers: 60 (at line 1), 65 (at line 6)

---

the tomb Horace's word is *Libitina*, the goddess who presided over funerals.

the logic of the shrinking heap when is a heap of sand not a heap? When I have taken one grain off? or two grains? or three? This argument is called *sorites*, from the Greek word *sōros* ('heap'), and is attributed to the fourth-century BC philosopher Eubulides of Miletus.

author Livius Livius Andronicus (not the same as the historian Livy), the earliest writer of Latin literature, composed plays for a festival in 240 BC, as well as a translation of the *Odyssey*. He is called 'author Livius' to distinguish him from the aristocratic family whose freedman he was.

An intimidating schoolteacher (Epistles 2.1.70). Relief from the Rhineland, second century AD.

is sometimes dated, mostly awkward, often inept,
it shows good sense, it thinks as I do and as heaven approves.
Myself, I don't assail the songs of Livius
or wish them lost. **Whacker Orbilius** I recall   70
dictating them at school. But this *is* strange –
that they're called 'polished', 'lovely', almost 'perfect'.
In fact, if one well-chosen word shines out, or if
a line or two seem somewhat neatly put,
that by itself quite wrongly sells the whole.   75

2.1.76–89   Horace says that archaic writing may be excused but should not be praised.
He gets into serious trouble for suggesting that old works might be improved
upon. Perhaps the older generation is simply unwilling to give way to the
younger; perhaps they simply don't want to admit that all that learning they
did when they were young was a waste of time.

2.1.90–2   If novelty in Greece had been as much deplored   90
as here, what would be left as old? Or what would pass
from hand to hand, worn out by popular demand?

Whacker Orbilius   a schoolmaster at Rome in Horace's youth. Rather too ready to use the cane ('Whacker'), he was still a good teacher and a generous man, honoured by his fellow citizens of Beneventum with a statue. He is known from Suetonius' book *On Grammarians.*

> 1 Lines 1–22. In *Epistles* 2.2 and 2.1 Horace is giving the same message, first to Florus, then to Augustus, but in very different tones. What is the message? What is the tone of each? Why does Horace change his tone? What would Horace say about Chaucer and Shakespeare?
>
> 2 Lines 34–49. What has Horace suggested is the motive behind those who call no one a hero until he's dead? **What implication does this have for Horace himself?** And how is Augustus' unique status used by Horace in his own cause?
>
> 3 In your humanities or literature courses, do you study the canonical 'great masterpieces', or modern literary works? What influences your instructor's choice of readings, do you think?
>
> 4 Can you think of any authors that are still studied and venerated because of their antiquity but who you don't think have any great literary talent?
>
> 5 Does Horace's defence of the new against the old imply that there is no point in studying Horace today?

2.1.93–102   In Greece peaceful times led to the development of a whole variety of cultural pursuits – sport, sculpture, painting, music, theatre – as a result of which Greeks lack concentration, flitting from one hobby to another.

2.1.103–38   At Rome by ancient pleasant custom men woke early,
worked **with closed doors**, gave clients benefit of law,
made well-secured advances to sound borrowers,   105
listened to elders, gave the young instruction how

What implication does this have for Horace himself?   in this context, consider *Epistles* 1.19.32–41. Horace is talking of the sixth-century Greek poet Alcaeus (p. 62), the principal model for his own lyric poetry:

> His words, till then unspoken, I, playing the Latin lyre,
> gave to the world. It's a joy to bring things never heard
> before, for free-born eyes to read and hands to hold.
> Why does the unkind reader call my works 'superb'
> at home and 'lovely', then go out and run them down?
> I don't go hunting for the fickle public's vote
> by offering dinners or a worn-out cloak.
> I deal with noble writers: hear them and avenge them,
> I won't address a Teachers' Union or a school.
> Hence all those tears.

The last line is a quotation from a comedy by the second-century playwright Terence (*hinc illae lacrimae*), which became a proverb for 'So that was what all the fuss was about.' Clearly Horace's *Odes* had not been received as he might have hoped.

with closed doors   unlike the Roman upper class of the day, as described by Virgil: 'The lofty house with its splendid doors vomits up early in the morning a whole wave of clients coming to pay their respects' (*Georgics* 2.461–2).

to increase wealth and cut back ruinous lust.
The people now has changed its fickle mind, and burns
with one desire: to write. Strict fathers and their boys
put on a wreath at dinner and dictate their works.   110
Myself, I claim I've not a single line to write,
then prove **less truthful than a Parthian**: before the sun
I'm up, demanding paper, pen and writing-box.
Untrained at sea you'll fear to sail; who'll dare prescribe
wormwood except a pharmacist? A doctor's skill   115
a doctor offers. Go to the smith for smithing.
But, taught or untaught, everyone writes poems now.
Of this mistake (or 'mild insanity') what is
the value? Hear me now: the poet's heart
is rarely greedy: verses he loves, and them alone.   120
Losses, absconding slaves, fires: he can laugh at them.
He never plots to cheat a partner or a ward
who's still a minor, lives on beans and coarsest bread,
an idle, useless soldier – but to the state a profit,
if you grant this: that small things are an aid to great ones.   125
The poet shapes the infant's tender, lisping mouth,
and from the start diverts his ear from smutty talk,
shaping his heart with principles of friendship,
correcting oafishness, resentment, anger.
His tales are of good deeds; he fills the coming age   130
with high examples, he consoles the poor and sick.
Unmarried girls, sound-hearted boys, where would they learn
to pray, did not the Muse provide the poet-priest?
The choir implores the gods' assistance, feels their presence,
in studied prayer begs and secures the rains from heaven,   135
averts disease, disperses dreadful dangers,
wins peace, wins harvests bountiful with fruits.
Songs charm the gods above, the gods below.

---

less truthful than a Parthian   compare *Odes* **3.5.33n**, p. 97.

wormwood   'used in the treatment of coughs, asthma and other ailments' (Rudd, p. 94, quoting Pliny, *Natural History* 21.160–2).

Unmarried girls, sound-hearted boys   the reference seems to be to the choir which sang the *Carmen Saeculare* at the Secular Games in June 17 BC; also perhaps to *Odes* 4.6, where Horace speaks proudly of having, in the name of Apollo, trained the choir for that occasion (lines 29–44).

From this point, the social value of literature, Horace now embarks on a highly selective history, beginning with ribald rustic entertainment which served as the basis upon which drama was later introduced. Roman writers of plays were not without talent, he writes, but they did lack persistence and craftsmanship, and the modern theatre has degenerated into mere spectacle. The question then arises, what literature *will* Augustus accept into his library on the Palatine, the literature which will become the Latin canon? Horace has already made his case for lyric poetry, and he now gives pride of place to epic and narrative verse, which allows him to put forward the names of his friends Virgil, who had died some seven years earlier, and Varius. It also allows him to conclude with a modest disclaimer of his own talent: he would like to write epic, but *sermones* **are all he can manage**, and to attempt anything else would see him writing poems which deserved merely to be used as wrapping paper for groceries.

---

1   In his magisterial work *Horace on Poetry*, C. O. Brink made this comment on the *Letter to Augustus*. 'The Letter … is a *command performance* executed with great *candour* and *skill*. It is also a personal poem designed to give voice to some of Horace's most cherished *convictions as to the relation of poetry and society*' (vol. 1, p. 191). (The italics are mine, and indicate what seem to be the key points.) How far do these selections from the poem bear out Brink's judgement?

2   Does poetry educate? And do you think writers have a duty to uplift their readers?

3   With the advent of new media (blogs, webpages) and on-demand printing, more people than ever are getting their writing published. Is this democratization of writing a good thing?

The *Art of Poetry*

As stated in the introduction to this chapter, the last letter of these three is addressed to three members of a family called Piso (see line 6): father and two sons who (to judge by comments in the poem not included here) appear to be on the verge of adulthood. It becomes clear that the family is that of the Calpurnii Pisones, one of the great families of the late republic and early empire. The ancient commentator Porphyrio tells us that the letter is written to the Lucius Piso who was subsequently **prefect of the city** and his

---

sermones **are all he can manage**   in saying this, he engages in some typical irony: in talking of the subject-matter of the epic poetry he cannot write, he refers to several passages of his own recently published fourth book of *Odes* (Hills, p. 133).

prefect of the city   a magistrate instituted by Augustus to be the emperor's deputy in Rome. This Piso held the office from AD 13 until his death in 32.

two sons. This Piso was son of another Lucius Piso, consul in 58 BC and father-in-law of Julius Caesar. He was a friend of the Epicurean philosopher Philodemus, **many of whose writings were discovered** in the eighteenth century in a magnificent villa at Herculaneum – the Villa of the Papyri. **It is not implausible** that this villa belonged to Piso and his sons, and that one of the sons is the Gaius Piso whose first shave is commemorated by the Greek writer of epigrams Apollonides. By a happy accident, one of the writings found at the villa refers to Varius, Plotius, Virgil and Quintilius Varus, all of them mentioned by Horace with approval as friends and critics (*Satires* 1.10.81 and especially, for Varus, *Art of Poetry* 438). Horace knew the towns of the Bay of Naples well – his horse was so familiar with the route there that he had trouble persuading it to go somewhere else (*Epistles* 1.15.10–12). It is an engaging thought that we can almost pinpoint a meeting-place for Horace and his favourite company.

The poem is generally regarded as Horace's most difficult. The problem lies not in its individual passages, which are, as will be seen, almost all both entertaining and intelligible. The most important question relates to the principle Horace announces in line 23: 'Let it be what it will, but let it be one.' **What is the overall unity of the poem?** How are the parts related to each other?

There is no point in doing more than touch on these issues when only a part of the poem is presented in translation. But it is worth asking the question: 'What is the poem?' As a letter, it is something of a monster – well over four times the length of the longest letters of Book 1, and roughly twice as long as each of the two in Book 2. Soon after it was written, it acquired the name *Ars Poetica*, the 'Art of Poetry'. This further obscured its character as a letter, turning it into a technical manual. But Horace ensures that it remains a letter by addressing the Pisos specifically on several occasions throughout the poem, and the reader is clearly intended to bear in mind the sort of poetic projects the youngsters have in hand.

---

many of whose writings were discovered   in the form of scrolls, many in a fragmentary state, which had been carbonized in the eruption of AD 79 and are now being deciphered using multispectral imaging.

It is not implausible   there was also a Calpurnius Piso who was consul in 23 BC, whom we know to have had two sons. Horace describes himself in line 306 as 'not currently writing anything', which seems to date the *Art of Poetry* after 23, when *Odes* 1–3 were published. This Piso's elder son was 21 or 20 by then.

What is the overall unity of the poem?   Andrew Laird speaks of a unity which depends less on overall structure than on the way each separate subject 'leads comfortably into what follows' by the principle of *akolouthia* (natural succession), which 'Porphyrio identified as the explicit concern of the poem's opening' (*CCH*, pp. 136–7).

In the letter, Horace shows the influence of the existing tradition of literary criticism going back to Aristotle's *Poetics* and *Rhetoric*, especially *Rhetoric* 2.12–14 and 3.7. Porphyrio also notes that the letter is a collection of the most important principles established by Neoptolemus of Parium, a Greek writer of the third century BC. Intriguingly, among the Herculaneum papyri is one where Philodemus, in his work 'On Poems', criticizes the observations of a writer whose name, otherwise illegible, ends in *-tolemos*. This author, generally identified as Neoptolemus, had divided the art of poetry into 'poet, poem, and poetry' (Greek *poētes, poēma, poēsis*). Considerable effort has been spent on attempts to identify this structure (and on the distinction in meaning of 'poem' and 'poetry') in the letter. But Horace is reluctant to be squeezed into the narrow confines of a textbook. Textbooks must set out their chapter headings clearly and divide chapters into sections and subsections. Conventional headings for literary issues (from Aristotle's *Poetics*) are plot, character, diction, thought, spectacle and lyric poetry. It is easy to see several of these discussed in the *Art of Poetry*. It is not at all so easy to decide exactly where discussion of one ends and the next begins, or to determine an overall pattern for the work. This may be the intended consequence of Horace sticking to the principle suggested in *Epistles* 2.2.124: art conceals itself.

A surprising feature of the *Art of Poetry* is the space devoted to writing plays. This is a branch of literature to which Horace never set his hand. We do, however, know that plays in the classical Greek style were being written: Ovid wrote a tragedy *Medea*, Horace's friend Varius a *Thyestes*, and in *Odes* **2.1** Horace encourages Asinius Pollio to return to tragedy after his history is completed. Augustus himself made some progress towards writing a tragedy on the subject of Ajax (Suetonius, *Augustus* 85.2). So it would be no surprise if the young Pisos were doing the same. A number of Horace's recommendations presuppose the idea that the play, when written, will be presented in the theatre and not simply read. Much of the literature of criticism is in any case concerned with plays (Plato, especially *Republic* 10, Aristotle *Poetics*), but it is clear that one of the crucial questions for Horace is 'will it work with a (discriminating) audience?' and this can most vividly come out if the imagined audience is a theatrical audience.

1–31   To a human head suppose a painter wished to fit
a horse's neck, and add on many-coloured feathers
and limbs assembled anywhere, all ending in
a horrid fish, with, up above, a lovely woman.
You're asked to view it. Could you contain your laughter, friends?   5
Believe me, Pisos, such a picture would be like
a book which, as a sick man's dream, was full

of strange imagined forms, not head, not foot
combinable. 'But painters, poets too,
have always had this freedom to break out at will.'   10
I know. This licence I concede and claim by turns,
but not for savage to lie down with meek, and not
for snakes to pair with birds, tigers with lambs.
In weighty enterprises, lofty schemes,
you often find, sewn in, a **purple patch** or two   15
to catch the eye: Diana's altar and her grove,
the sweet stream slipping swiftly o'er the sward.
The river Rhine's portrayed, a rainbow in the sky.
All out of place. Let's say you have the skill to paint
a **cypress tree.** What use, if you've been paid to show   20
a desperate shipwrecked sailor? You've begun
an **amphora.** The wheel goes round. Out comes a **bowl.**
In short, **let it be what it will, but let it be *one*.**

      We poets, Piso and those sons of whom you're proud,
are mostly fooled by what *seems* right. I would be brief,   25
but am obscure. I try for smoothness: what I write
lacks force and spirit. 'This will be grand.' It's pompous.
You're cautious? Scared of storms? You won't get off the ground.
Your theme is single and you're over-keen to vary it?
You'll paint your trees with dolphins, waves with boars.   30
To avoid a fault's a blunder where there is no skill.

---

purple patch   thanks to Horace, this phrase has become proverbial for inappropriate embellishment. This much is clear. But the metaphor is from the weaving of textiles, and it has not been settled what sort of process or decoration is here suggested.

the sweet stream slipping swiftly o'er the sward   Horace's line, with assonance and flowing rhythm, is at least as pretentious as this one.

cypress tree   ancient commentators say there was an artist who could only paint cypress trees. A sailor asked him to paint the shipwreck from which he had escaped. The artist asked if the sailor would like to have a cypress tree included in the painting. Horace's language brings out the point of the story.

amphora, bowl   an amphora is tall and has a narrow mouth. The clay has evidently collapsed on the wheel to produce a dumpy, wide-mouthed vessel.

let it be what it will, but let it be *one*   of course a bowl can have its own unity. The issue is not simply whether the object is consistent with itself, but consistent with its creator's intentions.

We poets   in the Latin, 'we' is not revealed until the next line, thereby including the Pisos with Horace more subtly.

32–98   Don't engage in a project unless you're competent at all aspects of it. Make a suitable choice of subject; then words and structure will come by themselves. Don't use odd words: achieve your effect by new combinations. For new ideas, new words may be invented, if carefully adapted from the Greek. As with all human enterprises, words which once were new fall out of use and die. Usage is all. Suit vocabulary to genre – epic, elegiac, iambic, lyric. (If you can't manage this you don't deserve the name of poet.) In works of drama vary the register to suit the character.

99–113   Poems must have more than beauty. They must charm
and draw the **listener**'s feelings where they will.   100
We smile when others smile, and when they weep
we do so too. If you would have me grieve, first you
must grieve yourself. Then I'll be hurt by your distress,
Peleus and Telephus. But if your words don't fit,

---

listener   not 'reader'. The primary method of getting to know new literature was to have it read to one, formally at a 'recitation' at the house of a well-to-do citizen or informally as Horace imagines the young Pisos reading to their father.

Peleus and Telephus   characters from tragedy, whose misery must be conveyed. Peleus was Achilles' father, and husband of the sea-goddess Thetis. There is a Latin tragedy *Hermiona* by Ennius' nephew Pacuvius (mid-second century BC) in a fragment of which Peleus is mentioned, after Achilles' death, as aged and childless. Telephus was wounded by Achilles. The wound could only be healed by the rust from Achilles' spear. Telephus as wretched suppliant is a familiar image in Greek art and figured in (lost) tragedies by Aeschylus, Sophocles and Euripides; also in *Telephus* by the second-century BC Roman tragedian Accius. In *Epistles* 2.1.55–6 Horace expresses at best half-hearted approval of Pacuvius and Accius; presumably it is their tragedies which he is criticizing for failure to convey feeling.

Achilles uses the rust from his spear to cure Telephus' wounded leg. From a relief at Herculaneum.

I'll either fall asleep or laugh. A mourning face   105
needs words of grief, an angry one, of menace;
a merry face – then playful words; solemn – then strict.
Nature prepares us inwardly for every kind
of fortune. She gives joy or drives us on to rage
or casts us to the ground in woe. Then she brings out   110
the heart's disturbance through the medium of the tongue.
If one should speak in words discordant with one's state,
the Romans, **knights and infantry**, will burst out laughing.

114–24   This is the range of characters to be coped with: old man, young man; *grande dame*, nursemaid; trader, farmer; **foreigners from two different countries; Greeks from two different cities**; figures of legend: Achilles, Medea, Ino, Ixion, Io, Orestes.

---

knights and infantry   Horace imagines a scene at a Roman theatre. The front 14 rows were reserved for the second-highest class in Roman society, the knights (*equites*). Although originally a military classification, the term no longer had any military significance; those who were not *equites* would be senators (for whom seats were reserved in the orchestra) or plebeians. It is Horace's joke to refer to the plebeians as 'infantry'.

foreigners from two different countries; Greeks from two different cities   the comic writer Plautus included a Carthaginian in his play *Poenulus*, clearly identified by his Punic speech. Aristophanes presented a Theban in *Acharnians*, also with Theban peculiarities. But one suspects that Horace is referring to techniques less blatant here.

125–88   If on the stage you put what's not been tried, and dare   125
to make new characters, let them be kept the same
from first to last, and be consistent with themselves.
It's hard to express the general by the particular.
Put the Troy story into acts: that's better than
to put on stage what was unknown, unsaid before.   130
You'll make what's **common property** your own
if you avoid the easy, trivial round
and don't think sound translation means mere word for word
rendition, nor in imitating land yourself
where diffidence or laws of genre leave you trapped.   135

It's hard to express the general by the particular   it is clear from line 129 that Horace is discouraging his readers from writing tragedies with plots and characters of their own invention. In lines 125–7 he has allowed for the possibility that they may. He has given the conditions under which it can be attempted, though perhaps only as a last resort after all the mythical subjects have been considered. Line 128, marking the change from hesitant encouragement to positive discouragement, must provide *a reason why* he is discouraging them. It may be that 'to express the general by the particular' is what all tragedians do, and by 'It's hard …' we should understand 'It's hard enough to write tragedy anyway, so better stick to tradition.' In that case 'the general' can refer to the tragedian's activity as described in Aristotle, *Poetics* 9: 'Poetry is more elevated than history, since poetry relates more of the universal.' The 'particular' will be the events, items and people of the story you are using (Medea, the poisoned robe, the murder of the children). Horace is thus concluding the point he has been so far making: it is much harder to achieve wholeness and consistency with themes and characters you have invented yourself. The line is the subject of a very great deal of discussion (Brink, vol. 2, pp. 432–40).

Put the Troy story into acts   Aeschylus described his plays as 'slices from Homer's banquet'. (Though most Greek tragedies – including the surviving ones by Aeschylus – did not overlap with the plots of the *Iliad* or *Odyssey* but drew on other sources of legend.)

common property   i.e. the material from legend which is available to all.

where diffidence or laws of genre leave you trapped   Horace himself has faced this sort of problem. In *Epistles* 1.19.22–5, contrasting himself with imitators ('herd of slaves') he says 'I did not tread in anyone else's footsteps. He who has confidence in himself will lead and rule the swarm. I was first to introduce the iambics of Paros into Latium' (*Epistles* **1.20.23–4**). Iambics constitute a genre with its rules. In introducing them to Latin, Horace faces the problem that 'personal attack' is part of the rules of that genre, but that if he goes in for personal attack (which he suggests in *Satires* **1.4**, pp. 19–27 he has no wish to do) he may fall foul of other rules, i.e. the law as expounded in *Satires* 2.1.82 by the great jurist Trebatius: 'Should anyone compose malicious songs against another, there is the law and there is a court.' Thus, in refraining from using iambics for personal attack, he has refused to be limited by 'diffidence' or 'laws of genre'.

Odysseus puts out the Cyclops' eye (Art of Poetry 145). From a cave-resort of the emperor Tiberius at Sperlonga on the coast south of Anxur (see pp. 31–2).

Nor will you open like a **cyclic poet** once:
'Of Priam's fortune and that glorious war I sing.'
Who could fulfil the promise of such bombast?
Mountains in labour will bring forth a joke – a mouse.
Far better he whose efforts never led to folly: 140
'**Of that Man tell me, Muse,** who, when Troy's fated time
had come, saw many men, their practices, their cities.'
Not smoke from flame, but light from smoke he plans
to bring, and show conspicuous marvels in what follows:
Antiphates, Charybdis; Scylla and the Cyclops.   145

---

cyclic poet   the 'cyclic' epics were post-Homeric compositions, which were organized by later scholars into a 'cycle' telling the whole story of the world. They exist only in small fragments. They were almost all held to be much inferior to Homer.

Mountains in labour will bring forth a joke – a mouse   this is Horace's famous line *parturient montes, nascetur ridiculus mus.* He is translating a Greek saying. Horace's line, like this one, ends with the little mouse, even smaller in Latin: *mus.*

Of that Man tell me, Muse   these two lines are a very close adaptation of the first lines of the *Odyssey*. Homer's qualities are being approved at the expense of the cyclic poet.

Antiphates, Charybdis; Scylla and the Cyclops   monsters encountered by Odysseus. Antiphates was king of the giant, man-eating Laestrygonians. The Cyclops was the one-eyed giant from whom Odysseus escaped by blinding him, then disguising himself and his men as the Cyclops' flock. Scylla and Charybdis were the monsters on either side of the straits through which Odysseus had to pass; Charybdis sucked her victims to the depths, Scylla grabbed them from up a cliff.

He won't start 'Diomede's Return' from the demise
of Meleager, nor Troy's tale from the twin egg.
Always he's speeding towards the end. He hurries
his listeners half-way in, as if they knew the story. What
he fears would be too dull to handle he omits,   150
inventing so, so mixing fantasy with fact,
that start agrees with middle, middle with end.

Hear now what I need, and your audience with me.
You want your claque to stay until the curtain, and remain
seated until the singer tells us 'please applaud'?   155
Mark how each age is different in its ways, and write
what's fit for changing natures and advancing years.
The child who's learned to speak, who now can walk
securely, longs to join his peers in play, gets in and out
of rages over nothing, changes from hour to hour.   160
The beardless youth, free of his guardian at last,
loves horses, hounds, the Campus, grass and sun –
wax to be shaped for wrong – resents advice,
is slow to make provision, squanders money,

Diomede's Return   this is evidently a real cyclic poem or one imagined by Horace. There was a collection of poems (*Nostoi*) covering the return journeys of the heroes from Troy, of which the *Odyssey* is the archetype. *Diomede's Return* will be one of them. Meleager was Diomedes' uncle. There are various accounts of his death, which in any case will have happened long before the Trojan war and, from an epic point of view, in a completely different story. It would be absurd to use it to begin the story of Diomedes' return from Troy.

twin egg   Helen of Troy and her twin sister Clytemnestra, Agamemnon's wife, were daughters of Leda, whom Jupiter had loved in the guise of a swan; hence the egg.

half-way in   this is the famous tag *in medias res*. When the *Odyssey* begins, Odysseus is already on Calypso's island, with only one more stage to go before he gets back home to Ithaca. We do not hear about his journey from Troy until Book 9. Virgil organizes the *Aeneid* similarly: at the beginning Aeneas is on (he thinks) the last stage of his journey to Italy.

the curtain   on a Roman stage the curtain did not fall, but was raised from a slot on the stage.

please applaud   all surviving Latin plays conclude with an instruction to the audience to applaud, delivered either by one of the actors in character, or by a representative member of the company, or by a person described as 'singer'.

guardian   a boy could expect to be accompanied in public everywhere by a slave (*paedagogus*) until he came of age at 16. Augustus was vexed, says Suetonius, when his grandson Gaius had the temerity to attend the theatre unsupervised.

Campus   the Campus Martius, see map, p. 4.

full of ideals and longings, falls in and out of love.   165
Other pursuits engage the full-grown man:
riches he wants, connections, honours; he's afraid
of doing what he later may find hard to change.
Around the old man many troubles swarm: he earns
but hoards his earnings, frightened to make use of them,   170
nervous and passionless in everything he does;
postpones, sits idle, hopeless, hoards his remaining days,
awkward, cantankerous, **praising the time long gone**
when he was young, harsh critic of his juniors.
The years bring many blessings as they come   175
and take them as they recede. For fear an old man's lines
be given to youth, or adult's lines to child,
we'll always keep to what **each age** demands.

      Events are acted out on stage or told in words.
The mind is slower to respond to what it hears   180
than what is offered to its **trusty eyes** and what
the viewer tells himself. But you will not present
on stage what's best to keep indoors, and you'll remove
much from our eyes for vivid narrative to offer.
Let not **Medea** kill her sons on open stage,   185
nor wicked **Atreus** cook a dish of human offal,

---

praising the time long gone   this is the well-known tag *laudator temporis acti*.

The years bring many blessings as they come / and take them as they recede   the idea seems to be that the younger man looks forward to the years which make him older, more prosperous, etc., while the older man looks only to the increasing number of years behind him.

each age   an extensive characterization of each age was offered by Aristotle, *Rhetoric* 2.12–14; this is said to have influenced Horace. Shakespeare may have Horace in mind when Jaques speaks of the seven ages of man in *As You Like It* 2.7: his speech begins 'All the world's a stage …'

trusty eyes   Horace is referring to a Greek proverb: 'the eye is more trustworthy than the ear'. Similarly, you believe what you have seen first-hand ('what / the viewer tells himself') sooner than what someone else tells you.

Medea   she helped Jason to win the Golden Fleece, but was obliged therefore to flee with him from her home in Colchis. When they came to Corinth, Jason proposed to marry the king's daughter. In revenge for his treachery, Medea murdered Jason's bride, the king and her own and Jason's children. In Euripides' play and in Ennius' Latin adaptation the children are killed offstage.

Atreus   father of Agamemnon. His wife Aerope slept with his brother Thyestes. Atreus killed Thyestes' children, cooked them and served them to their father. This is narrated by a messenger in Accius' play *Atreus*. Atreus on re-entering boasts that he has provided the children with a satisfactory burial place – inside their father.

nor **Procne** turn to bird, **Cadmus** to snake.
Such shows I find repellent and incredible.

Medea murdering one of her sons (Art of Poetry 185).
From a Campanian amphora, c.340–320 BC.

1   Can you think of poems which are, in Horace's terms (lines 99–113), beautiful without being satisfactory poems? In what are they not satisfactory?

2   The image in line 139 is vivid, but is it apt?

3   In what sense is the narrative of the *Odyssey* providing 'light from smoke' (line 143)?

4   In *Ajax*, Sophocles has Ajax kill himself on open stage. In Shakespeare's *King Lear*, Gloucester's eyes are gruesomely put out on open stage – 'Out, vile jelly!' Where does this leave Horace with his rule (lines 179–88)?

5   From your experience of reading fiction, do you find Horace's advice in the poem so far convincing?

Procne   a character in plays entitled *Tereus* by Sophocles and Accius. She married Tereus, king of Thrace. Tereus raped her sister Philomela and cut out her tongue. Philomela revealed this to Procne by weaving an illustration of the story onto a cloth. Procne took revenge by getting Tereus to eat their son Itys. In the event Tereus was turned into a hoopoe, Procne into a swallow and Philomela into a nightingale. The story is also in Ovid, *Metamorphoses* 6.424–674.

Cadmus   the mythical founder of Thebes. His son Pentheus came to a terrible end after acting contemptuously towards Dionysus, and Cadmus thereafter left Thebes with his wife Harmonia. At the end of their lives they were changed into snakes and transported to the Elysian Fields. In a surviving fragment of tragedy, Cadmus says: 'Alas, I am becoming a snake. Embrace what is left of me' (Euripides, Fr. 930). Unfortunately it is impossible to know whether this was spoken by Cadmus on stage or is a speech of Cadmus as reported by a messenger. This story too is in Ovid, *Metamorphoses* 4.562–603.

189–418   There should be no more and no fewer than **five acts**. The chorus should support and guide the actors. Music should not play too conspicuous a part. Modern instruments are too showy and loud.

The discussion of more vulgar entertainment moves Horace to talk of **satyr plays** and the different register required for them, for tragedy and comedy. Too vulgar a style may please the popcorn-buyer ('roasted chickpea and nuts', line 249) but alienate the better class of spectator.

Horace now discusses metrical matters, which seem a digression until he moves to what he considers the incompetent metrical practice of the Romans and uses this to insist on the value of the close study of Greek poetry. This leads him to a rapid and selective summary of the history of drama, whose purpose appears to be to contrast ancient (Greek) standards with modern (Roman) ones.

He explains that these days poets think natural talent is all that matters; hard work is too much for them. But without it, poetry is valueless. The hard work must include the understanding of ethical and practical matters, and careful reading. Romans, with their generally philistine education, have no notion of the effort required. When you have the knowledge, you must impart it in a way which gives pleasure, and you must learn from your mistakes. A moderately good orator has his use, a moderately good poet does not. Forgetting this, these days everyone is in a hurry to write verse. And, correspondingly, they all have their hired admirers.

419–76   Like auctioneers, who gather crowds of purchasers,
the poet calls the **flatterers** 'Want some pickings?'   420

---

five acts   Greek tragedy and early comedy show no evidence of a five-act prescription. But it is likely that the comic writer Menander (late fourth century BC) divided his plays into five sections, and the tragedies of Seneca, written in the mid-first century AD, can also be divided into five. Later grammarians prescribed five acts for all plays, and attempted unconvincingly so to divide the comedies of Plautus and Terence. It seems that Horace's authority here (probably deriving from an unknown Greek theorist) has played its part in establishing a rule which lasted until the eighteenth century.

satyr plays   it was the rule, at the Athenian festival of the City Dionysia, for each tragedian to present, in a single day, three tragedies and, last of all, a satyr play. These were similar to tragedy in structure and language, but distinguished from it in that the chorus consisted of satyrs (conventionally goat-legged, human-bodied semi-divinities of the wild) and that the tone tended to burlesque. One complete satyr play, *Cyclops*, survives among the tragedies of Euripides. In 1988 the writer Tony Harrison presented *The Trackers of Oxyrhynchus*, his own adaptation of the fragments of Sophocles' satyr play *Ichneutae*. The idea that satyr plays were being performed in Augustan Rome is a surprise.

flatterers   interestingly, among the papyri from Herculaneum (see p. 176) there are three containing discussion of flattery.

(he's rich in land and rich in money out on loan).
If he can host a splendid feast, and offer
bail for a poor uncreditworthy client
enmeshed in lawsuits, I'll be staggered if he can,
fine fellow, tell a genuine from a lying friend.   425
If you have made, or wish to make a man a gift
don't ask him 'Come and hear my verses' when he's all
excited. 'Great!' he'll cry, 'Bravo! Magnificent!'
One line will turn him pale, another make his eyes
drop friendly moisture; he'll jump up, **strike foot to ground.**   430
At funerals hired mourners say and do almost more
than those whose grief is heartfelt. So the sycophant
shows more emotion than the one whose praise is true.
Kings, so they say, press **many flagons full**
of unmixed wine on those of whom they seek to know –   435
should they be made their friends? If you're a poet,
the fox's hidden heart must not deceive you.
Quintilius, if you read to him, said 'Please correct
just this, and this.' You'd say 'I can't do better.
Twice, yes, three times I've tried, in vain.' 'Then cross it out.   440
Back to the anvil with a verse that's badly turned.'
If you preferred to justify, not change, the fault,
he wouldn't waste another word, another second.
Yourself, your poems – you could love them on your own.
A thoughtful, good man will condemn a lifeless line;   445
reject a coarse one; on untidy ones he'll mark
a black line crossways; sprawling ornament
he'll prune and force to let in light where it's too dark.

---

he's rich in land and rich in money out on loan   this line had been used earlier by Horace in *Satires* 1.2.13 of someone whose wealth was simultaneously enormous and secure.

fine fellow   the phrase is ironical.

strike foot to ground   stamping seems to have been a way of reacting when one was being carried away by a speech. Cicero speaks of a courtroom speech as having fallen flat when no one stamped during it.

many flagons full / of unmixed wine   hence the proverb 'truth in wine' (*in vino veritas*).

Quintilius   almost certainly the Quintilius of the Herculaneum discussions (see the introduction to the *Art of Poetry*) and the subject of *Odes* 1.24. In the ode, Virgil is being consoled for the death of Quintilius, who is remembered for his 'naked truthfulness'. Virgil himself took ten years to write the *Aeneid*; this amounts to three lines a day.

a black line crossways   the mark known as *obelus*, which Aristarchus (line 450) used to mark lines he considered spurious. Aristarchus was a formidable critic, head of the Library of Alexandria in the mid-second century BC.

Obscurity he'll show up. What's to change, he'll mark –
an Aristarchus. This he won't say: 'Why do I cross a friend   450
over a nothing?' Suchlike nothings cause real harm
to one who's victim once of **spite and mockery**.
Like one who has the **royal illness** or **the scab**
or whom enraged **Diana** sends amuck,
men of good sense avoid **a crazy poet**, and fear   455
to touch him. Children are rash: they tease and harass him.
If he is staggering, belching lofty lines,
and like the fowler chasing blackbirds, falls
into some pit or well, though he may long cry 'Help!
Help, citizens!' there will be none to rescue him.   460
If one should care to offer help, to drop a line,
'And how do you know he didn't jump on purpose down,'
I'll say, 'not wanting to be saved?' I'll tell the tale
how the Sicilian poet died. '**Empedocles**,
wanting the title "god", leapt, **chilly**, into blazing   465
Etna. Poets must have the unfettered right to perish.
To save a man against his will amounts to murder.

---

spite and mockery   Horace knew very well what it was to be subject to these, to judge by
Satires 1.6.45–8 and **2.6.47–9** (pp. 44–5).

royal illness   this seems to be jaundice. One explanation for its name was that prescribed
treatments were vastly expensive.

the scab   this covered a number of diseases, including leprosy.

Diana   goddess associated with the moon (*luna*); 'lunatic' means 'mad' in Latin as in
English. Both Coleridge (in *Kubla Khan*, see p. 23) and Horace ironically present the poet as
possessed, though to rather different effect.

a crazy poet   the connection of thought appears to be that a poet who has been indulged
by flattering friends will come to believe in his own superiority and thus lose contact with
the real world.

Empedocles, / wanting the title "god"   Empedocles appeared in *Epistles* **1.12.20** (p. 160) as
a Sicilian cosmological philosopher. He wrote a work called *Purifications* and seems to have
believed that, by following the principles of this work, human beings could escape the
cycle of rebirth (known also from Pythagoras) and become divine. A fragment attributed
to him runs: 'I walk among you as an immortal god.' Bertrand Russell quoted the couplet:
'The great Empedocles, that ardent soul, / Leapt into Etna and was roasted whole.'

chilly   the contrast between 'chilly' and 'blazing' perhaps represents Empedocles' belief
(see *Epistles* **1.12.19n**, p. 160) that the world was governed by conflicting principles, of
which 'hot' and 'cold' were two. The (cold) philosopher challenges the (hot) volcano.
But 'chilly' is also a word used for ideas or poems which fall flat, so Horace may here be
offering a (not too serious) comment on Empedocles as poet and philosopher. In Latin
the word 'chilly' comes between 'blazing' and 'Etna', thereby creating a pictorial effect
impossible in English.

'*Blazing Etna*' *(Art of Poetry 465–6)*.

It's not the first time. If you pull him out, he won't
turn human and renounce his longing for a famous death.
Indeed, it's not quite clear why he writes verses. Did he   470
piss on his father's ashes? Did he foully disturb
a **lightning-shrine**? He's raving, sure, and like a bear
who's had the strength to break the cage-bars in his way,
ruthless reciter, scares schooled and unschooled away.
But those he grabs, he grips and kills with reading.   475
He'll not drop off their flesh till full of blood – a leech.'

---

1 What sort of poetry are the sons of Piso expected to write? For what purpose
   might they write so? (It may be worth looking at *Odes* **2.1**, pp. 86–9 again in
   this context.)

2 The last scene in the *Art of Poetry*, and probably the last scene in all Horace's
   poetry, is the mad poet down the well. Does this caricature have any serious
   purpose, or is it merely a piece of flamboyant decoration like the fantastic
   creature of lines 1–5?

3 Does the *Art of Poetry* set out standards which would be useful to you in
   assessing a modern work of literature?

---

lightning-shrine   a place where lightning had struck (*puteal*) was held sacred and fenced
off.

Further reading

For the reader without Latin, a close approach to Horace is possible in the following works, all of which have Latin text, English translation and a full and interesting commentary.

The editions of *Odes* by **David West** are: *Horace Odes I: Carpe Diem* (Oxford, 1995); *Horace Odes II: Vatis Amici* (Oxford, 1998); *Horace Odes III: Dulce Periculum* (Oxford, 2002). David West has also tranlated the *Odes* and *Epodes* (Oxford, World's Classics, 2008).

Michael Putnam's edition of Book 4 is *Artifices of Eternity* (Ithaca, NY, 1986).

For the *Satires*, there is **Michael Brown**, *Horace Satires I* (Oxford, 1993), and **Francis Muecke**, *Horace Satires II* (Oxford, 1993).

For the *Epodes, Epistles* and the *Art of Poetry*, conditions are a little less favourable, but text with accompanying translation is available in the Loeb Classical Library's editions: **Niall Rudd**, *Horace: Odes and Epodes* (Cambridge, Mass., 2004), and **Rushton Fairclough**, *Horace: Satires, Epistles and Ars Poetica* (Cambridge, Mass., 1929).

For a general introduction to Horace and an excellent overview of his work, there is *Reading Horace* by **David West** (Edinburgh, 1967), and *Horace* by **Philip Hills** (London, 2005). *The Cambridge Companion to Horace* (*CCH*), edited by **Stephen Harrison** (Cambridge, 2007) and *Horace, Odes and Epodes*, edited by **Michele Lowrie** (Oxford, 2009), consist of a very useful collection of essays summarizing the state of Horatian studies at present and dealing extensively with the poet's reception in the Middle Ages, the Renaissance and the modern era. For studies of Roman poetry and culture of this period, see **R. O. A. M. Lyne**, *The Latin Love Poets from Catullus to Ovid* (Oxford, 1980), **Jasper Griffin**, *Latin Poets and Roman Life* (London, 1998) and **Susanna Braund**, *The Roman Satirists and their Masks* (Bristol, 1996). For discussion of genre, see **Francis Cairns**, *Generic Composition in Greek and Roman Poetry* (Edinburgh, 1971).

For politics and society in the Augustan period, **Andrew Wallace-Hadrill**, *Augustan Rome* (London, 1993) makes an excellent introduction. For more detailed studies, **Josiah Osgood**, *Caesar's Legacy* (Cambridge, 2006), gives an excellent new discussion of the 30s BC, while for the rest of the period, see **Karl Galinsky** (ed.), *Cambridge Companion to the Age of Augustus* (Cambridge, 2005).

The principal ancient sources for the period, quoted quite often in the notes, are Velleius Paterculus, who served in the army under Tiberius, Augustus' biographer Suetonius, and the early third-century historian Dio Cassius. They are all available in the Loeb Library, Dio translated by **Earnest Cary**, Suetonius by **John Rolfe**,

and Velleius by **Frederick Shipley**. These translations can also be accessed on the admirable website Lacus Curtius:
http://penelope.uchicago.edu/Thayer/E/Roman/home.html

For general reference, the *Oxford Classical Dictionary* (*OCD*), 3rd edition revised, eds. **Simon Hornblower** and **Antony Spawforth** (Oxford, 2003) is invaluable. For the mythological background which forms such a large part of the stock-in-trade of ancient poets, the *Dictionary of Classical Mythology* by **Jenny March** (London, 1998) is both entertaining and extremely useful.

The editions of the Latin text of Horace without translation are: **R. G. M. Nisbet** and **Margaret Hubbard**, *A Commentary on Horace: Odes Book 1* (Oxford, 1970) and *Odes Book II* (Oxford, 1978); **R. G. M. Nisbet** and **Niall Rudd**, *A Commentary on Horace Odes, Book III* (Oxford, 2004); **David Mankin**, *Horace Epodes* (Cambridge, 1995); **T. E. Page**, *Horace, Odes and Epodes* (London, 1883); **A. Palmer**, *Horace Satires* (London, 1883); **Roland Mayer**, *Horace, Epistles Book 1* (Cambridge, 1994); **Niall Rudd**, *Horace, Epistles II and Ars Poetica* (Cambridge, 1989).

Authors mentioned in the text but not referred to above:

Mary Beard, *The Roman Triumph* (Cambridge, Mass., 2007)

Susanna Braund, *Satire and Society in Ancient Rome* (Exeter, 1989)

C. O. Brink, *Horace on Poetry*, 3 vols (Cambridge, 1963, 1971, 1982)

D. S. Carne-Ross and **Kenneth Haynes**, *Horace in English* (Harmondsworth, 1996)

Eduard Fraenkel, *Horace* (Oxford, 1957)

James Michie, *The Odes of Horace*, text and translation (London, 1963)

Llewelyn Morgan, 'The One and Only *Fons Bandusiae*', *Classical Quarterly* (NS), 59 (2009), 132–41

Denys Page, *Sappho and Alcaeus* (Oxford, 1955)

Ronald Syme, *The Roman Revolution* (Oxford, 1939)

H. P. Syndikus, *Die Lyrik des Horaz* (Darmstadt, 1973)

Richard Thomas (ed.), *Virgil, Georgics III–IV* (Cambridge, 1988)

B. H. Warmington (trans.), *Remains of Old Latin* (Loeb Classical Library, London, 1938)

Gordon Williams, *Tradition and Originality in Roman Poetry* (Oxford, 1968)

Paul Zanker, *The Power of Images in the Age of Augustus* (Ann Arbor, Mich., 1990)

List of passages discussed

Acknowledgements

The author and publishers acknowledge the following sources of copyright material and are grateful for the permissions granted. While every effort has been made, it has not always been possible to identify the sources of all the material used, or to trace all copyright holders. If any omissions are brought to our notice we will be happy to include the appropriate acknowledgement on reprinting.

Cover: A Roman Scribe Writing Dispatches, 1865 (oil on panel), Alma-Tadema, Sir Lawrence (1836-1912)/Private Collection/The Bridgeman Art Library; p. 10 sarcophagus depicting Jason and the fire breathing bull at Colchis, 753-476 BC (marble), Roman/Louvre, Paris, France/Lauros/Giraudon/The Bridgeman Art Library; p. 13 *Relief of a banqueter*, Roman, Late Republican period, about 50 B.C., marble from Carrara in northwest Italy, height 29 cm (11 1/6 in), width (max.) 23.5 cm (9 ¼ in), Museum of Fine Arts, Boston, Henry Lillie Pierce Fund, 00.311 Photograph © 2010 Museum of Fine Arts, Boston; pp. 16, 60, 79, 92, 121 © The Trustees of the British Museum; p. 18 Relief depicting Menander with theatrical masks, copy of a Greek original (marble), Roman/Museo Gregoriano Profano, Vatican Museums, Vatican City/Alinari/The Bridgeman Art Library; p. 30 MM, Foto taken himself, Wikipedia; pp. 32, 134, 157, 182 Keith Maclennan; p. 38 Statuette of a donkey braying, Roman, 1st-2nd century AD (bronze)/British Museum, London, UK /The Bridgeman Art Library; p. 42 Eric Dugdale; p. 52 © Donald Cooper/Photostage; p. 53 The Art Archive/Bibliotheque des Arts Decoratifs Paris/Gianni Dagli Orti; p. 64 Greek vase painting, Antikenslg. & Glyptothek., Staatl., Munch, akg-images, London/Erich Lessing; p. 66 Fighting outside Troy, frieze from the Siphnian Treasury, c.525 BC (marble), Greek, (6th century BC)/Archaeological Museum, Delphi, Greece/Bernard Cox/The Bridgeman Art Library; p. 70 Cgheyne, Wikipedia; p. 77 Attic Black-figure amphora depicting Athena, 5th century BC (pottery),/© Ashmolean Museum, University of Oxford, UK/The Bridgeman Art Library; p. 88 Alexander the Great (356-323 BC) from 'The Alexander Mosaic', depicting the Battle of Issus between Alexander and Darius III (399-330 BC) in 333 BC, floor mosaic removed from the Casa del Fauno (House of the Faun) at Pompeii, after a 4th century BC Hellenistic painting by Philoxenos of Eritrea (mosaic) (detail of 154003), Roman, (1st century BC)/Museo Archeologico Nazionale, Naples, Italy/Alinari/The Bridgeman Art Library; p. 96 John Ross/Robert Harding World Imagery; p. 101 Apollo Belvedere, Roman copy of a Greek 4th century BC original (marble), Roman/Vatican Museums and Galleries, Vatican City, Italy/Photo © Anatoly Pronin/The Bridgeman Art Library; p. 103 Franz-Marc Frei/Corbis

p. 124 Primavera, c.1478, (tempera on panel) (detail of 558), Botticelli, Sandro (1444/5-1510)/Galleria degli Uffizi, Florence, Italy/The Bridgeman Art Library; p. 131 © RMN/Herve Lewandowski; p. 139 Statue of an old market woman, 1st century A.D. New York, Metropolitan Museum of Art, Marble, Pentelic, H. 49 5/8 in. (125.98 cm), Rogers Fund, 1909, Acc.n.: 09.39 © 2010 Image copyright The Metropolitan Museum of Art/Art Resource/Scala, Florence; p. 141 Chimaera of Arezzo or the Chimaera wounded by Bellerophon, Etruscan, 380-360 BC (bronze)/Museo Archeologico, Florence, Italy/The Bridgeman Art Library; p. 152 Epicurus, Musee du Louvre, Paris, akg-images, London/Erich Lessing; p. 159 Bust of Agrippa (63-12 BC) (marble), Roman, (1st century BC)/Louvre, Paris, France/Giraudon/The Bridgeman Art Library; p. 169 cameo, akg-images/Erich Lessing; p. 172 Relief depicting a school scene, from Neumagen (stone), Gallo-Roman, (2nd century AD)/Rheinisches Landesmuseum, Trier, Germany/Lauros/Giraudon/The Bridgeman Art Library; p. 180 Telephus relief, Herculaneum (Italy), akg-images, London/Rainer Hackenberg; p. 185 vase painting, Musee du Louvre, Paris, akg-images, London/Erich Lessing; p. 189 Bernhard Edmaier/Science Photo Library